Proverbs
to
Live By

ENDORCEMENTS

Proverbs to Live By is exactly what is needed for the body of Christ today. Dr. Harry Heinrichs Has not only packed each day's devotional with serious, reliable, and understandable content, but he has taken us to the Old Testament book of Proverbs, a book that was given to the people of God for just such an occasion and just such a time as this. May our Lord be pleased to use it in the hearts and lives of multitudes.

Dr. Walter C. Kaiser. Jr., Ph.D.
President Emeritus
Gordon Conwell Theological Seminary
Hamilton, MA

Harry Heinrichs provides the reader with devotions and practical ways to interpret and implement the teachings of Proverbs. His insights into the Lord's wisdom and moral coaching are excellently written, easily understood and ever so timely. Enjoy Harry's day by day encounter with Proverbs.

Dr. Howard A. Tryon Jr.
President, Proverbial Coaching
Founder, Christian Actualism

Wisdom is a skill we are not given at birth, but must be learned over a lifetime. Wisdom is the art of extracting the gifts found in the God has given us. The book of Solomon's Proverbs is a curriculum for life.

Dr. Heinrichs has given us a gift of access to his daily dosage of wisdom. With his practical approach we can all embrace these truths into a daily devotional habit which honors God.

Dr. Darryl Del Housaye, Ph.D.
President, Phoenix Seminary

The world today is drowning in data. Knowledge on virtually any subject is just a computer click away. But while knowledge is increasing exponentially, wisdom is not. If anything, mastering the skill off living life successfully is becoming a lost art. And that's why the Book of Proverbs – and this daily devotional – are so important. Dr. Harry Heinrichs takes his audience on a one-year journey of discovery through a book specifically written to offer "prudence to the simple, knowledge and discretion to the young" (Prov. 1:4). Harry combines his own study of Proverbs with his years of pastoral experience to help readers access God's practical wisdom of life.

Dr. Charlie Dyer, Ph.D.
Associate pastor, Grace Bible Church
Sun City, Arizona

Are you searching for wisdom? Most of us certainly need to! Life is often full of discouragements. Our faith gets tested, and others may offer little help, quoting aphorisms and flippant comments which never reach our souls. There are days when we ache for certainty and even well-meaning pious platitudes produce little or no encouragement.

Perhaps others look to you for wisdom and you're worried a day Will come when your knowledge and wisdom will be of little help? The solution, as with most things in life, is found in God's Word. In His grace, He has concentrated wisdom, based in His own holy and loving character, in the Book of Proverbs. Here we find the wisdom of God as mediated to us by King Solomon – arguably the wisest man who ever lived. And there are insights from other sages too.

Dr. Bing Hunter, Ph.D.
Executive Vice President & Academic Dean
Phoenix Seminary

Harry Heinrichs has been a ministry associate of mine and a dear friend for a number of years. It is a joy for me to commend this devotional book to you that has flowed from Harry's heart and his walk with God. I believe that you will be encouraged, blessed and strengthened as you read it day by day.

Dr. Paul Cedar
Honorary Chairman, Mission America Coalition

DR. HARRY HEINRICHS

Proverbs
to
Live By

Miniature Life Lessons for Daily Living

BALBOA
PRESS
A DIVISION OF HAY HOUSE

Balboa Press books may be ordered through booksellers or by contacting:

Balboa Press
A Division of Hay House
1663 Liberty Drive
Bloomington, IN 47403
www.balboapress.com
1 (877) 407-4847

Because of the dynamic nature of the Internet, any web addresses or links contained in this book may have changed since publication and may no longer be valid. The views expressed in this work are solely those of the author and do not necessarily reflect the views of the publisher, and the publisher hereby disclaims any responsibility for them.

The author of this book does not dispense medical advice or prescribe the use of any technique as a form of treatment for physical, emotional, or medical problems without the advice of a physician, either directly or indirectly. The intent of the author is only to offer information of a general nature to help you in your quest for emotional and spiritual well-being. In the event you use any of the information in this book for yourself, which is your constitutional right, the author and the publisher assume no responsibility for your actions.

Scriptures taken from the Holy Bible, New International Version®, NIV®. Copyright © 1973, 1978, 1984, 2011 by Biblica, Inc.™ Used by permission of Zondervan. All rights reserved worldwide. www.zondervan.com The "NIV" and "New International Version" are trademarks registered in the United States Patent and Trademark Office by Biblica, Inc.™ All rights reserved.

Print information available on the last page.

ISBN: 978-1-9822-0393-1 (sc)
ISBN: 978-1-9822-0395-5 (hc)
ISBN: 978-1-9822-0394-8 (e)

Library of Congress Control Number: 2018905545

Balboa Press rev. date: 11/08/2019

Contents

Preface ix

Introduction... xi

January 1

February.. 32

March 60

April.. 91

May...121

June...152

July 182

August 213

September 244

October...274

November 305

December..336

Preface

Initially these "Proverbs to Live By" were designed to serve the local church constituency where I served as the temporary Associate Pastor. From the very beginning, the distribution was via email only. Soon after their initial appearance, the email list began to expand to include family and friends, and friends of friends. Many of the recipients are now distributing them by various means to their friends and email lists. It seems the time has now come to collect these devotionals into a book, making them available to the public.

This author will assume that all readers of this book are already wise and discerning, but that none of us are "all-wise." Therefore, it is a logical conclusion that all of us continually need the "learning" and the "guidance" provided in the Book of Proverbs. These devotionals will not attempt to provide any new contributions to wisdom and guidance per se, but rather to help us focus on that, provided in the holy text. Any references to personal experiences and insights are simply intended to help us understand and apply the teachings of the ancient text in our current life-situations.

The materials included in the pages that follow, were written over a period of several years in different contexts. Nevertheless, since these devotionals have proved to be a help and encouragement to many through the years, it is the prayer of this author that they will continue to serve as a help and encouragement to readers in this present format.

"All Scripture is God-breathed and is useful for teaching, rebuking, correction and training in righteousness so that the man (or woman) may be thoroughly equipped for every good work." 2 Timothy 3:16-27.

Introduction
For Pastor Harry Heinrichs Book

"Getting wisdom is the wisest thing to do." That's the advice Proverbs 4:7 offers in the *New Living Translation*. The entire book abounds with such helpful gems, as one might expect since its stated purpose is "to teach people wisdom" (Prov. 1:2). Most of us run short of wisdom no matter how bright or learned we may be. The chief reason for our lack is that regard, according to Proverbs, is that wisdom is God's gift to us (Prov. 2:6) which we acquire as we "fear" (i.e., revere, trust, obey, submit to) the Lord (Prov. 9:10).

The Book of Proverbs is accordingly worthy of being read, studied, and applied. My friend and colleague Pastor Harry Heinrichs, has provided an enlightening and practical tool in this handy volume of devotional meditations to extract and enjoy its God breathed treasures. *"May Proverbs to Live By"* be just that in your walk with God and trek through life; pithy pointers from God Himself on how on how to cope and, beyond that on how to conquer! Yes, "seek His will in all you do, and He will show you which path to take." (Prove. 3:6).

In His tender grip,

Dr. William G. Bjork
Grace Bible Church
19280 N. 99th Avenue
Sun City, AZ 85373-1401

As we begin our devotional studies in Proverbs, let us note that the purpose of the book is given in chapter 1:2-6. It is for attaining wisdom and discipline, for understanding words of insight, and to acquire a disciplined life. In other words, by reading and heeding, our behavior will change for the better; we will gain wisdom and self-control, or discipline. Let me suggest that you read the whole book of Proverbs. It has 31 chapters. That is one chapter a day for a month. We will pick out individual verses to focus on for each day. By the grace of God, may this produce wise behavior in our everyday living.

"The fear of the Lord is the beginning of knowledge, but fools despise wisdom and discipline." The word knowledge here is not an accumulation of facts, but rather it is a life-changing knowledge. This knowledge is obtained through "the fear of the Lord," but what exactly is this fear of the Lord? How about this? It is a reverential respect for God that leads to trust and obedience. You probably had the reverence and respect, and maybe awe, in your thinking already. So did I. But how do we score in the obedience part of it? If we, like some, take the attitude that says I know I'm saved and going to heaven even if I ignore this prompting, then we have much too low a view of God.

None of us obey perfectly at all times, but when our attitude toward obedience becomes lax, then we are the biggest losers. We may indeed still know Him as Savior, but lacking "the fear of the Lord", and we really do not know Him as <u>Lord</u>. To acknowledge Him as Lord is to yield the control of our lives to Him. According to our text, the relational aspect of the Christian life begins here. Without that, this Scripture would class us as fools.

Have a year of growing in wisdom and knowledge!

*"**Let the wise listen and add to their learning, and let the discerning get guidance.**"*

I don't know if by a strict definition of the words in verse five, this would truly qualify as a "proverb," but its teaching definitely qualifies as fodder for a devotional on wisdom. In its broadest sense of course, all information can add to our learning. I believe Solomon is applying it specifically to reading the Proverbs. Very often specific proverbs will prove more helpful to some people than to others, but the verse is given to all listeners. We are not instructed to listen only to "wise" people; there is wisdom in the listening itself. When I took classes in learning to listen, their immediate purpose was to add to sales ability. However, I discovered very quickly their value applied to life in general, and to ministry in particular. The Apostle James said in 1:19: ***Everyone should be quick to listen, slow to speak and slow to become angry.***

The last half of the verse speaks to what happens after listening. For the wise, they will be discerning, and the result will be guidance. Since not every speaker we listen to is wise, and since even the ones who are wise are not infallible, the listeners—you and I, need to be discerning. When we discern an error in what is being said, we are not automatically "ordained" to correct the speaker or the error. Correction may at times be in order, but our text instructs us to get guidance from what we have just heard. It may be guidance in what <u>not</u> to do, or in the <u>way</u> to do or not do something or other. The point is, wise people will listen and add to their learning, and they will discern and get guidance from what they have heard. Furthermore, listening, learning and getting guidance will make us wiser still.

"The fear of the Lord is the beginning of knowledge, but fools despise wisdom and discipline."

Knowledge is essential to wisdom, but knowledge alone does not constitute wisdom. So, the verse continues: "fools despise wisdom and discipline." These fools may indeed have knowledge and by some even thought to be wise. Knowledge alone might help one win at Jeopardy but not at successful living. Obviously then, there can be an academic knowledge of truth which, unapplied, does not contribute to wisdom. Therefore Proverbs 9:10, "The fear of the Lord is the beginning of wisdom, and knowledge of the Holy One, is understanding," can serve as a commentary on 1:7.

I suspect that most true Christians are still pursuing a deeper knowledge of the Scriptures, as we all should be. Let's just make sure we apply that knowledge to daily living and to a more intimate knowledge of the Lord Himself. Our text says the fear of the Lord is the beginning of knowledge; other Scriptures say the fear of the Lord is the beginning of wisdom, see Psalm 111:10 and Proverbs 9:10. Obviously then, the two are closely related and in some contexts may be almost identical. Since the "fear of the Lord" is critical to both, let's examine that phrase. Often this fear has been defined as "awe, reverence, and worship or praise." I would like to insert the word "trust" as well. "When I am afraid, I will trust" says Psalm 56:3. Fear of anything else is mitigated by trust in God. Fear of God then, would mean wanting to please and obey Him at all costs, because He loves us.

God so loved the world that He gave Jesus to redeem us. Having received Jesus as Savior and Lord, all our sins are forgiven. So, let's get to know Him better through the teaching of His Word.

"Listen, my son, to your father's instruction and do not forsake your mother's teaching. They will be a garland to grace your head and a chain to adorn your neck."

The whole book of Proverbs seems to assume a family structure as God originally designed it, such that the parents will properly teach their children in the ways of righteousness. However, back then as today, this was not always the case.

At first glance, this Scripture is directed to children who are beginning to question their parent's omniscience; those who are learning to make their own decisions and to find their own way in life (teen agers?). For many this could now be the grandchildren, and their own children would be the ones providing the instructions. Unfortunately, even the wisest and most godly parents make mistakes in judgment. We see that both in Scripture and in personal experience. The truth however, does not change regardless of age or current culture. God's principles are eternal.

For children of any age, do not forsake the values and the godly principles your parents are, and have been, seeking to cultivate in you. They have made some mistakes in details or specifics, and those are not worthy of much attention. For parents and grandparents, the teaching continues. Corrections and discipline definitely come to an end at some point, and to try to continue these practices, becomes interference and is counterproductive. The teaching then is restricted to a demonstration of their own values and godliness. Actual advice can be carefully given—only when asked for.

The reward in this life for both those giving and receiving such instructions, is a "garland of grace on your head and an ornamental chain around your neck." The eternal reward is still future for all who are reading this page.

Proverbs 1:10

"My son, if sinners entice you, do not give in to them."

Actually, to get the context for this verse we need to read vss. 11-16 as well. Unless there is a principle here that goes deeper than the surface, this section might not have much relevance for most of us. And yet, in recent years the so-called "demonstrations" in America which have turned violent have followed that exact path. Nor has this violence been restricted to the foolishness of youth. These events were well planned and funded by an older segment of society. But who among us would tend to yield to invitations like those in this section? Well, let's look for the broader principle.

Where do enticements to any kind of sin come from? Since God cannot be tempted by sin and He does not tempt anyone, James 1: 14 says "each one is tempted when, by his own evil desires, he is dragged away and enticed." And where do those enticements come from? I'm glad you asked. James answers that as well in the very next verse. Any given desire may or may not be intrinsically evil, but "after desire has conceived, (after the desire has dragged you away) it gives birth to sin." Desire for some material objects may be quite legitimate, but if you cannot afford it, or if you just don't have the Lord's peace about the matter, and you let desire entice you over your "better judgment," your desire has conceived. In matters of thoughts and actions it may become much more subtle than related to material objects. After all, no one else knows your thoughts, and your actions can be camouflaged. James says when desire has conceived it give birth to sin.

In the Living paraphrase Proverbs 4:23 reads, "guard your affections." I'd like to say: also guard your desires. Don't let them entice you.

Proverbs 1:19

"Such is the end of all who go after ill-gotten gain; it takes away the lives of those who get it."

If your Bible has section divisions and headings, it possibly shows verses 8-19 as one section and a heading such as exhortations to wisdom with a sub-title to warn against enticement. Such divisions are not necessarily inspired by the Holy Spirit, but can be helpful to the reader. My NIV makes these verses one division and as such, verse 19 can serve as kind of a summary for the section, a "raison d'etre," if you like.

God never gives a prohibition for the purpose of "cramping our style;" it is always given for our benefit. In the section just ahead of our text, we have a vivid picture of self-destruction. The plans laid out by sinners who want to entice us would all appear—on the surface, to get us what we want. In verse 13 the plan is to get "all sorts of valuable things." Come join us, they say, and share in the profits. Of course, we may not like the idea of lying "in wait for someone's blood" in order to get it, but hey, there may be some less violent way to get it. Maybe for some there really is a non-violent, even legal way of obtaining what does not honorably belong to us. Verse 10 says don't do it. Not even if there is no likelihood of ever getting caught. To do so would be to fight against your own best interests. You will end up in a trap you have laid for yourself. You cannot get away from yourself.

Verses 17-18 show how schemes to get from others what you want to have, really just entangle yourself. Our text simply shows that **all** who go after ill-gotten gain will end up in trouble. No one can get away with it. To those who think they can or may even have gotten away with it, just remember that God is in control. He will see that justice is done and that righteousness will prevail.

Proverbs 1:20 – 21

'Wisdom calls out in the street, she raises her voice in the public squares; at the head of the noisy streets she cries out, in the gateways of the city she makes her speech."

Some of us might want to obtain great wisdom with the snap of a finger. It just does not work that way. Wisdom begins with a "fear of the Lord" and grows or matures with an increasing fear and knowledge of God. But our text says wisdom is calling out to us, and can be heard even in the din of busy, noisy living. How so?

Well, for one thing, wisdom is not learned or achieved by reading a textbook or attending a class. James 1:5-6 would tell us that we must first of all recognize a personal lack of, and need for wisdom. Then we must ask God for it and He will give it generously and without criticism, but we must ask in faith. But many could say "I have asked, and He still has not given me any wisdom at all, let alone giving it generously." And what is all this about wisdom calling out in the street and city square? Good question!

We can expect to learn wisdom at every juncture of life; it is there and available. We learn to recognize wisdom gradually as we follow the Lord in obedience. In his book **In His Steps,** Charles Sheldon urged his readers (and his congregation) to ask "What would Jesus do?" prior to taking any action. That's the easy part. After that comes a determination and a commitment to proceed to obey what He tells you.

The fear of the Lord, which is the beginning of wisdom, consists of awe, reverence, worship, praise and trust. The fear of the Lord is simultaneously a growing love relationship with the One who took your place at Calvary.

"If you had responded to my rebuke, I would have poured out my heart to you and made my thoughts known to you."

I would encourage you to read the rest of chapter 1 before you proceed from here. But remember, this is not God talking about your salvation or about answering prayer; this is wisdom warning you against rejecting wisdom.

Wisdom is calling to us all the time, wanting us to notice and pay attention, vs. 20. For those who fail to heed, and that is all of us at one time or another, there can be dire consequences. Galatians 6:7 states unequivocally "a man reaps what he sows". Therefore, before venturing into an unknown situation we need to ask for, listen for, and seek for wisdom. Our text assures us that wisdom wants to, and longs for opportunity to, "pour out (its) heart to you." Wisdom wants to make its thoughts known to you. Jeremiah 33:3 reads *"Call to me and I will answer you and tell you great and unsearchable things you do not know."* Certainly, that includes wisdom, guidance and direction. The promise in Philippians 4:19 is God **will** supply.

Notice our text says "if you would have" responded . . . That means that since you did not, you brought the consequences on yourself. Wisdom wanted to spare you the embarrassment, the cost, the pain, or whatever else the consequences of a particular unwise action are. You cannot blame anyone but yourself. On the flip side, all the blessings and promises of God apply to those who wait to find wisdom's direction. So, if we are at the place of having made the error, and we then heed the rebuke, God's grace covers the mistake and "wisdom" will again make its thoughts known to you. Hallelujah!

Proverbs 1:32-33

"The waywardness of the simple will kill them, and the complacency of fools will destroy them; but whoever listens to me will live in safety and be at ease without fear of harm."

These verses summarize this section of warnings. Much of 22 through 32 is negative because these are warnings. They focus on the foolish and their ways, and the consequences thereof. To paraphrase just some of it, "how long will you remain foolish, how long will you delight in mockery and hate knowledge? If you had responded I (wisdom) would have told you what to do, told you the best way to do it etc. But since you rejected me . . . I will laugh at your disaster."

Why are some people seemingly "hell-bent" on pursuing evil and serving self, while others are pursuing personal holiness and righteous living? Let's take a look. Have you ever noticed how we often refer to someone who insists on doing something the wrong way? We say something like "You are way out in left field," and we respond to others with "Right on!" It is a heart issue. The song writer asks "Is your heart right with God?" It is sin that has changed our direction. The Old Testament recognized frequently, but Ecclesiastes 10:2 says it in plain language. "The heart of the wise turns to the **right**, but the heart of the fool turns to the **left**." The Bible talks about God's righteous right hand." The fear of the Lord is the beginning of wisdom, so those who pursue a wisdom deeper than their own can be called wise, even though they have not yet fully achieved. Therefore, "whoever listens to me (wisdom) will live in safety and be at ease, without fear of harm." To turn right is to turn toward God, and to turn left is to turn away from God. So, whenever any of us turn left, it is time to repent and turn right for grace and mercy.

Proverbs 2:1-5

"My son, if you accept my words and store up my commands within you, . . . then you will understand the fear of the Lord and find the knowledge of God."

Whereas chapter 1 gave us the warnings against rejecting wisdom, this section gives us the benefits of wisdom and its pursuit. Here we have phrases like "turning your ear to wisdom, applying your heart to understanding, search for its hidden treasure." This absolutely implies effort and determination on our part. Yes, James 1:5 says if we lack wisdom we have but to ask, and that it true—that is the beginning point. But God will not then generously pour out His wisdom without any participation on our part. He told Joshua Do not let this book of the Law depart, but meditate on it "day and night." It was only on that condition that he was promised success.

You would do well to read all five verses today; not just the two quoted above. All of the first four verses are the conditions upon which we can claim the promises that follow. If we meet those conditions, **_THEN_** we will understand the fear of the Lord. It seems to me that until we fully meet the conditions, we will not fully understand. And it is only in meeting these conditions that we will "find the knowledge of God." So, it is a process. The Apostle Paul told the Corinthians that now we only "know in part, but then I shall know fully." In other words, again we are in process—in every area of our Christian life! When it comes to understanding the fear of the Lord, and finding the knowledge of God, we can expect to advance and grow in direct proportion to meeting the conditions laid out in our text. Without any selfish pride or super-spirituality, we can objectively determine whether or not we are making progress. We can and should get to know the Lord better as time goes by. To do so is wisdom.

Proverbs 2:6-7

"For the Lord gives wisdom, and from his mouth come knowledge and understanding, He holds victory in store for the upright, he is a shield to those whose walk is blameless."

This text begins with "The Lord gives wisdom." We knew that already, but the verse continues with "from His mouth come knowledge and understanding." I dare say none of us have ever heard "words from His mouth" in the way that Moses heard them at the burning bush. For us then, this means that we get His words from the written Word. Have you ever read the entire Bible? It is all His Word. The knowledge and understanding in this verse refer primarily, I believe, to know the word by reading, and understand it through meditation and prayer. He opens our understanding of the word and of Himself as we draw near to Him.

He, the LORD, holds victory in store for the upright. Any time we can choose between victory and defeat in any area of our lives, we would naturally choose victory. So, what does it mean to be "upright"? It does not mean those who are perfectly sinless; rather, it refers to those who walk in integrity. It means when we stumble and fall, we quickly repent, confess and return. The very sin that just tripped you up, is now turned into a victory. Furthermore, he is a shield to those whose walk is as just described. That is to say, He is our Protector and our ongoing protection. He guards the course and protects the way of his faithful ones. Remember what Jesus said to Peter in Luke 22? He said "Satan has asked to sift you like wheat, but I have prayed for you." That is true for you and me as well. Think of it, Jesus is praying for you and for me.

"The name of the Lord is a strong tower; the righteous run to it and are safe." You know what? I think Jesus loves you. In fact, I know He does; and me too.

The LORD *"guards the course of the just and protects the way of his faithful ones."*

Verse 8 continues the thought of the previous verse. In our English translations it is even a continuation of the same sentence. So, let's take a closer look.

We are familiar with the idea of the Lord protecting us, although I don't believe we fully appreciate it. Nevertheless, it is true and in that we rejoice. We probably believe that means if we get into trouble or are in danger etc., He will protect us, and of course He does. He has done that countless times in the past, and we may marvel at His faithfulness. We have promises like Psalm 55:22 *"Cast your cares on the Lord and he will sustain you; he will never let the righteous fall."* To me though, this text adds another dimension. All His promises to never leave us are wonderful, and we can never depend on them too much. They are true. They are dependable. They will never fail us. But this text says that He guards our **course** and He protects the **way** of His faithful ones. We may travel a road that is relatively smooth, but we cannot see the dangers lurking in the shadows.

Here is an abbreviated story about a missionary who had to go into town every month. It was an overnight trip since there was no road. Coming out of the bank he noticed several men eyeing him, but went on to the place where he bedded down. It was an uneventful trip. The next month the same people were there and asked him about 16 the soldiers who had guarded him when they came to rob him. He told the experience to his home church on his next furlough, and the pastor asked those who had prayed for the missionary that day to stand. There were 16 who stood. God had sent his angels to guard the way of His faithful one. We may not always know it, but He guards **us**, our **course**, and protects us on our **way**.

Proverbs 2:9-10

Then you will understand what is right and just and fair—every good path. For wisdom will enter your heart, and knowledge will be pleasant to your soul.

Every once in a while, we may have one of those "aha!" moments. We may hear or read something, and it is almost like the last piece of a puzzle. It fits. Now we finally "get it." We understand. More often however, understanding probably comes to us more gradually. Our text says "then." So, when is "then?" When you begin to see the benefits of wisdom as presented in this section. Then you will finally understand . . . When we see that the Lord guards our course and protects our way, we will understand what is right and just and fair—every good path. We may have known about this before, but we really haven't experienced it; we haven't yet lived it, at least not consistently.

Let me suggest that in life, and especially in our spiritual life, we often know intellectually a lot more than we understand. Our text says **then** you will understand. Why "then?" The next verse answers that. "For (or because,) "wisdom will enter your heart." That is God's doing. "Then" also the knowledge will become "pleasant to your soul." "Then" is when we've been asking God for wisdom, James 1:5, and He is answering. He is answering because we are earnestly seeking. OK, but besides asking, how can we truly seek for wisdom? By getting to know the Giver of wisdom better. Wisdom is not the ultimate goal. It is a by-product of getting to know God. God Himself said "you will seek me and find me when you seek me with all your heart." Jeremiah 29:13.

An old A.B. Simpson song says "once it was the gift I sought, now the Giver own." The question then is: are we after the gift, or the Giver?

Proverbs 2:11

"Discretion will protect you and understanding will guard you."

Along with a heart in tune with God, verses 9-10, the writer now turns his attention in verse 11 to that which needs to accompany the heart, namely practical living.

Have you ever met someone whose heart seems to be right with God, but their speech seems "out of place" at times? They may say things that are not particularly wrong, but just inappropriate at the time. My Webster's dictionary defines discretion in part as: "ability to make responsible decisions" and judgment calls. This would include our speech, decisions and actions. Discretion and understanding are tied together in our text, with the promise that they will protect and guard us. I don't know about you, but I need protecting and guarding.

Lacking in discretion, or speaking indiscreetly, will very likely be offensive to someone. True, we may regret saying it later, but we cannot unsay what we have once said. We can apologize and confess and receive forgiveness, but if we are lacking discretion it will happen again and again, and we will reap the consequences. Probably we will lose friends. Certainly, we will lose opportunity to have our life be a light pointing to Jesus. Discretion, says God, will protect us. The way that understanding ties in here is that we need to understand what we are doing, and what the potential consequences are. Such understanding will guard us against repeating our folly. So, when praying for wisdom, we may also wish to, or need to pray for discretion and understanding.

Proverbs 2:12 (-19)

"Wisdom will save you from the ways of wicked men,
from men whose words are perverse, . . ."

These verses all belong together but we'll look at verse 12 only for now. Wisdom will save you it will keep you, it will protect you—not from wicked men, but from their ways. Since we are still sinful people, even after we are born-again, we will all continue to fall into some sin from time to time. This verse does not claim otherwise. As born-again children of God, "the blood of Jesus Christ, God's Son, purifies (**keeps on** purifying) us from all sin." (1 Jn. 1:7) These "wicked men" are not necessarily vile criminals, murderers, robbers, adulterers etc. but "their ways" and their "words are perverse." In the course of life, we will associate with some of them, do business with them and perhaps golf with them. Hopefully we will also befriend some of them. Wisdom however, will save us, keep us and protect us from adopting their ways.

The wickedness and perverseness of such people is primarily their godlessness. This can certainly *lead* to vile sinfulness, but may not necessarily always reflect such a lifestyle. They need not be anti-God at all; they may even go to church regularly. They have just never yielded the control of their lives to God through Jesus Christ. They are too self-sufficient. That is where the need for wisdom becomes evident. The first Psalm declares the blessedness of those who do not walk "in the counsel of the wicked." Now read the rest of the text.

Too much of modern Christianity focuses on cultural, if not political, correctness, and not enough on personal holiness. What is required here is wisdom; wisdom that comes only from God.

Proverbs 2:20-22

"Thus, you will walk in the ways of good men and keep to the paths of the righteous . . ."

These last verses of this section look at the other side of the coin. Not only will wisdom protect and guard you against the negative aspects of life, wisdom will also provide the positive benefits. We used to sing a song that said in part, "to shun the wrong and do the right; to live a pure and holy life, I want the Lord to have His way with me." 1 Corinthians 1:30 assures us that Christ Jesus "has become for us wisdom from God." So, wisdom will guide us into keeping company with "good people," and will also keep us on the paths of righteousness.

This of course is not to say that we should avoid keeping company with non-Christians. Absolutely not! "Red and yellow, black and white, all are precious in His sight." But Proverbs is not here talking about evangelism; it is talking about how to shun the wrong and do the right in our own lives. It is only when we walk in wisdom that we can honestly say, as my pastor is fond of saying, that "Jesus is my very best friend." It is only when Jesus is our very best friend that our lives will radiate the love of God to both fellow-Christians and to non-Christians.

From here, the next verse implies that walking in wisdom will also result in life being enjoyable, prosperous, meaningful fulfilling for us in the here and now. "The upright will live in the land and . . . remain in it." We will then be equipped to deal with and to handle difficulties and whatever else may come our way.

I guess we can conclude that it is wise to obtain wisdom.

Proverbs 3:1-2

"My son, do not forget my teaching, but keep my commands in your heat, for they will prolong your life many years and bring prosperity."

That is a reminder of Exodus 20:12 to "honor your father and mother, so that you may live long in the land the Lord your God is giving you." Initially this is a father giving advice specifically regarding his earlier teaching, which has a broader application to include us today. The teaching is a teaching of the truths of God in His word, and not so much academic teaching. It is a teaching of godly life principles and values.

The first verse admonishes us to remember these teachings and to keep them in our hearts. How often do we know and even remember, but yet fail to keep these commands in practice? Keeping them "in our hearts" is live by them; to do them. Jesus told the disciples in John 13:17 (ESV) "If you know these things, blessed are you if you do them." This is a reminder we cannot hear too often. Nor can we heed it too carefully.

The second verse goes on to show us the benefits of following this advice. First of all, as in the fifth commandment, "they will prolong your life many years." Even when we are quite ready for the Lord to come back, until He does, we still seek to avoid ending our life on earth. Life is precious. Then the second benefit is that following this advice will "bring you prosperity." Unfortunately, our culture has programmed us to think prosperity is always or only measured in financial terms. This is talking about having a prosperous life. Our life itself will be successful and satisfying, and will accomplish the purpose for which God gave it to us in the first place.

"Let love and faithfulness never leave you; bind them around your neck, write them on your heart. Then you will win favor and a good name in the sight of God and man."

It is interesting that though these verses were written 1,000 years before the New Testament, they teach the same truths. Galatians 5:22 teaches that love and faithfulness are part of the fruit of the Holy Spirit.

The first word to catch my attention is one that has been challenging me for a few years now, and it is the word "let." God has made us to be loving and faithful, but sin interrupted. However, that is still God's plan for us. The problem is we can no longer fulfill that purpose; we cannot make ourselves to be loving and faithful. However, by implication God is already in process of producing these graces in us. Our text says do not let them leave you. By itself, this text does not provide a full answer to the dilemma; it simply tells us to allow this to be the case. Let it, allow it, do not let it stop. However, it also points to our involvement in the process by giving us instructions as to our part. The words "bind them" and "write them" are instructive. What this text does not clearly provide is where to find this love and faithfulness to begin with.

Many Old Testament texts, especially in the Psalms, repeatedly tell us to Trust in the Lord, as does the New Testament. It is only since the Resurrection, however, that we can have both the Source and the enabling in the person of the Holy Spirit who is dwelling within us. He is the One producing the love and faithfulness, which we then need to allow Him, or let Him make functional in our lives. As we allow love and faithfulness to become a part of our lives, we get the blessing of favor with God and man.

Proverbs 3:5-6

"Trust in the Lord with all your heart and lean not on your own understanding; in all your ways acknowledge him, and he will make your paths straight."

These verses are perhaps the most memorized and quoted verses in all of Proverbs. Among Bible believing Christians, none would disagree with the truth of these verses. At the same time, none of us could claim to fully and completely practice these truths at all times.

What do these verses teach us? Certainly, we do trust in the Lord with all our hearts in regard to salvation. That's how our relationship with the Lord began. From there we have a tendency, like most infants to say "me do it myself." The proverbs therefore, are there to teach us practical truths for daily living.

How often do we earnestly pray about a circumstance or an issue and then proceed to figure out for ourselves what to do about it? This verse teaches us to "lean not on your own understanding." We are pre-programmed to lean on our own understanding, and we need to be re-programmed. This is not to say that we must abandon human understanding, but rather to acknowledge Him in "all your ways." Yes, we are involved in the whole process, but ours is not the final word. Often God has no intention of removing obstacles and difficulties; He wants to "guide us through them." As we follow Him, "he will make your paths straight."

To acknowledge Him in all the vicissitudes of life is to know Him so intimately that we expect Him and allow Him to take charge.

"Do not be wise in your own eyes; fear the Lord and shun evil. This will bring health to your body and nourishment to your bones."

I wonder if the Apostle Paul had his devotions in these verses the day he wrote Romans 12. In verse three he wrote "do not think of yourself more highly than you ought, but rather think of yourself with sober judgment." Some of us grew up in a culture where we were taught to denigrate ourselves. Perhaps that was seen as the solution to pride and self-exaltation. Wrong! Our text cautions against self-aggrandizement. To this 1 Corinthians 4:7 replies with "what do you have that you did not receive?" So that leaves no room for boasting, but the other extreme is self-deprecation. The balance, in my view, is given in the Romans passage above. The late Dr. L. E Maxwell used to say "it is the hardest thing in the world to keep balanced." That came to be known in college as Maxwell 1:1.

True wisdom is to "fear the Lord and shun evil." The wise person will be constantly impressed with who God is, resulting in worship. In full dependence on Him, he will shun evil and do good. This is the essence of spiritual health, and interestingly, this also leads to physical health. Elsewhere we read that a merry heart is good medicine. Ultimate and total health will be ours in glory, but in the meantime, according to our text, a right relationship with the Lord now contributes to health and well-being down here.

Proverbs 3:9

"Honor the Lord with your wealth, with the first-fruits of all your crops."

I used to include this Scripture in my teaching when I did financial seminars around the country. Normally, I would delete the coma after "wealth" and replace it with the word "and" to emphasize the two aspects of giving. Our wealth is the sum total of our accumulated assets, whereas the first-fruits speaks of our income. We can honor the Lord with our giving; from our income as well as the disposition of our estates—our accumulated wealth. However, to honor the Lord with wealth and income speaks to the totality of our "money management," not just the giving aspects.

There is a reason why the Bible speaks more about money than it does about heaven and hell. The reason is not God's concern with filling the coffers of churches and church related ministries. Our total money management reflects our personal relationship with the Lord. Financial advisers will talk about "financial freedom" as it relates to some mysterious "amount" of money. Biblically there can be no financial freedom until 100 percent of our money management is brought under the Lordship of Jesus Christ. Our money management reflects the degree to which we are surrendered to the Lordship of Jesus Christ.

The promised blessings of verse 10 cannot be bought with our giving; they reflect our living. These blessings come as a result of our faithfulness in honoring the Lord, not just with words but with life. Promises that say "when you give more to *our ministry*, God will give 30, 60 or 100 times more to you" are not God's promises. None of God's grace and mercy is for sale, but God does bless and expect our faithfulness. In fact, faithfulness "is required," 1 Corinthians 4:2.

Proverbs 3:10

"Then your barns will be filled to overflowing, and your vats will brim over with new wine."

In this section, verse 9 is the condition on which the promised result or consequence of verse 10 rests. The condition is not tithing, not even in the Old Testament economy. Rather, the condition is the Lordship of the LORD, and since money tends to present one of the most enticing temptations, teaching on the subject is required. The Lord does not **need** our wealth or the first-fruits of our earnings; we just need to give it. For our own benefit. Honoring the Lord by our giving will protect us from greed and from becoming too self-sufficient. Even if we could acquire the world's wealth (Mark 8:36), it would not matter where it counts. As I'm writing this, I just heard of a TV personality who is leaving a $24 million a year career to make more money elsewhere. I can neither judge nor give counsel, but I do know that riches for riches sake have no intrinsic value.

We do not need barns or wine vats for the promise of verse 10 to be fulfilled for us. The promise is that God will provide. He will provide abundantly when the heart condition of verse 9 is met. He will give us just as much wealth as He intends for us to have. Let me give you a simple exercise to test your own heart attitude toward money and honoring the Lord with it. Whether you tithe, or give offerings, or both, try making this declaration to the Lord in conjunction with each gift: "Lord, I acknowledge that all that I am and have is already yours, so along with this gift I now surrender my life and my possessions to You afresh. Please give me the needed wisdom and guidance to manage your assets, currently under my management, for your glory." This will apply to your spending, your saving and/or investing, and your giving in support of Kingdom work. Just try it for a while.

Proverbs 3:11-12

"My son, do not despise the Lord's discipline and do not resent his rebuke, because the Lord disciplines those he loves, as a father the son he delights in."

There is more to the Christian life than assurance of salvation and blessings. Our text brings to light an aspect of Christian living that we most generally want to avoid—unless it is applied to others who deserve it. Who of us wants to be disciplined? The writer of Hebrews had it right: "No discipline seems pleasant at the time, but painful." (Heb. 12:11). We didn't like it as children, and we don't like it now. Of course, as children we needed it and often deserved it. But is it any different now?

We have to keep in mind that the words discipline and punishment are not synonymous. The basic motive for each is different. The motive, the purpose of discipline is correction and training. The purpose of punishment is to demonstrate or teach consequences. When a man is sentenced to imprisonment it is considered a paying of debt to society.

The Lord's discipline may often be administered as punishment, but it is for the purpose of correcting and training. God told Solomon that if His people sinned, He would punish them with the rod, and later He called conquering nations "the rod of His wrath." But look back at the text to see whom the Lord disciplines: He *"disciplines those he loves."* So, the first thing to pay attention to when He administers discipline, painful or otherwise, is His love. So, don't resent it. But read on. He also rebukes, which, if heeded, may not involve painful punishment. Now let's skip ahead a few hundred pages to 2 Timothy 3:16 and see that all Scripture is given to correct and train the child of God. I have learned that it is one thing to want my own way, and quite another thing to insist on it.

Let's not resent the Lord's discipline; it is for our good.

PROVERBS TO LIVE BY

"Blessed is the man who finds wisdom, the man who gains understanding."

That verse may have a Proverbs address, but it is a beatitude similar to those in Matthew chapter 5. My dictionary says a beatitude is "a state of utmost bliss." Not bad. ***Blessed is the man who finds wisdom.*** Now let's put it all together.

If we do not despise or scorn or shun the Lord's discipline, we will gain wisdom. Great! That is precisely what we wanted in the first place. Now we have got what we wanted. Isn't that reward enough? Not in God's economy. Jesus said that the one who has, will be given more. The one who finds wisdom by receiving the Lord's discipline now has both the wisdom he was after, and has also has entered a "state of utmost bliss," courtesy of a loving heavenly Father. But the goodies keep piling up. According to our text, as we find wisdom, we also gain understanding. And tomorrow will be just like today, only better.

Now let's go back to our Hebrews text of yesterday and read on. "Later on, (discipline) produces a harvest of righteousness and peace for those who have been trained by it." In other words, God is not yet finished with me. We are still in process. If you are like me, you sometimes become impatient with your "slow spiritual progress," right? Cheer up. You are not making yourself more Christ-like, that is God's doing. You have the promise of Philippians 1:6: He who began a good work in you will carry it on to completion until the day of Jesus Christ. Hallelujah! God is making progress in our lives. We may not yet be what we're going to be, but we are no longer what we once were.

Proverbs 3:14-15

"Wisdom is more profitable than silver and yields better returns than gold. She is more precious than rubies; nothing you desire can compare with her."

Again, as at other times in Proverbs, wisdom is seen as a lady. A gorgeously beautiful, and most desirable lady. You may have heard people say they know money cannot buy happiness, but they would like to have just enough of it to prove it. In fact, it would be fair to say that most people strongly desire material wealth. Our text does not argue that, but points out that wisdom is more desirable than silver, fine gold and jewels. There is nothing wrong with having enough money to be able to buy the jewels, but keep in mind that silver and gold, and any other forms of wealth, fades into insignificance when compared to God-given wisdom. It is none of my business how you might answer, but I'll ask the question. How would you compare the amount of time and effort you spend pursuing wisdom as opposed to pursuing wealth? Just asking!

The patriarch, Job, has some very interesting and enlightening things to say about wisdom. In fact, it would be worth your while to read Job 28:12ff. In verse 23 he says "God understands the way to it (wisdom), God . . . alone knows where it dwells." By human effort, man is able to accumulate wealth providing he also has the God-given abilities required. Faithfulness comes into play here as well. However, man cannot obtain true wisdom by any human means; education, yes, but not wisdom.

Now note the last phrase of our text: "nothing you desire compares with her." Nothing! Nothing in human relationships, nothing in human comforts, nothing in possessions, absolutely nothing in all creation can compare with wisdom.

And nothing can separate us from the love of God.

Proverbs 3:16-18

"Long life is in her right hand; in her left hand are riches and honor. Her ways are pleasant ways, and all her paths are peace. She is a tree of life to those who embrace her; those who lay hold of her will be blessed."

True, nothing is as valuable as wisdom, but other things too have value. Nothing you desire compares with her, but wisdom itself will bring you some of these other valuable gifts as well. The first of these is long life. The fifth commandment says honor your father and mother, so that you may live long in the land. So, it is wise to honor our parents, and that is confirmed in this Proverb. The next valuable gift listed here is riches, and with that also comes honor. The previous verses do not seek to denigrate riches and honor; only to exalt wisdom. And it keeps getting better. Now we learn that wisdom's ways are pleasant. To some of you this may seem an oxymoron, but the ways of wisdom are more pleasant than a good game of golf. In fact, wisdom will make the game more pleasant. Then all wisdom's ways are peace. So, when we don't experience pleasant ways and peace, we must be lacking wisdom. All but two of the New Testament books speak of peace; Jesus often used it as a greeting, but at the same time He bestows peace. In fact, Jesus, the personification of peace, says "my peace I give you." Wisdom is also a tree of life to those who embrace her, and finally, those who lay hold of wisdom will be blessed.

If Webster's definition of "blessed" is correct, then to gain wisdom is to enter into a state of "utmost bliss." These verses are absolutely profound. Most of us would be hesitant to claim great wisdom, and that's OK. Just know this; as we gain in wisdom we will proportionately gain in the blessings of wisdom's gifts and bliss.

Proverbs 3:19-20

"By wisdom the Lord laid out the earth's foundations, by understanding he set the heavens in place; by his knowledge the deeps were divided, and the clouds let drop the dew."

After a glimpse in verses 17-18 at the benefits of wisdom to humans, the author now turns to look at what wisdom does/did to the Lord, or rather what the Lord did by wisdom. The text says He laid the earth's foundations. The earth is sphere, floating through space, does it have a foundation? If it does, then do all the planetary objects also have foundations? It would seem that way. He set the heavens in place. But it is not the kind of foundation we use when placing a building on the earth so it won't move.

Some translations say "by wisdom He **founded** the earth," but that still suggests some kind of an anchor to keep it on course. Earth travels one orbit around the sun annually, (about 584 million miles) and each of the planets throughout the universe has its own specific orbit. What keeps everything from becoming a chaotic, incoherent mess? How about this; they are all anchored, or have their foundations on His wisdom, knowledge and understanding. If so, they were not only set in place by His wisdom, they are held, kept, and sustained in place by, in, and on His wisdom.

Now, coming back to earth for a while, verse 20 tells us "by His knowledge the deeps were divided." Does that mean the Atlantic and Pacific oceans were divided? I don't know, but in Genesis 10:25 we read that in the time of Peleg the earth was divided. Could the Proverbs text and the one in Genesis be referring to the same event?

It doesn't really matter. What does matter is that the all wise, omnipotent God of the universe is in control. And He can take care of any little (or big) issue in your life today, and all year.

Proverbs 3:21-22

*"My son, preserve sound judgment and discernment,
do not let them out of your sight; they will be life for
you, an ornament to grace your neck."*

In this section we are exhorted to be diligent in pursuing wisdom. Obviously, we will not attain to the level of wisdom displayed in the previous verses. God has and is absolute wisdom, and is therefore the source of all the wisdom we may aspire to. What is more, that wisdom is available to us. Remember James 1:5: "if any of you lacks wisdom, he should ask God." Simple, yet profound!

But look at the opening words of our text; *preserve* sound judgment. It is not so much a matter of how much wisdom you have, as it is to preserve what you do have. Remember it; maintain it; use it; don't let it out of your sight. When you encounter a situation, whether it is new or a repeat, what wisdom did God give you then, and how did you receive it? So, how does it apply here and now? What God has already given you is yours, so take it and put it to work for you today.

In Romans 8:24 the question is "Who hopes for what he already has?" With that same logic, who asks for wisdom that he already has? Don't let the wisdom you have out of your sight; you never know when you're going to need it. It is too easy to hide behind a screen of false humility which says "I'm not that smart, I don't have that kind of wisdom" etc. So now look back at James 1:5. If you lack wisdom, ask God; if you have wisdom, use it. That, I believe is the thrust of verse 20. Sound judgment and discernment will be life for you; it will be an ornament of grace.

Use boldly for His glory the wisdom God has given you, and it will increase. So will be fulfilled the words of Jesus: to him who has more will be given. It will continue to grow and increase.

Proverbs 3:23-25

"Then you will go on your way in safety, and your foot will not stumble; when you lie down, you will not be afraid; when you lie down, your sleep will be sweet. Have no fear of sudden disaster or the ruin that overtakes the wicked.

For those who heed wisdom's advice, these are powerful and precious promises. First there is promise of safety. That of course is not just a daily but a constant need for everyone. Since the wisdom taught in Proverbs is for ordinary, everyday living, that is its first application. Wisdom will enable you to recognize potential physical danger. Wisdom will also enable us to recognize spiritual and relational dangers. Many times, wisdom will enable us to avoid temptations to sin, and if we do sin, wisdom will help us to recognize it before we become enslaved. Also, wisdom can help us keep our mouth shut so as not to endanger a relationship, and sometimes to avoid a potentially bad relationship.

At times we all have to go through difficult and unpleasant experiences where wisdom will keep us from stumbling. Perhaps the real need here is "focus," and wisdom will provide that.

Then there is the matter of unfounded and pervasive fear. Fear of the dark and the unknown is not only a children's lot, nor is it restricted to women among adults. Who among us is as brave as military-aged young men? This section of Scripture is addressed to "my son," presumably a virile young man going out on his own into the world. Such young men, and all of us, can lie down unafraid, sleep peacefully, having no fear of sudden disaster or the ruin that overtakes the wicked, but it takes the confidence found only in the Lord. And it takes wisdom, it takes divine wisdom, to experience and enjoy the peace and security to be found only in the Rock of our salvation, and to keep our confidence in Him.

Proverbs 3:27-28

"Do not withhold good from those who deserve it, when it is in your power to act. Do not say to your neighbor 'come back later; I'll give it tomorrow' when you now have it with you."

We all know we should not do bad/evil things. The Bible gives sufficient teaching on that so it is always clear—not that we "always" refrain from doing bad, but at least we know we should. Perhaps Scripture speaks a little less frequently to the matter of failing to do good. James may have had his devotions in Proverbs 3 the day he wrote: "Anyone, then, who knows the good he ought to do and doesn't do it, sins." James 4:17. These verses in Proverbs, written about 3000 years ago, speak to the sins of omission.

Verse 27 presents both sides of the coin: do not withhold good and do not feel overly compelled by a need. It is not always possible to do what needs to be done. The good here is generic. It does not differentiate between different kinds of good. If the person needs some physical assistance, giving money instead is inadequate, and just saying I'll pray for you is not a substitute. But this is not applied to every person in every encounter. It says to "those who deserve it." That means, if you have a moral obligation to help. Wisdom will frequently be your only guide here. There is no Bible verse that clarifies every detail of every situation. No one can give to every worthy cause, and no one can assist in every situation. Furthermore, it applies only when it is in your power to do something about it.

But verse 28 says in essence "don't put it off." A saying that was common in my Bible School days was "delayed obedience is disobedience." This verse would underscore that and we've probably all been guilty at some time or other. To simply say "I will pray about that" is good—if that is all that is required. It can also be an excuse to not do what is needed, even though one is able, or to be an excuse for disobedience. Heart attitude is often the real issue. Thinking through these verses has just clarified a matter for me. I hope it helps you as well.

Proverbs 3:29-30

"Do not plot harm against your neighbor, who lives trustfully near you. Do not accuse a man for no reason—when he has done you no harm."

In the previous two verses we had reference to sins of omission. Things we could have done and should have done but failed to do. In these two the issue is very much a matter of sins of commission. Do not do these things! But who would ever want to harm someone else, unless perhaps it were for some personal gain or advantage? How about anyone who has selfish tendencies? How about if someone were to start, or just pass on, an unsubstantiated rumor that would reflect poorly on the unsuspecting neighbor in order to make themselves appear in a better light? These kinds of things happen all too frequently, even among Christians. Certainly, a direct physical or even verbal assault would be seen as "doing a sin" but to do it secretly or by insinuation is just as much a sin of commission.

People sometimes say things like "I don't know if it is true, but I sure wouldn't put it past him/her." Have you ever said things similar to that? Have you heard others do it? Who actually benefits from such statements? Far as I can tell, the devil is the only one who gains. All of us lose. Any damage we do in tearing someone else down hurts us more than the victim. On the other hand, Jude verse 29 says "But you, dear friends, build yourselves up in your most holy faith." So, while these verses have a negative message, learning from them is a very positive thing. The way to build ourselves up, as Jude teaches, certainly includes building others up as well. *"Therefore, as we have opportunity, let us do good to people, especially to those who belong to the family of believers." Galatians 6:10.*

Proverbs 3:31-32

*"Do not envy a violent man or choose any of his ways
for the Lord detests a perverse man but takes the
upright man into his confidence."*

These verses give us the clear "command" in this section of Proverbs.
Do we need to be told "Do not envy a violent man."? We already
know that. That is the tenth commandment in Exodus 20. OK, the tenth
commandment is a general principle, it is theology, it is God's command;
but we still do it. I think Proverbs is slightly different, though in no way
contradictory. We tend to think of the commandments in a spiritual sense;
it is a sin to violate or disobey them. True. But without a period or even a
comma, verse 32 continues on to say "or choose any of his ways." So, we
may reason: I am not envying the person, but since he was so successful in
what he did, I'll just learn from his ways.

I was taught years ago that "successful people hang out with successful
people." There is a lot of truth to that, and maybe some wisdom as well.
High school kids are learning by observation that losers tend to hang out
with losers as well. "Birds of a feather . . .

Solomon is giving us practical wisdom when he says "or choose any
of his ways." Choosing one or more of his ways might indeed bring us
material increase or status or whatever we use to measure success. But at
what cost? What good is honor if we did not obtain it honorably? God
loves to bless His faithful children with many different gifts. Proverbs
10:22 seems to fit here; "The blessing of the Lord brings wealth, and he
adds no trouble to it."

When we have an honorable President, it would seem an honor to
be taken into his confidence. So, take a look at the next verse. "The Lord
detests a perverse man, but **takes the upright into his confidence.**"
WOAH!! He takes the upright into His confidence. That's us! We are
taken into His confidence. What would you not trade for that? Solomon
might have commented, "I'm just telling you how it is." You deal with it.

Proverbs 3:33-35

"The Lord's curse is on the house of the wicked, but he blesses the house of the righteousness. He mocks proud mockers but gives grace to the humble. The wise inherit honor but fools he holds up in shame."

In the immediate context here in Proverbs, the Lord's curse is on the house of the wicked, not so much *because* they are wicked, though that is true, but more because they are not wise. Similarly, His blessings on the righteous here is *because* they are wise. Obviously, the first step of true wisdom is to move into the family of God "by grace, through faith." Remember, we are dealing with wisdom or lack thereof as it relates to life as we live it here and now. Unwise (i.e. wicked) actions in this life will bring results in this life, as will wise actions. Eternity and heaven or hell is not in view here.

It is interesting to see the New Testament writers use Old Testament Scriptures to make their points. Probably Galatians 6:7 has these Proverbs verses in mind when it says "A man reaps what he sows." So too does James 4:6, which is an actual quote: "God opposes the proud but gives grace to the humble." Selfish pride is foolish, and we see this throughout Proverbs. God has so created and ordered the universe that there are natural consequences to what we say, think or do. So, if I drive through a red light and receive a ticket, God is not meting out vengeance on me; I am reaping the results of my action. God's grace to the humble is equally handed out as the natural harvest of our actions. God's grace, however, goes beyond the natural harvest to provide forgiveness and blessings and eternal rewards.

We need to take personal responsibility and blame neither God or the devil for our actions. The devil did not "make me do it," and God allowed me freedom to choose.

Hallelujah! What a Savior.

PROVERBS TO LIVE BY

Psalm 37:16

"Better the little that the righteous have than the wealth of many wicked."

Today's Proverb is found in the book of Psalms which, while it is not a book of proverbs, has some proverbs in it. Remember, proverbs are wise sayings.

First of all, this proverb is not suggesting that all the righteous are poor or have very limited wealth. Nor is it suggesting that to have wealth makes one less righteous. In no way is it suggesting that "poverty is next to godliness," as some have taught. The main point of the proverb is to say that even with very limited material resources, a righteous person is better off than the very wealthy who are "wicked," or unrighteous or foolish. It is saying that one poor man with God is better off than the combined wealth of **"many"** wicked. It is saying that for the Christ-follower, true wealth must not be measured in material assets.

The "many wicked" are not likely to be reading or heeding the Scriptures anyway, so this verse is for all of us who name the name of Christ. We need to ask ourselves wherein lies the true value of all that we have. What does our wealth do for us? What does it provide? Wealth provides power, and many people, both wise and unwise, both righteous and wicked, both godly and ungodly want it for the power it provides. The next verse provides some helpful insight. The power will be broken. Yes, the verse narrows it a little by saying "the power of the wicked," but it is the **power** that will be broken. If not before, that power will be broken at death.

We are studying the proverbs for the purpose of becoming wise in relation to life on earth, as well as for obtaining "a rich welcome" into our eternal home, so the wise, and those seeking to become more wise, need to pay more heed to our use of wealth than to our accumulation of wealth.

PROVERBS TO LIVE BY

Psalm 131:1-2

"I do not concern myself with great matters or things too wonderful for me. But I have stilled and quieted my soul like a weaned child."

When I read that, I see a toddler, about 2 or 3 years old who is within sight of his mother. Not a worry in the world. This child is able to get around on his own 2 feet and go exploring as long as mother is close by. This child is learning to express himself—to some extent. He has no idea where the next meal is coming from, but that's OK, mother takes care of that. At times there are other people around, and that may be interesting, but mother is the one that matters.

King David, many years older than the toddler, has a very similar attitude toward his Provider and Caretaker. "My heart is not proud," he says; "my eyes are not haughty." But wait a minute, he is king in an era and a culture where the king's word was absolute law and he was free to do anything and everything he wanted, and he is not proud? His eyes are not haughty? He is the only one in the whole country who lives in a palace. We tend to find the flimsiest reasons to be haughty and to think we are superior. What makes the difference? When David made his opening statement, he said **"O Lord."** He considered himself blessed, not better. When he wrote "I have stilled and quieted my soul," he is saying that it was/is a learning process. He learned to trust the Lord as implicitly as a weaned child trusts his mother. Not only is he not proud, he is not worried. And furthermore, even though he could not see beyond today, he knew that God can. So therefore, he had hope. He had strength for today and bright hope for tomorrow. And he calls on us, as the people of God, to put our hope in God as well. The more we can learn to become like a weaned child in our trusting, even while living as mature adults, the more we will become like Jesus.

Proverbs 4:1-2

*"Listen, my sons, to a father's instruction; pay attention
and gain understanding. I give you sound learning, so
do not forsake my teaching."*

Notice first of all that wisdom begins when children are given parental instruction and guidance. In these verses the words are <u>instruction,</u> <u>understanding</u>, <u>sound learning</u> and <u>teaching</u>. Most of us bemoan the corruption permeating our whole culture. Corruption is found in (both parties of) government, in education, in business, in entertainment in the media and (hold on to your seats) in churches. Many of us would point the accusing finger at one or two of these as the primary culprits. The Word of God does not.

I think our text reflects the teaching of Deuteronomy 4:9: "teach them to your children and to your children's children." The writer of Proverbs is passing on to his children what he learned from his own father, their grandfather. That is what is, and has been, missing in our culture for a long time. We, the people of God have not been properly teaching our children for several generations. So, where do we go for an answer? It can't come from the corrupt institutions. So, should we pray for God to raise up a great leader who can usher in a spiritual revival? We already have great preachers and institutions. The breakdown is further up the line. Our text tells us it is the fathers and grandfathers who must personally provide the "wise teaching."

In a welfare society, the populace wants others to pay the bills. In cultural Christianity we want others to have the revival, to do the works of righteousness. We expect others to do teaching and to instill the values. The answer is for you and me, the readers of this devotional, to genuinely return to God in repentance and to lead our families. Pastors have their place, and we have ours. It begins with the family. Ours.

Proverbs 4:3-5

"When I was a boy in my father's house, still tender, and an only child of my mother, he taught me and said 'lay hold of my words with all your heart; keep my commands and you will live. Get wisdom, get understanding, do not forget my words or swerve from them.'"

A few millennia after these verses were written, I was a boy in my father's house and still tender. He taught us children individually, he also taught all of us together and, particularly on Sundays, he also taught the neighborhood. He used the words of Scripture in his teaching and he also used his own words which often echoed the principles of Scripture. When I was very young, my father's own words were more understandable to me, and when I did not obey them, he had ways of improving my understanding.

All in all, I learned that if I would keep his commands, which were paraphrases of God's commands, I would live. At times I was not so sure I was going to live if I disobeyed, but I did. With more maturity I began to see how my father's teaching and discipline had trained me to heed my Heavenly Father's teaching and discipline. Not only did that contribute to my living into "old age," but I also have assurance of living in eternity. I'm sure many of my readers can relate to this, so the question is: How well have you and I passed this teaching and training on to our children and grandchildren?

Further questions would be: "How well are we <u>living</u> by the teaching of the Heavenly Father?" "How well are we <u>obeying</u> His commands now?" "How much wisdom have we attained to, by living according to His teaching and training and discipline?" How much?" I have also learned that wisdom is obeying out of love and worship, rather than obeying out of fear or threat of punishment.

Proverbs 4:6-7

"Do not forsake wisdom, and she will protect you; love her, and she will watch over you. Wisdom is supreme; therefore, get wisdom. Though it cost all you have get understanding."

The picture is still that of wisdom as a treasured bride. In that era and culture, a dowry had to be paid to obtain a bride/wife. Wisdom does not come for free nor does it come easily. True, James 1:5 says that when we recognize our need for wisdom, we have but to ask God for it, and He will give it generously—but at a cost. He gives it proportionately as we "trust and obey." From verse five forward, James teaches us wisdom. We must **learn** wisdom.

Once learned and acquired however, as with a bride, wisdom can be neglected to one's personal hurt and loss. This proverb gives both warning and promise. The warning is: don't forsake her—that is not wise, in fact that is stupid. The promise is: rather nurture and cultivate her and she will protect you; love her, and she will watch over you. In fact, if you truly love wisdom, you should constantly want more and more of her. The danger is that we have a tendency to slack off our pursuit of wisdom; we begin to coast, we become complacent or even careless.

Our text reminds us that wisdom is supreme. Don't reconsider the price of the dowry. "Though it cost you all you have," go for it. It is worth it. It will continue to be worth it. If indeed wisdom is supreme, and you have already acquired a measure of it, don't forsake or neglect it, and its dividends will increase exponentially. The "cost" is not measured in dollars and cents. At times the cost may be keeping our mouth shut when we wish to speak. The cost will include measuring our words and attitudes and actions, and keeping constant vigilance.

Proverbs 4:8-9

"Esteem her, [wisdom] *and she will exalt you; embrace her, and she will honor you. She will set a garland of grace on your head and present you with a crown of splendor."*

Isn't it interesting how we, in our humanness, often go after things backwards! This text promises exaltation, honor, a garland of grace and a crown of splendor, and these are all very admirable and desirable qualities. These are promised as benefits or results of wisdom. So, what do we often do? We simply go after the benefits, rather than the product. We go after honor instead of wisdom. We've all met people like that. It seems they just want to be seen and known for being something they are not. In fact, some of us probably meet someone like that whenever we look in a mirror. Maybe we all do. We want to be exalted; we want the honor; we want grace and splendor. But we are going about it backwards. I often think of the old A.B. Simpson song: *once I sought the blessing; now I seek the Lord.* (not an exact quote.)

Has it ever occurred to you that the pursuit of wisdom and the pursuit of God are very much intertwined? That is because wisdom comes from God. I see that more and more clearly all the time. The Moody Bible Commentary says of this text "one must seek wisdom, but when one finds it, one realizes that it was not because of the effort, but because it was a gift of God." That agrees, I believe, with the teaching of James: if any of you lacks wisdom, let him ask of God who gives generously." The acquisition of an education and knowledge are commendable. With God-given intellect we can learn, both in school and in life, but we cannot by personal effort convert knowledge into godly wisdom. It is a "God-thing." So, with all our getting, let's get wisdom.

"Listen, my son, accept what I say, and the years of your life will be many. I guide you in the way of wisdom and lead you along straight paths. When you walk, your steps will not be hampered; when you run, you will not stumble."

Let us note first of all that there are general promises and principles in Scripture that apply generally. The fifth commandment is not saying that every human on earth who honors his parents will live to old age; neither is that the promise of our text. Meeting the conditions of promises will, however, put one in a position to receive the fulfillment of the promise. An unconditional promise like Romans 10:9 is specific: whoever will "confess with your mouth 'Jesus is Lord' and believe in your heart that God raised him from the dead will be saved."

Benefits of following wise teaching include a longer life. To some perhaps, a smoother life would be more important than a longer one. OK, look at verses 11-12. The path of wisdom is generally straighter and smoother than a path of unwise and ungodly council. When we are making foolish decisions and choices, we bring much trouble and turmoil on ourselves. Decisions and actions have consequences, which sometimes take years to come to fruition, but they will come. The consequences of wisdom become evident both immediately and throughout life, and on into eternity.

A fundamentally wise decision is to turn the control of our lives over to the Lord Jesus Christ. Thereafter, allow the (then indwelling) Holy Spirit to guide and direct our daily affairs of life. The text says "when you walk, your steps will not be hampered and when you run you will not stumble." He will save us <u>from</u> many disastrous situations, and help us <u>through</u> all the difficulties that still arise.

Proverbs 4:14-15

"Do not set foot on the path of the wicked or walk in the way of evil men. Avoid it, do not travel on it; turn from it and go your way."

At first glance, this may seem to apply to young men and women, and it does. When Solomon wrote this to or for his sons, (4:1) they probably were in their teens and twenties. Grandparents can quite possibly think of one or more of their grandchildren for whom they are praying, asking God to keep them from such paths. Many of us are thankful to God that they are doing as well as they are. Yet we understand that they are never fully "out of danger." So, we dare not lighten up on our prayer concern. The warning of this text is very stern; do not set foot on that path! Do not walk in that way! It may not *look* dangerous, but it is. So, avoid it like you would the plague.

This warning is to "my sons," but it is by no means **only** for young people. Consider the author, Solomon. At the dedication of the Temple he was a man who sought after God, but we might seriously question the wisdom of some of his activities in later years. How many people have we known, or known about, who in their later years in fact did walk on the path of the wicked? How many have indeed "set foot" on that path, never intending to become one of them, but thinking it can't hurt to just go along with them as long as we do it in moderation.

The fact is, none of us are safe and secure while relying on our own good intentions and our past track record. We do not have it in ourselves to keep off every evil way. There are some paths "of the wicked" that have special appeal to specific people "our age," no matter what age that is. At every age, our only security is the Lord.

Proverbs 4:18-19

"The path of the righteous is like the first gleam of dawn, shining ever brighter till the full light of day. But the way of the wicked is like deep darkness; they do not know what makes them stumble."

This text concludes a comparison between two paths: that of light and darkness. Recently, when I went walking in the morning it was dark outside (except for street lights). Pretty soon however, the sky began to turn bright, and by the time I got home it was fairly light out. Even the street lights were going off. It kept on getting lighter and brighter as the sun rose till the full light of day.

That is the picture the writer of Proverbs is painting for us in these verses as it relates to the path of the righteous as opposed to the way of the wicked. Since Jesus IS the light, the more we learn to walk close to Him, keeping our eyes focused on Him, the brighter the path becomes. Things that we could not, as a new Christian, see clearly – if at all, become clearer the longer we walk with the Lord. Notice that the text does not refer to how long you have known the Lord. It makes no reference to *when* you came to a saving faith. It does not consider Christian parentage or regular church attendance. The path gets ever brighter as you walk the path of righteousness. By contrast, *"the way of the wicked is like deep darkness."*

A claim to being a Christian, or regular church attendance will not brighten the path automatically. It is a relational issue; it is a matter of a consistent walk with Him who is the light. "If we walk in the light as he is in the light" as 1 John 1:7 puts it, then the path will increasingly become brighter until the full light of eternal day. Let's keep walking.

42

Proverbs 4:20-21

"My son, pay attention to what I say; listen closely to my words. Do not let them out of your sight, keep them within your heart, for they are live to those who find them and health to a man's whole body."

In the early chapters of the book, Solomon keeps calling us to listen, to pay attention. Why does he keep repeating that call? Probably because of our failure to listen, or our short attention span and memory. It is too easy to hear words without listening to what they are saying. We hear without paying attention. In school a lack of attention is reflected in the grade; in life it is reflected in our living. When it comes to the Word of God, this is very serious business. How often have you read a passage of Scripture without really paying attention to what you are reading? Too often, I'm sure. But when you suddenly do see it, that is no time to berate yourself for past failure; rather that is the time to thank God and get busy becoming a doer of the word.

Our text calls us to not let such words "out of your sight." That tells me that when a truth of Scripture "jumps out at you," whether in your reading, or in a message, keep referring back to it until it until you know it. Really know it. But the text goes on and tells us to "keep these words in your heart." That means until they become an integral part of your very life. You just can't forget them because you are now living them.

If you forget how many miles the sun is from the earth, that's not too serious; you weren't going there anyway. But if we ever forget the word of God it is very serious, because His words "are life to those who find them."

Proverbs 4:23

"Above all else, guard your heart, for it is the wellspring of life."

This is an interesting statement. You could also read it as "you must guard your own heart." Yet Philippians 4:7 assures us that if we remain in contact with the Lord, verses 4-6, then "the peace of God, . . . will guard your hearts and your minds." So which is it? Philippians was written later and is New Testament, so is that It. However, the Old Testament is equally God's Word. How about they are both right, and they can be seen to be in agreement.

Let us notice first of all that the heart needs guarding. Have you recently, or ever carefully guarded your words and actions to keep from sinning? Me too. The Psalms frequently quote David as telling the Lord in his prayers that he had "determined not to sin with his lips". When that is true for us, that is good praying. Keep in mind that Jesus said out of the abundance, or overflow of the heart the mouth speaks. Matthew 2:34.

Now notice why this is important for everyday normal living. Even though this present life is a preparation ground for eternal living, the wisdom that Proverbs has us strive for is for time and space living. So, when it says your heart is the wellspring of life, it is talking the here and now. Eternity comes later. So, guarding your heart will enhance life here and now.

Remember that the word "heart" in scripture rarely refers to the blood pump, but rather the real person, beginning with motivation and attitude. When we adequately guard that, words and actions will pretty well take care of themselves. We teach young children "be careful little eyes what you see." For gown-ups we could say "be careful little mind what you think."

"Put away perversity from your mouth; keep corrupt talk far from your lips. Let your eyes look straight ahead, fix your gaze directly before you. Make level paths for your feet and take only ways that are firm. Do not swerve to the right or the left; keep your foot from evil."

Have you ever purchased an item where the package says "some assembly required?" That sounds like instructions that will be simple and easy to complete. I'm sure for some people that is true, for others, not so much. What we have in this text is something like that. These verses are the "how to" manual for the previous verse about guarding your heart. So read the verses again.

When Jesus said "apart from me you can do nothing" in John 15:5, I believe He included this Proverbs construct. None of us can do the assembly of this construct, let alone the operation of it, apart from the enabling and guidance of the indwelling Holy Spirit. Look at it line by line. Put away perversity—all perversity; keep corrupt talk far from your mouth. Look where you are heading. If we fail to do that in driving a car, it may quickly lead to disaster. In life it is even more disastrous, if not as quickly. Can you see where you are heading? We must fix our eyes on Jesus, Hebrews 12:2. Then, make level paths for your feet and take only ways that are firm. At first glance this might sound like "take the easy way out," but that is not the thought here. This is talking about taking the right way, the one (in New Testament lingo) where Jesus is leading. In one of her *Jesus Is Calling* devotionals, Sarah Young calls on us to follow Jesus, allowing Him "to direct your path," realizing that the path may in fact be rough and uphill at times. But it is safe. So do not swerve right or left so your foot will not slip into evil.

Proverbs 5:1-2

"My son, pay attention to my wisdom, listen well to my words of insight, that you may maintain discretion and your lips may preserve knowledge."

Both actions and inactions, both obedience and disobedience have consequences. When we combine paying attention and listening well, as in this text, we get to the point of what this Scripture is saying. This means we are beginning to both put into practice and understand what the communication is. We find in 2 Timothy 3:16 that all Scripture is given to change and transform our lives which is precisely what today's text is intending to do in one specific area of life. All of Proverbs chapter 5 is a warning against adultery.

The desired result of knowing and doing right will begin to take place. That result in this text is to "maintain discretion" and to "preserve knowledge." Discretion means to be able to make responsible decisions, and this, the father says to his son, comes from listening well to my words of wisdom. The word "responsible" indicates a serious consideration of the options before making the decision. Have you ever said to yourself, or others, "I hope I made the right decision?" Since we are all finite and make mistakes, the counter question to that would have to be "did you seriously consider the options and the consequences?"

The rest of the chapter shows some of the possible consequences of a wrong decision on this subject. We can easily extrapolate and see that in other areas of life and in facing different temptations there are likely to be equally devastating consequences. Adultery is not the "unpardonable sin" but it is a very costly one. But then again, there are no inconsequential sins. So, let's learn to pay attention and to listen well.

Proverbs 5:12-14

"You will say, How I hated discipline! How my heart spurned correction! I would not obey my teachers or listen to my instructors. I have come to the brink of utter ruin."

Such a projected consequence is correctly set in the context of the harvest of adultery. The previous verse indicates this to come "at the end of your life." It may of course also come earlier. Unfortunately, there are people in all walks of life, whether Christians or not, who have this to look forward to. The only remaining hope for all such people is in genuine repentance and confession, resulting in forgiveness by a gracious, loving, Heavenly Father.

My concern here is also for those who are not guilty of this particular sin. While details may well differ, similar results will apply equally for those who have spurned wisdom in other aspects of life. Those who spurn wisdom as a lifestyle will find in later years that certain forms of foolish selfishness fade into insignificance and lose their appeal. That may merely reflect biological changes that come with age.

The point is, in God's economy it is never too late to begin the pursuit of wisdom. There are human teachers and instructors who can help but above and beyond that, since "the fear of God is the beginning of wisdom," our real source for learning wisdom is the Word of God. Read it. And since Proverbs is a book of wisdom relating to every aspect of life, that is a good place to begin. Just a chapter a day gets one through the book in a month. Young people would do well to make this an ongoing practice all through high school and college. It is a truism that "sin will keep you from the Bible and the Bible will keep you from sin." That is true for children and seniors as well.

Proverbs 5:21

"A man's ways are in full view of the Lord, and he examines all his paths."

To the unregenerate, this should be a frightening thought; they just can't get away with anything. To the Christian it should be a delight and a comfort. The writer has just been warning against adultery, but here he assures us that God examines <u>all</u> our paths. So you have a day when the path is rough and difficult, and maybe discouraging. When have you last had such a day? But the whole way is in full view of the Lord. He sees. He knows. He cares. In fact, He "examines" is said strictly for our benefit. He does not need to examine for the purpose of trying to figure it out. He examines all our ways to ensure that nothing can be on your way that is beyond your endurance. So, does that encourage you? It should. If some other person or evil power is causing the problems, God has it all on record; He'll take care of it – in His own good time. In the meantime, He will not allow you to be tested, tempted or distraught beyond the capacity of your endurance. He will always "provide a way out so that you can stand up under it." (1Corinthians 19:13). And He will reward your and my faithfulness in availing ourselves of His provision.

Can you imagine what it would be like to go to the Lord at the end of the day and telling Him what went on, if He were then to say "No, really? How in the world did that happen? Somehow I sure didn't see that one coming." Thank God, all our ways are in full view of the Lord. He knows. He cares. He provides He and protects. While Job was going through his "intolerable" ordeal he told his friend, Eliphaz, that God "knows the way that I take {and} when he has tested me, I will come forth as gold." (Job 23:10) At times we may not *feel* that He is or will be sufficient, but we can *know* and be assured that He is sufficient and more than sufficient.

Our ways—yours and mine, are in full view of the Lord.

Praise the Lord!

Proverbs 6:1-5

"My son, if you have put up security for your neighbor,
If you have struck hands in pledge for another," . . .
then do this, *free yourself like a gazelle from the hand*
of the hunter, like a bird from the snare of the fowler."

What better way to teach wisdom than the "if-then" method, the method so often used in Proverbs. Much of education at all levels is merely a matter of passing on information, and that does provide "knowledge." Wisdom requires a level of understanding. Our text says "If you have done this, then here is what you need to do." That is information. But by the time we see the "what and why" of the consequences, we begin to understand. Wisdom is in figuring out how to obtain the desired outcome.

The Bible has much to say about money management, and today we have a very important principle to consider. Because it begins with a warning not to put up security for a neighbor or "another," many people have figured that is the only way this applies. Consequently, some people have done great harm to adult family members. Well-meaning parents sometimes provide for their adult children what they should provide for themselves. Often then the children become more and more dependent, and less and less responsible individuals. There needs to be a balance here. In 2 Thessalonians 3:10 we read that if a man will not work, he shall not eat, but 1Timothy 5:8 says "if anyone does not provide for . . . his immediate family . . . he is worse than an unbeliever." So, the issue really has less to do with actual money and more with teaching principles of money management. Why should anyone impoverish or endanger themselves for the benefit of someone, family or neighbor, who is unwilling to take care of themselves.

Talking to a wealthy businessman about his estate plan, he told me right up front "I do not want to make my children rich," so we talked about a plan to provide generously for ministries and leave his children love gifts. He had it right. He had taught his children to provide for their own needs.

Proverbs 6:6 (+7-11)

"Go to the ant you sluggard; consider its ways and be wise!"

Can the ant really teach us wisdom? OK, it can maybe teach us a little about diligence and planning ahead in relation to work and earning a living etc., but what about wisdom for daily living? What about those who are no longer in the work force? What about life goals? What, if anything, can it teach about our spiritual life and our walk with the Lord? Well, thank you for asking.

First of all, it is not for the ant to teach us knowledge; most of us already know more than an ant, but wisdom, yes. So, what does the ant do that is wise enough for us to take notice? Well, the ant does not even know it is wise; it merely does what God made it to do. Think about that: the ant does what God made it to do. God has not given it the sense it would take to figure out it has to store up food.

God has given us both the intelligence to figure things out, and a freedom of choice to go with it. I don't know why God created ants at all, nor, since He did, why He created them the way He did. But I do know why He created people. He created us for His pleasure; He created us to glorify Him; He created us to be objects of His love. He created us in order to have fellowship with Him, and with each other. Since He created us for fellowship, He also gave us the capacity to choose for or against. The ant does not have that capacity, so it merely does what it is made to do and thus it fulfills its purpose.

For us to be wise, we need to, like the ant, do what God made us to do. But the choice is ours. And because of sin we often choose unwisely to do things our way. What a shame!

PROVERBS TO LIVE BY

"A scoundrel and villain, who goes about with a corrupt mouth . . . always stirs up dissention."

In the Moody Bible Commentary this section is headed as "Warning concerning troublemakers." Unfortunately, we all know too many such troublemakers.

God places a high premium on unity. Psalm 133:1 says *"How good and pleasant it is when brothers live together in unity."* In John 17 Jesus prayed that we (as believers) might "be one, as we are one. . . May they be brought to complete unity." And why not? We are made in His image, we are redeemed and have been brought into His family, we have the Holy Spirit indwelling us. But such unity is a process. The words of Jesus are "may they be **brought**," (not transported) into complete unity. Jesus' prayer will be fully answered when we are brought into His presence, but in the meantime, we should be approaching that goal.

One problem we encounter along the way is the scoundrels and villains who are working dissension. They are not named but are at least partially described in these verses. They are the ones who use deceit and corrupt or deceitful speech to cause division and dissension. Their overt purpose may well be to simply get their own way, which they assume to be superior. But the result is disunity, division and dissension.

My concern with this proverb is not so much that we make sure we identify *them* so as not to be taken in by their deception, but rather that we take a good look in the mirror of Scripture to identify our personal selfishness. Each of us has enough selfishness left in us to actually be, or become, one of "them." By the grace of God and the help of the Holy Spirit, we can seek to become part of the answer to Jesus' prayer to "be brought to complete unity."

Proverbs 6:16-19

"There are six things the Lord hates, seven that are detestable to Him: haughty eyes, a lying tongue, hands that shed innocent blood, a heart that devises wicked schemes, feet that are quick to rush into evil, a false witness who pours out lies, and a man who stirs up dissension."

"There are seven things that are detestable to him," and going through the list we can readily see why, but what is there for us to learn? To some of those things, like murder, most of us can quickly plead not guilty— until we look at Jesus' definition of murder in Matthew 5:22. Jesus looked deeper than what law can do. According to Jesus, it is not only the "act" but the heart attitude that counts. In fact, the act is merely the outward expression of what is already in the heart. Jesus further said "The things that . . . come from the heart . . . make him unclean. For out of the heart come evil thoughts, murder," etc. Matthew 15:18-19. So yes, we have a lot to learn from our text.

Staying with the murder issue, of which few, if any of us are legally guilty, let's try to look at it from Jesus' point of view. The act of killing someone is against the law in Western culture, and it is sin; but it should not be in that order. It is sin regardless of civil law or culture. Jesus said it comes from the heart and that is where the sin is, whether it is carried out in a physical act or not. If it is not, it carries no jail or execution sentence, but we have already been judged and found guilty. So how can we deal with it? Confession, yes; asking forgiveness, also yes, BUT these must be accompanied by repentance. With the help of the Holy Spirit and by the grace of God we must repent and turn from the heart attitude to God. Repentance is turning from our own way to God. Now we also need to ask God to search our hearts concerning each of the items on that list. And we may need to do this often.

Proverbs 6:20-22

My son, keep your father's command and do not forsake your mother's teaching. Bind them upon your heart forever fasten them around your neck. When you walk, they will guide you; when you sleep, they will watch over you; when you awake, they will speak to you.

When Solomon did his devotions, he did not have the New Testament. In fact, the day he wrote these verses, he may well have had his devotions in Deuteronomy 6:6-9 where God told Israel to teach His commands to their children. So, when Solomon referred to his own commands to his son, and to his mother's teaching, he probably had specific reference to God's Word – not to his son's responsibility to take out the garbage or muck the cattle stall. It is God's Word we most need to heed, and children obeying their parents' specific duties around the house is really training for heeding God's commands in everyday living.

I like the admonition to bind them upon your heart and fasten them around your neck. Upon your heart refers not so much to memorization as it does to gaining an understanding of what it means. The Psalmist said *"I have hidden your word in my heart that I might not sin against you,"* 119:11. Just knowing the words and the reference does not keep one from sinning, but understanding the word might. Then fastening them around your neck indicates a plan for keeping yourself constantly reminded. For me, this is the part that includes memorization.

Then verse 22 gives us the purpose of such learning and constant awareness. For us to obtain constant guidance and protection in life's activities, we need to know and understand the commands of God and plan to be constantly reminded thereof. This speaks, I believe to our having fellowship with God. Most of us never hear God speak to us in an audible voice, but each of us can and should hear Him speak to us in His Word. This last verse speaks to us of a certain constancy; when you walk, when you sleep and when you awake.

Proverbs 6:23-24

"For these commands are a lamp, this teaching is a light, and the corrections of discipline are the way to life, keeping you from the immoral woman, from the smooth tongue of the wayward wife.

Chapter 6:20 through chapter 7 consists of warnings and teachings concerning adultery. If you read the whole section you can readily see that is indeed the teaching, and that is how it needs to be applied. However, the same principles apply equally to other areas of sin and temptation; lust points in more than one direction. Therefore, we need to look at the principles taught and the results of bad choices in other areas of life as well. The King James version summarizes all sin in three categories as: "the lust of the flesh, the lust of the eyes, and the pride of life" in 1 John 2:16.

The liberal media says murder is Ok if done to a pre-born baby and then rename it, and Hollywood says adultery is OK if it is by mutual consent. Human reason always seeks to justify its actions, but God says "all unrighteousness is sin," 1 John 5:17. If we think we can make murder or adultery or any other sin OK by simply renaming it, we are very unwise. And yet we all do it with our own favorite sins. Our text says "these (wise) commands are a lamp, this teaching is a light, and the corrections of discipline are the way of life." That is pretty much a paraphrase of Psalm 119:105.

1 Corinthians 11:31 tells us that if we "judged ourselves, we would not come under judgment." Let me bring that into our context: if we disciplined ourselves, we would not come under God's corrective discipline. We don't need to reap the harvest of unrighteousness if only we wisely avoid the unrighteousness in the first place. The key is in the Word of God.

Proverbs 7:1-3

"My son, keep my words and store up my commands within you. Keep my commands and you will live; guard my teachings as the apple of your eye. Bind them on your fingers; write them on the tablet of your heart."

These verses echo 6:20-22, so they are obviously worth repeating. But the question comes to mind, can we learn something beyond what we got from those verses in chapter six? Since it is God's word, we could not possibly have exhausted it last time, so we can safely expect to get a word from the Lord again this time.

In his 2nd letter Peter said: *"this is now my second letter to you. I have written both of them as reminders . . ."* I spent significant time in Psalm 119 this morning, and as you may have already noticed, practically every verse, out of 176, has direct reference to the word or the law of God. (Now that's repetition!) Verse 34 for instance, prays *"Give me understanding,* (that is wisdom) *and I will keep your law and obey it with all my heart."*

But we are in Proverbs. Why the repeated call to "my son, keep your father's commands"? I am reminded of the 6-year-old who, when asked to describe love, said "if you love someone you have to tell them often, because people forget." We simply need reminders. Every proverb in the book, every caution, every reminder is followed by a declaration of consequences of heeding and/or ignoring the wise advice.

OK, so you and I have that pretty well nailed down. (We do, don't we?) We know full well that obeying God's word keeps us from sin, and sin has consequences; we understand that. But how are we in consistently heeding God's instructions? Is God's word at our finger-tips as instructed in our text when someone cuts us off in traffic, or when someone deliberately infringes on our rights? How often do we think bad thoughts without using bad words? How often do we flirt with temptation because we just like to think about it, even though we are mentally committed to never follow through? Oh, we know we are "skating on thin ice," but at the time we think it'll hold us. *"Keep my words and you will live."*

55

Proverbs 7:4-5

"Say to wisdom, you are my sister, and call understanding your kinsman; they will keep you from the adulteress, from the wayward wife with her seductive words."

If you read the rest of the chapter you see a young man who was not necessarily looking for sin; he was just foolishly walking down the wrong street. Had he been thinking and talking wisdom and understanding, he would have turned the other way several streets earlier. Verse 7 says he "lacked judgment," he didn't figure it out. We do not need to be in the wrong part of town to demonstrate a lack of judgment. To foolishly and without proper judgment make a decision, or make a statement, or take an action, does not necessarily mean we are heading toward sin. It may simply mean that difficulties or unpleasant circumstances or even disaster will result. Wisdom is first for living this life, and then living it as preparation for the next life.

Verse four is written in Hebrew poetry when it says to call wisdom my sister and understanding my kinsman. That is not to differentiate between wisdom and understanding, ascribing one to the sister and the other to a kinsman. Here, wisdom and understanding are one and the same, and "sister" could also refer to wife. In that case, it would indicate that we should not seek to be wise in secret. Rather, it is attained and developed in close association with those who are near and dear to us. The ones who know us best will best be able to detect any false or assumed wisdom. To the extent that it is real, it will also become evident to those beyond our immediate circle of family and close friends. The remainder of chapter seven describes the consequences of poor judgment and a lack of true wisdom.

Still the fear of the Lord is the beginning of wisdom.

Psalm 50:15

"Call upon me in the day of trouble; I will deliver you, and you will honor me."

During the past few days wisdom has given us warnings and advice, and explaining the (sometimes dire) consequences of not heeding the warnings, but in spite of that, many of us have, either recently or not so recently, followed some unwise ways. For some the consequences were less serious than for others and for some the consequences continue. Today's Scripture is for all of us, whether we are in a quagmire or not. And, the promise is not given by *wisdom* speaking, but rather by the Source of all wisdom, by God Himself.

Asaph, the Psalmist, begins by pointing us to **"The Mighty One, the Lord, speaks and summons the earth"** (that is you and me). It is as if God is calling very personally and saying: "Hey George, hey Suzie, I know all about the trouble you are in. You failed to heed wisdom, you gave in to temptation, you tried to take a short-cut, you thought you knew best, you tried to figure it out on your own, you made the wrong choice, so now you are in trouble. I saw it coming and I tried to keep you from going that way, but you weren't listening. Now are you ready? OK then. Call upon me and I will deliver you. That's it. You call, I will answer. Simple as that! It is not too late. It is never too late to repent and turn to Me."

It is true that choices have consequences and we reap what we sow. But when God forgives, the guilt is gone. Psalm 32 is David's confession after sinning grievously. In verse 5 he says to God: You forgave the guilt of my sin. Ta Da! fellowship is restored. If certain "guilt feelings" remain, they are not the Lord's doing. You are free! Fellowship is restored! Guilt is gone!

And all we had to do was "Call." This honors God.

Proverbs 8:1-3

"Does not wisdom call out? Does not understanding raise her voice? On the heights along the way, where the paths meet, she takes her stand; beside the gates leading into the city, at the entrance, she cries aloud.

Several things jumped out at me: wisdom and understanding are trying to reach us—that is, God is trying to impart wisdom and understanding to us. He is placing them right in our path, and yet often we simply stumble over them or walk around them. Notice the effort to reach us: wisdom *"calls out, she raises her voice, she gets up on top of the heights"* so we just have to take note, *"she stands where the paths meet, beside the city gate, at the entrance she cries aloud."* Then to top all that off, James urges "if anyone lacks wisdom, let him ask." So, wisdom is not elusive, nor is it reserved for the select few. It is always within our reach.

I know Solomon wrote what he did under the inspiration of the Holy Spirit, but I don't think he had in mind only "spiritual" applications. He was talking daily living, not "having daily devotions." He was talking the wisdom and understanding that we need in day-to-day routines. So why do we miss it? Why do we lack wisdom? Let me suggest that when we lack wisdom, at least some of the time—and maybe most of the time, it is because we tend to make a distinction between the secular and the spiritual. The late Dr. Calvin B. Hanson used to say: "if Jesus Christ is Lord, then nothing is secular." I always admired Dr. Hanson, but at first, I could not see how changing the oil in your car could be "spiritual"? How can scrubbing the floor or cleaning the toilets be spiritual? Think about this: these things are neither spiritual nor secular. They are a part of living. But when Jesus Christ is my Lord, then I am spiritual, and that makes everything I do spiritual. How about that?

So, wisdom will enable us to live this, that we often call secular life, with greater joy and efficiency. At the same time, since under the Lordship of Jesus Christ this life is spiritual and is a preparation for eternity, wisdom will give us a better perspective on our sure-to-come trials and difficulties.

PROVERBS TO LIVE BY

Proverbs 8:4-5

"To you, O men, I call out; I raise my voice to all mankind. You who are simple, gain prudence; you who are foolish, gain understanding."

At this point it is no longer a father calling to his sons as in previous chapters. Here it is wisdom itself calling. When our children are under our care, it is our duty to instruct them and to seek to impart wisdom to them; once they've established their own homes and families, our role changes. Young people need to be exposed to, and learn the ways of, wisdom as found in the Word of God from their parents. Grandparents need to retain their concern for their children, and now also their grandchildren, but their teaching, their advice is now much more restricted to responding when requested. However, now more than ever it is the consistency of living and modeling that will provide wisdom and guidance.

Obviously, since we are human, none of us were perfect in our "telling." We certainly were not perfect living examples or models. That's what grace is for. But when our grandchildren see inconsistencies in us now that (they may think) we should have it all sorted out, they have our failures to add to their own struggles in trying to sort out the issues of life and wisdom. Again, God's grace is sufficient, but Oh, how they need to see consistency in us.

That is why in our text wisdom calls out "to all mankind." Often too much of our concern for young people is focused on "their music" or their dress or other expressions of youth. As we pray for our nations, we certainly need to include prayer for our youth. However, we need to pray, and do more than pray, to ensure that we—at whatever stage of life we are in, will "gain in understanding," and do a better job of modeling wisdom and godliness.

Proverbs 8:6-8

"Listen for I have worthy things to say; I open my lips to speak what is right. My mouth speaks what is true, for my lips detest wickedness. All the words of my mouth are just; none of them is crooked or perverse."

In the opening verses of this chapter, wisdom was trying to reach us; In this section wisdom is talking to us, so we had better listen. *To the discerning all of them* (the words of my mouth) *are right; they are faultless to those who have knowledge.* If I had a pulpit available right now, I think I would start preaching. This is powerful. "My lips speak what is true." All the time? Or just some of the time? "My lips detest wickedness." Same questions. "All the words of my mouth are just." Aw come on, let's get back down to earth. Literally none of them is crooked or perverse? Get real! Oh, I just noticed, that is <u>wisdom</u> talking, —not some politician, not even Solomon personally, nor your pastor, and not the writer of this devotional.

So, is there, or should there be a disconnect between us in real life and the Scriptures? Or do we have some adjustments to make. Better yet, is the Holy Spirit actually doing—or trying to do, a work in us? Galatians 5:22-23 tells us what will happen if we actually <u>allow</u> the Holy Spirit to do His work in us. He changes <u>us</u>—not just our circumstances or our perspective. That moves us to verse 9, and the matter of discernment. It seems to come down to our discerning between the Word of God, here known as wisdom, and our personal perspective on things.

If "all" the words of wisdom are just, and none are crooked or perverse, then does it not follow that whenever we speak in wisdom our words too will be right? And does it not also follow that when we speak unwisely, all of our words will at least be suspect? In verse 7 we read "my lips detest wickedness." That should increasingly be our condition. The degree to which that is our experience is the degree to which the Holy Spirit is making progress in conforming us to the image of Jesus Christ.

Proverbs 8:10-11

"Choose my instruction instead of silver, knowledge rather than choice gold, for wisdom is more precious than rubies, and nothing you desire compares with her."

These verses demand that we make a choice. OK but what is the choice? We choose between wisdom and wealth, or anything else we value. Nothing we desire compares with wisdom, says our text. So how do we choose? 1 Corinthians 1:20 asks us "Has not God made foolish the wisdom of this world"? Then verse 30 tells us "Christ Jesus has become for us wisdom from God." He is our wisdom. For those who have been born-again and have Jesus Christ living within by His Holy Spirit, that should be an easy choice. Wisdom is right there, He is right there, as near as breathing. So, what will we choose? Will we choose wisely? Will we choose Jesus Christ who is made for us "the wisdom of God? Oh, I know you may already have chosen Him as Savior, but will you now choose Him as our Wisdom? You can.

The fact is, we will choose and we do choose all the time, so it would be best to choose wisely. And we do choose wisely—often times. The teaching of wisdom is better than silver, and better than 24 karat gold, and more precious than rubies. Can you believe that? Christ Jesus IS our wisdom, and He is right here within. Once, when nickels and dimes were worth something, I asked some teen agers which they would choose: a bright shiny larger nickel, or a not so shiny smaller dime. They had no trouble with that one. Our choice should be even more obvious. Yet too often, we still fail to make right choices. Since Christ Jesus is our wisdom, let's ask Him.

Look at that last verse again; nothing you desire compares with wisdom. Not wealth, not power or prestige or popularity, not good looks, not leisure, not even our health, (although that may not be our choice) nothing! Nothing compares with wisdom. Jesus said "seek first the kingdom of God and his righteousness, and all these things will be given you as well." In this life He will give us whatever is best for us.

"I, wisdom, dwell together with prudence; I possess know-ledge and discretion. To fear the Lord is to hate evil; I hate pride and arrogance, evil behavior and perverse speech."

Wisdom is continuing to reveal itself. Here it is closely associated with prudence. Prudence, in my dictionary, is defined as "the ability to govern and discipline oneself by the use of reason." Accordingly, one dimension of wisdom is reasonable self-control. That may not sound particularly profound, until you look at the alternative: lack of self-control. A temper tantrum in a three-year old is one thing, but in a 43 year old it is a sad commentary on the man's character.

As the verse continues, we learn that wisdom has both knowledge and discretion. In other words, the wise person can obtain knowledge apart from learning it in class. And, wisdom also has discretion within it.

Psalm 111:10 tells us "the fear of the Lord is the beginning of wisdom, and here verse 13 reads: "To fear the Lord is to hate evil." So, it is time for a closer look.

I find it quite easy to hate certain evils and those who perpetrate evils. But that is not what wisdom is saying. When we lump the evil and the evil-doer together we are really acting out of pride, and that too is hated by wisdom. We are really taking the attitude that says: "I may not be perfect, but I'm certainly not <u>that</u> bad. We easily forget that I'm only a sinner, saved by grace. Wisdom would say that a holy hatred of evil is produced by a genuine "fear of the Lord."

On the subject of Holy Fear, The New Bible Dictionary says in part: "Holy fear is God given, enabling men to reverence God's authority, obey His commandments, and hate and shun all forms of evil." Philippians 2:13 says "it is God who works in you to will and to act according to His good purpose."

Proverbs 8:14

"Counsel and sound judgment are mine; I have understanding and power."

I have a friend who said years ago that he prays for wisdom every day. (I don't know if he still does.) Personally, I need it every day, but I can't say that I ask for it every day. But why not? Is there ever a day when you don't need sound judgment? I need it every day, and here wisdom is saying that *sound judgment belongs to me.* So, if we ask for wisdom every day, then we are given wisdom every day, and when we encounter a need to make sound judgment about something, wisdom is already there and we just need to exercise it.

In this context we might say that when we need to make a judgment about something, and even though we asked for wisdom in the morning we are not sure about how to call it up, wisdom is there to provide counsel. Let wisdom counsel you about making the best call in a given situation because not only sound judgment, but counsel also belongs to wisdom. Admittedly there are times when two alternatives seem equally good and/ or wise and yet a decision has to be made. Fortunately for us, wisdom also has understanding. Since wisdom comes from our Sovereign God, wisdom has perfect understanding of past, present and future—even as it relates to my circumstances in life, even though I don't.

Another thing about wisdom in this one verse, it also has power. Again, in this immediate context this is not so much power to exert over others, nor physical or mental power, so much as it is power to make the tough decisions; power over my own weaknesses. This would be power to agree with the counsel of wisdom, even when that is not to our personal liking. We could call that power over our own will, and that is precisely where the power is so often needed.

"By me (wisdom) ***kings reign and rulers make laws that are just; by me princes govern, and all nobles who rule on earth.***"

First of all, that speaks to the ideal. Both Bible history as well as secular history has shown that many kings did not reign by wisdom. The final King will. Many rulers and princes, congresses, and legislatures do make laws that are just, but at times these very same people also make laws that are unjust. But again, the final King will, in absolute wisdom, reign in perfect righteousness and justice. So, where does that leave the ordinary Christian individual who honestly seeks wisdom?

Each of us in fact does have a kingdom to rule, consisting of at least one person. So, let's begin there. When there are dependent children involved, parents rule the household together, and that is an awesome responsibility. Some people are elected to rule, and others are hired. But before anyone is ready to begin to rule over anyone at all one must learn to rule themselves. Jesus is the only One who did this perfectly, but don't despair, even Jesus "grew in wisdom," Luke 2:52. So let's learn to "rule" ourselves. What, in our lives, do we need to rule?

Each of course is unique, and in unique circumstances, some specifics will vary. For example, we talk about controlling our temper. That is "ruling," but that does not mean to eliminate temper, just don't let it rule your life. We have many different needs and desires which are good. and need to be met. But we must rule over them—not indiscriminately indulge them. And that takes wisdom. What is good for one may not be good for someone else. So, by wisdom we rule and reign, and Jesus said that the one who is faithful in little (things) will also be faithful in much. Luke 16:10.

Proverbs 8:17-19

"I love those who love me, and those who seek me find me. With me are riches and honor, enduring wealth and prosperity. My fruit is better than gold, what I yield surpasses choice silver."

Just for a moment, think of wisdom as a person, and then read the verses again. That is wisdom speaking. Doesn't that make you feel like you want to fall in love all over again? Let me tell you about a few friends, who in my opinion, plugged into wisdom and became very wealthy in material terms. A few did it by selling cars, another started a chain of grocery stores, others by starting a trucking business etc. They loved wisdom and wisdom loved to give them wealth. Verse 18 adds the word "enduring" to wealth and prosperity. I believe in each of these cases, if it had ever come to choose between their accumulated material wealth or the "enduring" wealth of verse 18, each would have unhesitatingly chosen the later. The point is, our friend, wisdom, wants us to have both.

However, let's not confuse this with the so-called prosperity Gospel. The reality is that wisdom, being wise, knows who can handle material wealth and who cannot; wisdom knows for whom material wealth is good and for whom it is not. It has never been God's plan that every Christian should be wealthy by this world's standards. It is His plan, however, that each of us should lay up treasure in heaven. As far as the few short years of this life are concerned, it will take wisdom to know and become all that God has planned for us to be.

The motto of the U.S. army, "Be all that you can be" would be a good one for us to adopt as members of God's army. Wisdom loves us so much that it wants to take us all the way to God's goal for us in this life, and then on to inherit all that He has for us in the next.

Proverbs 8:20-22

"I walk in the way of righteousness, along the paths of justice, bestowing wealth on those who love me and making their treasuries full. The Lord brought me forth as the first his works, before his deeds of old."

Theologically, this is a difficult passage right through the rest of the chapter. I will not attempt to do what scholars have been unable to do, and that is to fully explain this. To start with, wisdom is saying "I walk in the way of righteousness." We know the Bible declares that we are robbed in Christ's righteousness; when He takes our sin, He gives us His righteousness. So, God sees us as righteous in Him. However, that is not to say that our walk is therefore always righteous. Whether for a short time or long, we are sometimes not "in the way of righteousness" or "along the path of justice." According to this text, we will not find wisdom there.

We understand that one cannot learn to swim unless one gets into the water, but just getting into the water does not mean we can swim. Once Christ has saved us, means we now have access to divine wisdom, but in itself, that does not make us wise. We still have to ask, James 1:5, and we still have to learn to walk in the way of righteousness, along the paths of justice, and heed wisdom's advice and obey His Word. That is the process of becoming wise, for those who love wisdom. Wisdom itself wants to bestow a wealth of itself on us, making our treasuries full.

I take that last verse to mean that God, while He is Himself wisdom, created wisdom as a separate entity, apart from Himself. He did this before He created the heavens and the earth. If all that is correct, then He planned to provide wisdom to you and me from before the beginning of time and space. What an awesome God! Let's boldly ask for wisdom.

Psalm 37:30

"The mouth of the righteous man utters wisdom, and his tongue speaks what is just."

While yesterday's proverb talked about the "walk" and the "path" of wisdom, it was really talking about "being" rather than "doing." Wisdom is, therefore wisdom does. It is not talking about any physical activity like walking.

Today's text pursues that same theme. Let's look again at our verse of the day and try to think it through. The mouth of the "righteous" speaks wisdom and justice. Why? How? Well, not because the mouth wants people to think it is righteous, but because it **is**. It is the expression of righteousness, or the righteous one. The tongue speaks justice, not because it wants to become a judge, but because it is righteous or just. The tongue expresses what the person is. True, one can pretend to be what one is not, but that's all it is—a pretense.

To paraphrase what Jesus said in Matthew 12:34, what the heart **is**, the mouth speaks. In the NIV it reads like this: "Out of the overflow of the heart the mouth speaks." Because of the work of Christ, we are declared "righteous." God declares us so. Therefore, it is not mere wishful thinking. It is so! Yet our experience does not consistently reflect the reality of righteousness. The truth is, in our experience we are **becoming** what the finished work of Christ has made us positionally.

So, I ask myself: How full of Christ is my heart? How full of righteousness? How full of wisdom? Is it overflowing? I can test that by listening to the overflow. To the degree that I **am** becoming righteous in my present life, my mouth will utter wisdom and justice. Also, to that same degree I will be joyful, "rejoicing in the Lord always."

Proverbs 8:23-31

"I was appointed from eternity, from before the world began. . . before the mountains were settled in place, before the hills, I was given birth."

We are not going to quote the whole lengthy section, but please read it. It all speaks to wisdom having a beginning, as a separate entity, being born at some point before time began.

Genesis 1:1 clearly states that "In the beginning, God created the heavens and the earth." Therefore, according to our text, wisdom was born before "the beginning." If you want to know exactly how that all fits together, you will have to wait with me to ask for the explanation when we see Him face-to-face. To me, this opens the door a tiny crack into the awesomeness and the Sovereignty of our great God. It is relatively easy to sing "Our God is an awesome God" whether our worship is private or public. We just cannot comprehend the magnitude of that statement— maybe not even in eternity.

But while we cannot comprehend, we can nevertheless contemplate, so let's do that today. You may want to use Scriptures like Job chapters 39 and 40, or Isaiah chapter 40, especially verses 12 through the end, or others of your favorite Scriptures to guide your contemplation.

For example, "who has measured the waters (of the world) in the hollow of his hand?" (While keeping the salt water from mixing with the fresh.) That would take a pretty BIG God. "Who has understood the mind of God?" Science can explain a lot of what the human mind is capable of doing, and what it is designed to do, but they can't understand it well enough to make a human mind—with nothing more than the dust of the earth to work with. Dear reader, we have an awesome God, and He is in process of teaching us wisdom. No better Teacher can be imagined.

       PROVERBS TO LIVE BY

Proverbs 8:32-34

"Now then, my sons, listen to me; blessed are those who keep my ways. Listen to my instruction and be wise; do not ignore it. Blessed is the man who listens to me."

First of all, this is not Solomon talking to his sons; this is wisdom talking and calling the readers "sons." Earlier in this chapter wisdom has been telling us about itself and giving us its credentials. Wisdom was brought forth by God, before He created the heavens and the earth, and has therefore always resided with God. Wisdom speaks to us in many different ways, including of course the Word of God. However, it also speaks to us in our experiences, both when we fail at something and when we succeed, and it speaks to us through other people, whether young or old, whether well educated, or not so well educated, and it also speaks in and through nature.

With credentials like that, accommodated to reach the average person, it should hardly be necessary to call potential listeners to attention. We should be clamoring to hear what wisdom is saying. Yet the grace of God is always calling us to go the right way and to do the right things. Yes, it is wisdom that repeatedly calls out: "please listen to me," but it is the grace of God that enables us to listen and then to understand and act. Just listening alone is of little or no value, but here wisdom is asking/calling us to listen **because** God has promised a special blessing to those who keep the ways of wisdom.

These blessings are promised in verse 32 and in verse 34. Verse 34 promises blessing for listening and then eagerly looking for opportunities to hear some more. But there are right and wrong places to search. This verse teaches us to wait daily at wisdom's doors, and to wait daily at wisdom's doorway, not at another place of our choosing. We must look for wisdom where it is. Jesus said "knock, and the door will be opened to you" Matthew 7:7. Let's keep on knocking.

Proverbs 8:34-36

"Blessed is the man who listens to me, watching daily at my doors, waiting at my doorway. For whoever finds me finds life and receives favor from the Lord. But whoever fails to find me harms himself; all who hate me love death."

Here the blessing is promised, it would seem at first glance, just for listening to wisdom. But take a closer look. There is a coma, not a period, after "listens to me." It is listening to understand, not just to hear. Sometimes we may listen to someone just to be polite; we may listen primarily to reply or to get to have our say. Too often we may listen just to gain information that we can pass on as knowledge. In fact, many people obtain a college degree by that kind of listening. What we have here is much more important than a mere college degree. Here the purpose of listening is to **become**, not to achieve or obtain. We are to become wise, and the blessing promised for those who do, wisdom is life.

Whoever finds wisdom, finds life. That is not saying they are the ones who will go to heaven, they find life here and now. Furthermore, they also "receive" favor from the Lord. What does it mean to "receive favor from the Lord"? It does not mean He will love you more; He loves you completely now, and there is nothing anyone of us can do to make Him love us more—or less. The change that comes through wisdom is a change in us, not in God. The change will become more and more evident and fruitful in our relationships. Our relationship with God will improve because we will be more aware of His constant presence with us and we will see more clearly that "God's will is good, pleasing and perfect" Romans 12:3. This will then translate into more favorable relationships with others. That, at least in part, is the favor of God.

"Wisdom has built her house; she has hewn out its seven pillars. She has prepared her meat and mixed her wine; she has also set her table."

These verses describe wisdom's preparation of the banquet she has prepared for her guests. It looks like whatever time and effort we may have put in to find wisdom will be well rewarded. Let's take a closer look.

We are familiar with Jesus' promise in John 14 that He is preparing a place for us in heaven. Wonderful! But that is for when this life is over. The Book of Proverbs teaches us how to pursue and obtain practical wisdom in this life. That is its primary purpose. Wisdom will of course help us in this life to prepare for the next, but it also has its intrinsic benefits for the here and now. I see the place Jesus is preparing as analogous to a dwelling here. While it will be totally different and immeasurably superior, it will be our abode or dwelling place.

In the opening words of our text, wisdom has also built a house for us, but not a dwelling. This house will be a place, a resort, to go to when we need to deal with issues and work through situations and make decisions. But it is not primarily a place for solving problems; it is a place of rest, and relaxation and yes, celebration. Look at the next verse. It is a place for a banquet. It is a place of celebrating party style. It is a place where wisdom dwells, and to which we can go at any time. We are always welcome. When you are facing a new situation, just duck in at wisdom's house and obtain whatever you need. And while you're there, indulge in a little feasting. The table is set, the steak is done to your liking, and the coffee is on, and she has a little take-along bag packed for you. And as to location, this place is as near as a prayer, so it is never "out of the way," no matter where your journey takes you.

"(Wisdom) has sent out her maids, and she calls from the highest point of the city. Let all who are simple come in here! She says to those who lack judgment, Come eat my food and drink the wine I have mixed. Leave your simple ways and you will live; walk in the way of understanding."

Wisdom has not only put up a big sign beside the freeway and placed an ad in the newspaper, she has sent out her deputies with a personal invitation to everyone in the city: "come in here and pick up your desired amount of free wisdom. It is dispensed in the form of a banquet." We may not be flattered to be thought of as "simple" and to be lacking in judgment. If so, we can of course refuse the invitation and go our own way.

Wisdom is something like salvation in the sense that we have to recognize our need for it before we can ask, and even seek, for it. Probably the number one reason we most often fail to recognize our own need is personal pride. In our attitude toward God we are often like a three-year old: "Me do it myself." Perhaps that is why Jesus said: "Without Me you can do nothing."

What can complicate the matter for us is that we do already have a measure of wisdom. God has endowed us with it. We have learned it growing up. We have learned a little more of it in the process of life experiences. But I have to ask: by what standard are you measuring your wisdom? A corollary question would be, by what standard do you measure your need for wisdom?

It seems to me, the closer you walk with the Lord, the more you love Him, the sweeter your fellowship with Him, the more you will desire and seek for greater wisdom.

Proverbs 9:7-9

"Whoever corrects a mocker invites insult; whoever rebukes a wicked man incurs abuse. Do not rebuke a mocker or he will hate you; rebuke a wise man and he will love you. Instruct a wise man and he will be wiser still; teach a righteous man and he will add to his learning."

This section deals with correcting and rebuking. There is some question about whether this is directed at a teacher (not necessarily a classroom teacher,) or at a student also not necessarily in a classroom setting. Perhaps, it is a little of each. In the course of relating to people, we all have opportunity (and experience?) to correct, rebuke and instruct. The verse that comes to mind is Proverbs 26:17. If we are too quick to correct or instruct, our response may well have results "like one who grabs a stray dog by the ears." In that regard at least, these verses apply to us in a teaching role. Don't be too quick to offer even a suggestion, never mind a correction.

On the other hand, when we are the recipients of the comment, let's not be too quick to consider it invalid or inappropriate. If we hold our temper, as well as our retort, we may in fact be able to learn something. Some time ago I had a discussion with an attorney friend about a ministry project opportunity for me; OK, he was a public relations lawyer so that gave him credence, OK he was a high-powered PR attorney so he was smart, and he had experience, but he knew nothing about this ministry opportunity involving me – or did he? At first, I listened because I wanted to be polite, knowing full well that he had no idea about my ministry opportunity. Well, as I listened politely, I soon began to see he did have a valuable perspective, even though he may not have fully understood my ministry opportunity, and would you believe it, I truly benefited as a result.

James 1:19 advises everyone to be "quick to listen, slow to speak, and slow to become angry." That could include receiving solicited as well as unsolicited advice and opinions. Even corrections. We will personally be the beneficiaries.

Proverbs 9:10

"The fear of the Lord is the beginning of wisdom, and knowledge of the Holy One is understanding."

In my Bible, the heading for chapter 9 is "Invitations of Wisdom and of Folly." The experience of every true believer is that both wisdom and folly offer constant invitations to respond to their wares. We want to do God's will, but sin does have its allure, so there is the age-old conflict. Romans 7 teaches us that too often we fail to do what we know is right and what we in fact want to do. On the other hand, we find ourselves doing what we know is wrong and what we truly do not want to do. Still on the subject of wisdom and the fear of the Lord, our text reads: *"The fear of the Lord is the beginning of wisdom, and knowledge of the Holy One is understanding."*

For your consideration, how does one learn the "fear of the Lord and knowledge of the Holy One?" How do we move from a Romans 7 experience to Romans 8:1-2? Topping the list has got to be His written word. Truly, the word of God is living and powerful, but the word must be heeded to do its work. I've heard of people placing a Bible under their pillow so they can get a better night's sleep. To me, that sounds like using the Bible as a "lucky charm," and that is not what it is. How many times do we read the word without paying it much heed? How often do we fail to "get the message"?

Jesus said "Blessed are those who hunger and thirst for righteousness, for they will be filled. When we are truly hungry and food is set before us, we are wise enough to eat. We must be wise enough to want, bold enough to ask, and hungry enough to eat the spiritual food of the word He sets before us and humble enough to take God at His word. After all, Father does know best.

"Be still and know that I am God, I will be exalted among the nations, I will be exalted in the earth."

This is not exactly a Proverb, but it is "a word in season." At least it is for me. I read this verse in my quiet time with the Lord this morning before writing this devotional. After pondering this for a bit, I came across Zechariah 2: 13: *"Be still before the Lord, all mankind, because he has roused himself from his holy dwelling."* Why do we (I) find it so difficult to get quiet before the Lord at times, and wait for Him to take action? Why must we always be so feverishly active? Of course, we really would not want it any other way.

Sometimes those of us who are healthy and always doing something, even if we are doing it "for the Lord," really miss out because of our activity. Yet we can't seem to learn. Isaiah 40:31 promises that those who "wait upon the Lord," (get still before Him) will renew their strength. Yet we often choose to complete our little project that we have set for ourselves first, and then sit back on the recliner and renew our strength that way. Often when I sit in my recliner, and my wife is just a few feet away, I am unaware of her presence because my mind is working on a sermon or on another devotional. Be still, wait. Then the Lord will be exalted.

Sometimes, the Lord may have to slow us down through circumstances we would never have chosen, such as a heart attack or some other incapacity. In some related reading I came across another line, applying to just such a situation. "Limitations can be liberating when your strongest desire is living" closer to the Lord. That same piece talked about the fact that sometimes God has done His greatest work through people with significant limitations.

We just need to learn to wait on the Lord, and let Him measure our significance and achievements.

Proverbs 9:11-12

"For through me (wisdom) *your days will be many and years will be added to your life. If you are wise, your wisdom will reward you; if you are a mocker, you alone will suffer."*

There are consequences. Always there are consequences. For everything we do, or don't do, there are consequences. Of course, we know that wise thing to do is to choose to follow the path of righteousness. We know that, but unfortunately, we don't necessarily always believe what we know. Our text says that wisdom will add years to our lives. That is given as general good advice; it is not an ironclad promise. So, if we focus on the remote possibility that it might not work for us today, then we might convince ourselves that "much as I would like to consult the Lord about this, right now I just don't have the time. If I don't get going right now, I'll be late for my appointment." And so, we rush on.

But wait a minute, don't you have two appointments? Are you willing to skip the first one entirely, in order to keep the second? And so, we rush through life. Of course, things are going to happen. God knows that. Schedules will need to change. Even our time with the Lord may need to come earlier or perhaps later some days. Our text is merely saying that wisdom is the better course, and ignoring (mocking) the right choice will come at a price. Wisdom will not tie us up in bondage to schedules or rituals; rather it will tend to free us up. Our text says wisdom will add years to our lives, and I can assure you, it will certainly add life to your years.

Wisdom always chooses righteousness. Lack of wisdom generally chooses convenience or expediency.

PROVERBS TO LIVE BY

Proverbs 9:13-15

"The woman, Folly is loud; she is undisciplined and without knowledge. She sits at the door of her house, on a seat at the highest point of the city, calling out to those who pass by, who go straight on their way."

The enemy of God is Satan, the enemy of Righteousness is Unrighteousness, the enemy of Wisdom is Folly. The better we get to know God the more readily will we recognize any counterfeit and deceit that the devil can throw at us. The more we walk/live in the ways of righteousness, the more quickly we will recognize that which is unrighteous. The more we grow in wisdom, the more clearly we will see the subtle ways of folly.

Chapter 9 of Proverbs opens with Wisdom calling out to us through her maids, her messengers; calling even from "the highest points of the city." In today's text we find folly, not as a horned monster, but as a very attractive woman. While wisdom has built her house, so has folly, and her invitations also go out to "all who pass by." And like wisdom, she too calls from the highest point of the city. Folly is undisciplined, so she can speak "out of both sides of her mouth." She can make her appeal seem both wise and attractive, and often with a promised short-cut to the desired destination, while actually leading to folly and destruction.

We will never achieve such a degree of wisdom in this life that we can always successfully spot and defeat folly at every turn. Nor will we get better at it by studying folly and her ways. So, let's never think we have achieved immunity. Our safety is in getting to know wisdom better, getting to know righteousness experientially, getting to know God in His fullness. Let's study Truth, and falsehood will become evident.

PROVERBS TO LIVE BY

Proverbs 9:16-18

"Let all who are simple come in here! she says to those who lack judgment. Stolen water is sweet; food eaten in secret is delicious! But little do they know that the dead are there, that her guests are in the depths of the grave."

Some of the words used by the woman Folly, are identical to those used by Wisdom. Fortunately for us, the writer also gives us insight to what Folly is really saying; that her words are deceptive. It is very doubtful that Folly actually tells her intended "guests" they are simple and lack judgment. But she certainly invites them in to her dwelling. And the "simple" and those who "lack judgment" do not bother to properly vet the source and intent of the invitation, so they gladly accept. It is also doubtful that Folly ever tells her guests where this good water can be had, or why the delicious food needs to be eaten in secret. A little mystique adds to the thrill. Notice that both Wisdom and Folly appeal to the same audience.

It is not only politicians who are members of the other party who fit the above description of folly. Nor is it only those who vote for the other party who are simple, and lacking in judgment. Too often it is we who are wise, (at least in our own estimation) who are deceived. The master-deceiver, is very adept at deceiving people at every level. None of us are beyond his reach. When we are deceived, we cannot possibly imagine the severity of the end result. So, let's look at the last verse again.

Those who accept Folly's invitation are unwittingly pursuing the way of death and the grave. But those who accept Wisdom's invitation have the assurance of life, Proverbs 8:35. *"Whoever finds me* (wisdom) *finds life."*

Now, this may be a good time to sing "Wonderful grace of Jesus."

PROVERBS TO LIVE BY

Psalm 49:1-3

"Hear this, all you peoples; listen, all who live in this world, both high and low alike: My mouth will speak words of wisdom; the utterance from my heart will give you understanding."

This Psalm is sometimes called a wisdom Psalm, and you can see why. It is not written by Solomon, but by the sons of Korah, but it is somewhat in the style the Book Proverbs.

First, we have a call to listen, and this call is to all mankind. To make sure the intent is clear it is specified to all who live in this world, both high and low, rich and poor alike. I suppose every culture has its own share of people who think themselves above the law, or above the need to listen to advice from anyone. Some think they already know more than just about anyone else. Some think their wealth exempts them from any need to listen to ordinary people.

So, let's forget those who think themselves to be big-shots, and do some listening of our own. The words from "my mouth' in this text are words from God. These words may be delivered by a pastor/teacher, by an ordinary fellow-lay person, by a radio or television preacher, by a boss or a co-worker, or just by some personal Bible reading. Too often we may "hear" the words without hearing the message. What is worse, we may actually hear the words **and** the message but fail to act on it. When that happens, we may quickly try to rationalize why this is not for me at the present time, or perhaps we try to think of someone else to whom these words could apply.

I believe if we fail to listen and pay attention when God speaks to us, and just try to ignore it and go on with our lives, it is at that point that our spiritual life begins to stagnate, and our fellowship with the Lord loses its luster. Wisdom is to listen and obey when God speaks.

Isaiah 32:8

"But the noble man makes noble plans, and by noble deeds he stands."

Proverbs are often found in Scriptures, other than the Book of Proverbs. This one found in Isaiah is written in the style of the Book of Proverbs in that it has the positive in verse 8 contrasted with the negative in verse 5-7. The book of Proverbs does that frequently.

This Isaiah passage in 32:1-8 has as a section heading in my Bible: *The Kingdom of Righteousness.*

The word "noble" as used here is not related to the idea of nobility as if referring to a monarch or other esteemed position, but rather it refers to character qualities. The antitheses of this "noble" person then is the scoundrel of verse 7. The New King James version has "generous" instead of noble. Among the high and mighty, the wealthy, the power brokers and philanthropists in our day and age can be found paupers in character, or scoundrels. Man looks at the outward appearance, but God looks at the heart.

What I find interesting here is that while fools and scoundrels may make plans to "appear" as something admirable, and possibly fool many, the noble person will make plans to "be" good and godly. In other words, no one will just fall into becoming noble by accident. Not even by wishful thinking. We need to "plan" to be right as well as to do right. Our text says the noble man makes noble plans. The plans themselves are noble and good and right. The scoundrel merely makes plans to do noble deeds in order to appear noble. It is the "impression" they are concerned about.

When the plans themselves are noble, then by those noble plans we can and will stand.

Proverbs 10: 1

"A wise son brings joy to his father but a foolish son grief to his mother."

The section heading *Proverbs of Solomon*, comprises the major section of the book. The title however, is not a part of the inspired Word of God. This simply lets us know that these are the Proverbs that Solomon wrote, as opposed to the copied work of someone else. Knowing who the human author was may be helpful to us in understanding the teaching. It allows us to see how the times and culture may have had an influence on the style of writing and the choice of specific words used by the author.

What is even more important however, is that we believe and accept the Divine Inspiration of every part of Holy Scripture, and therefore the inerrancy of the same. In the NIV, 2 Timothy 3:16 reads: *All Scripture is God-breathed and is useful for teaching, rebuking, correcting and training in righteousness.* That verse gives us the Divine purpose of the Book of Proverbs. This is vital for every believer in Jesus Christ to accept if we are to be "trained in righteousness."

Wisdom literature like Proverbs, especially in this section, uses mostly short one or two verse units instead of lengthier narrative. Because these units compare and contrast, most of these units have a "but" in the center, as is the case in this first verse. The contrast is between a wise and a foolish son (or daughter). The appeal itself is to the child on the basis of his/her love for the parents. Because of the human sinful nature, no child makes only wise choices just like their parents do not. However, in a godly home, there is the presence of supernatural love, as well as the natural love between parents and children. We all know from experience the hurt caused by foolish or unwise choices and we know the joys of wise choices. But a young child cannot know the depth of the joy, nor of the grief that their choices bring to their parents.

And neither parents nor children can know the depth of joy and of grief that we can and do bring to our heavenly Father.

PROVERBS TO LIVE BY

Proverbs 10: 2-3

"Ill-gotten treasures are of no value, but righteousness delivers from death. The Lord does not let the righteous go hungry but he thwarts the craving of the wicked."

To this point in the book, wisdom has been doing a lot of the talking, and chapter 9 gave the invitations of both wisdom and folly. In 9:4 wisdom addresses the "simple" as does folly in 9:16. Chapter 10 begins with: "The Proverbs of Solomon." So now we have a third voice. What follows in the next few chapters are brief proverbs on various topics. The first one deals with the values and limitations of wealth.

Investment advisers tend to think in terms of long-term gains, and Solomon does that too in Ecclesiastes. Here, however, he is including the value in eternity. That is true long-term. At the Judgment Seat of Christ, no one will be judged by the size of their investment portfolio. How we got it, or why we did not, is another matter. "Ill-gotten treasures" obviously refers to temporal gains, and does not refer only to the Bernie Madoff style of obtaining wealth through Ponzi schemes, although that is included. Nor does it refer only to wealth obtained illegally, according to man's laws. Rather it refers to anything that is unethical and unrighteous. Scriptures always place more emphasis on attitudes and motivations.

Since the times of Job and Abraham, Scriptures clearly show that God delights in blessing some people with tremendous amounts of wealth, but even that has zero value in eternity. It does have temporal value and *faithful stewardship* of wealth does have eternal value. In the final analysis, what counts is righteousness. Righteousness has no dollar value, but it does have God's promise of temporal and eternal provision. *"The Lord does not let the righteous go hungry."* Not a righteousness that we can conjure up, but that which is the righteousness of God, given to us through Jesus Christ. Confederate dollars lost their value at the end of the civil war; (American dollars may soon follow) but the righteousness of God lasts forever.

> *"Lazy hands make a man poor, but diligent hands bring wealth."*

While biblical principles apply to all people of all ages at all times, specific application of those principles will vary from one to another. How then would one apply a text like ours today to the elderly and perhaps somewhat infirm? Some might just shrug it off as applying only to those still in the labor-force. Others might think *"it's a good thing I was industrious when I was younger, so now I have accumulated a measure of wealth."* Young people might say I'll remember that for when I finish college. Such thinking assumes that accumulation of wealth is the primary goal in life. They would also contradict the concept of Scripture principles applying to all people at all times. So, let's take a closer look at the text.

In Luke 16:11 Jesus said *"If you have not been trustworthy in handling worldly wealth, who will trust you with true riches."* So, this text has a dual application, both temporal and spiritual. In our culture there are people who choose not to work, because welfare is available free-of-charge, and with virtually no effort on the part of the recipients; no effort at all if they receive it in the mail. However, the term "lazy hands" can also mean deceptive hands, in which case people may well accumulate material wealth at someone else's expense. And they may in fact **not** become poor financially. Yet the person who works diligently to earn his bread for today and accumulate some wealth for the tomorrows to come, will have the satisfaction of enjoying the fruit of his labors in this life, plus he will stand in line to receive "true riches" as well.

Now what about the spiritual application? Here I wish to focus on those who are, or soon will be, in the "retirement years" of their lives. If you have been able to make financial provisions for your retirement and perhaps for an inheritance for your children and grandchildren, then praise the Lord. Here is where you will face the opportunity, and perhaps the temptation to develop those "lazy hands." This should be a time to diligently "lay up for yourselves treasures of true riches in heaven.

Proverbs 10: 5

"He who gathers crops in summer is a wise son, but he who sleeps during harvest is a disgraceful son."

Sometimes I ask myself why Scripture talks so much about faithfulness in money matters. Why so much emphasis on hard work and diligence? It certainly can't be because God wants all His children to be wealthy, as some "blab it and grab it" preachers would have us believe. So why? I understand that within that context there is major emphasis on the agricultural aspect of accumulating wealth, because both Old and New Testaments were written to an agrarian culture, but still, why all this emphasis on accumulating wealth when we can't take with us into eternity? Even Solomon said that we don't know whether those who inherit our wealth will be wise or foolish.

How about this? Consider with me that this life is really a preparation for the next. The whole concept of the fruit of the Spirit is the work of the Holy Spirit to mold us into a greater degree of Christ-likeness; "Christ is being formed in us." Galatians 4:19. As a part of that process, Jesus said for us to "lay up for yourselves treasure in heaven," Matthew 6:20. OK, but how? Well now, that is a problem. How can you lay up invisible treasures in a place we can't see or even really visualize? What are these treasures?

Thank you for asking. If the work of the Holy Spirit is to make us Christ-like, it must surely refer to attitudes and values and the like. The accumulation period of our lives involves doing work which produces tangible results. In the process we learn what it takes to produce better returns for our efforts. Soon we see those results evidenced in the paycheck, and if the results are pleasing, we seek to improve. Those same principles will work in laying up treasures in heaven. We learn from what we can see materially and apply it to that which we can see only by faith. We learn faithfulness and diligence in the material realm, and then apply that learning to our daily walk with Christ." To do so is wise, and to fail to do it is disgraceful," says our text.

"Blessings crown the head of the righteous, but violence overwhelms the mouth of the wicked. The memory of the righteous will be a blessing, but the name of the wicked will rot."

The term "righteous" here is not talking about the righteousness of Christ that has been credited to the account of a believer. In Christ we are righteous, because when He took our sin upon Himself, He gave His righteousness to all those who receive Him. Here the righteousness is talking about the life-style that is observable by people who see and know us. His righteousness and eternal heaven are gifts given to us by His grace and mercy. The earthly right-living brings a blessing that is a reward to be experienced here and now.

When the text says blessings crown the head, this tells me first of all that it is plural. There are multiple advantages (blessings) in right living, and I will not attempt to name them. These would certainly include being able to look people in the face with nothing to hide. No hidden guilt. No hoping they won't find out about this that or the other. If we hope they never find out, we are living with a measure of anxiety which is a non-blessing. These are personal, hidden things that we hope will make us appear to live righteously. True right living (and of course nobody does it perfectly) also builds a reputation over time with others. Inner peace and joy come from righteous living. On the other hand, "violence overwhelms the wicked." Not that they necessarily have continual violent relationships, but peace and joy are missing.

Verse 7 promises that the memory of the righteous will be a blessing. True, that will be finally fulfilled in the next life, but it will apply to the here and now. God said so. However, the name of the wicked will rot. People will say the world would be better off without them. People will seek to avoid them; they won't trust them, and internally they will never be quite free from guilt feelings.

Right living has both temporal and eternal rewards; Wicked living has neither.

Proverbs 10:8

"The wise in heart accept commands, but a chattering fool comes to ruin."

This verse begins by referring to "the wise in heart." That verse tells me this is someone who is not trying to *appear* to be wise. This is one who is not overly concerned about what other people think. He may not even see himself as wise, but rather as one who is pursuing wisdom. This is one who regularly asks God for wisdom to meet life's challenges and vicissitudes. He is asking in faith, believing that God is and will be giving him, the wisdom he asks for, but not by some kind of an injection. Therefore, he is listening for wisdom, not knowing exactly when or where it may come.

The old saying: "if you have nothing good to say, don't say anything at all," reminds me of the private who complained to the captain about his sergeant, to which the captain replied with the old saying. Then he added "and frankly, I have nothing to say about your sergeant." In the context of our verse, if we truly listen, we can sometimes learn wisdom even from a fool. If nothing else, learn the wisdom of not saying anything. We cannot know where we will hear wisdom speak, so we just need to listen—but listen carefully. Wisdom may whisper to us at times saying "that comment, or that idea is for you; do it." Our text says that to the degree we are "wise in heart (we will) accept commands." Of course, our major source of wisdom will always be the Word of God, but He can speak in many ways.

The other side of the coin is the chattering fool who is so busy with himself and his own ideas that he often can't hear when wisdom speaks. That much I know from personal experience, and maybe so do some of you. Again, James 1:19 tells us to be "quick to listen, slow to speak, and slow to become angry."

So, in reverse order, to become wiser we must control and override our impulse to be a chattering fool, and listen for and to wisdom, and then accept and do what it requires.

> *"The man of integrity walks securely, but he who takes crooked paths will be found out. He who winks maliciously causes grief, and a chattering fool comes to ruin."*

This obviously is not talking about a material path which may possibly be dangerous and very insecure at times and in places. Rather this has to do with our character, and there we walk the path of our own choosing. This is not to imply that everything that happens is the result of our choosing—far from it. But no matter what happens or what unexpected and unforeseen issues arise, we always choose the way we deal with it.

The "man of integrity" is one who is committed to an honest lifestyle before the Lord. Isaiah 50:7 puts it this way: *"Because the Sovereign Lord helps me, I will not be disgraced. Therefore, have I set my face like flint, and I know I will not be put to shame."* We make the commitment, and He "helps me" to keep it. He is the One who enables us to live up to it. We must remember that the Christian "birth" is different from the Christian "walk." Birth is instantaneous at the moment we decide for Christ at salvation; the Christian walk is from that time forward all our earthly life. The walk requires multiple decisions as we repeatedly choose integrity at each juncture.

The rest of the text essentially says the one who takes crooked paths, the one who winks maliciously, the chattering fool, will not get away with it. In Numbers 32:23 God said "be sure your sin will find you out." Can or does a Christian ever do these sinful deeds? Obviously, yes, but take my advice, or better yet, take God's advice and don't try it. It's not worth it. Yes, there is forgiveness and restoration for failure, but at a cost to your own peace and joy. And reputation! And the Proverbs are given to help us better navigate this life.

Proverbs 10:11

"The mouth of the righteous is a fountain of life, but violence overwhelms the mouth of the wicked."

As we approach this one, I am reminded of the words of Jesus in Matthew 12:34 *"out of the overflow of the heart the mouth speaks."* What I think Jesus is telling us is simply that what is in the heart is more important than what comes out of the mouth.

On a television show featuring young children, I heard a four-year old tell the host "I'll pray for you so you won't cuss so much," to which the host replied "I don't use bad words when I'm with kids." In that I believe he may well have been right. Having watched that show numerous times, I don't recall ever hearing him "cuss." To a degree I'm sure all of us should be, and probably are, careful with what we say and that is as it should be. Some things are inappropriate to be spoken in a particular audience. But even more than monitoring our speech, we need to monitor the heart.

Having said that, let's look at that opening phrase again. *The mouth of the righteous is a fountain of life.* The righteous are the ones who are righteous of heart. Therefore, the bent of their life is to do, say and promote righteousness, and others are the direct beneficiaries of this righteousness. Just as he who would love God must love his brother, I John 4:21, so also, he who would live righteously before God must live righteously with his fellow-man. Righteousness in the heart WILL come out in speech and in deeds. It cannot remain hidden. Isaiah 50:4 has it *The Sovereign Lord has given me an instructed tongue, to know the word that sustains the weary.*

Isaiah and Solomon are saying the same thing here in different words. For the mouth to be a fountain of life or for the tongue to know the word that sustains the weary is one and the same thing and I want that. Do you?

Proverbs 10:12

"Hatred stirs up dissention, but love covers over all wrongs."

In contrast to the blessings brought on by the righteous, the wicked are here exposed in not-so-subtle words. In verses 6 and 11, "violence overwhelms the wicked," and here in verse 12 the hatred of the wicked "stirs up dissention." When Jesus said that the mouth speaks out of the overflow of the heart, (Matthew 12:34) that is true both of the righteous and the wicked. And while the wicked may try to mask their hatred with politically correct speech, the end result is still the same: they stir up dissention. All the while, their bottled-up hatred is bubbling and building up pressure until it explodes.

When a "righteous" person is then subjected to the brunt of this venom, the natural response is "like for like," and maybe in double dose. But God expects more than a "natural response" from us; He expects a super-natural response. And He also knows we are incapable of super-natural responses, which is why He gave us the Holy Spirit. Our text says love covers over all wrongs. In Matthew 5:44 Jesus said to "love your enemies, and pray for those who persecute you, and in a longer discussion, look at Romans 12:17-21. *"Do not repay anyone evil for evil. . . Do not take revenge. . . for it is written It is mine to avenge, I will repay, says the Lord. On the contrary: If your enemy is hungry feed him. . . In doing this you will heap burning coals on his head. Do not be overcome by evil, but overcome evil with good."*

So, our text concludes with "love covers over all wrongs;" it is fairly easy to believe this and even to do it when there is no conflict. When we are in the middle of a test it is another matter. It is still very much doable, but not in our own strength and not by our sheer determination. It will take full faith and trust and dependence on the Holy Spirit within.

PROVERBS TO LIVE BY

Proverbs 10:13-14

"Wisdom is found on the lips of the discerning, but a rod is for the back of him who lacks judgment. Wise men store up knowledge, but the mouth of a fool invites ruin."

Wisdom becomes evident in speech. However, there can be a vast chasm between the intelligent, educated people, and wise people. Wise people can be found among all classes of people, whether educated or uneducated, as can foolish people. Raw intelligence and education do not translate into wisdom, and wisdom does not exclude intelligence or education. We must always keep in mind that wisdom comes from God in answer to prayer, and it begins with a true fear of God. But wherever wisdom is, it will manifest itself.

On the other hand, the fool, or the one who lacks judgment, will have to bear the consequences. Our text says "a rod" (or punishment) will be needed. In our parlance we might say he will have to learn the hard way. One man said of a fellow Christian believer that "he used very poor judgment." At one time or another, that could probably be said of any one of us. If and when that is true, some kind of correction is probably needed. The way a wise person would handle that is found in 1Corinthians 11:31 *"if we judged ourselves, we would not come under judgment."* Persistent failure to correct ourselves may lead to external intervention.

Our text continues: *"wise men store up knowledge."* In other words, we learn from our mistakes, and remember them when a similar situation arises in the future. According to the last part of the verse, that is the real difference between a wise person and a fool. The fool persists in his folly; by the grace of God, and with divine help, the wise man turns away from folly. Let's not delay to confess and forsake foolishness when it is found to be present in ourselves.

"The wealth of the rich is their fortified city, but poverty is the ruin of the poor."

The Moody Bible Commentary begins comment on this verse with "Wealth certainly has its advantages." True. What it does not, and cannot claim, is that therefore wealth is the answer to everything. Our text says that wealth is a fortification, and it can certainly provide protection from some types of disasters. A no-so-wealthy person may say they understand that money can't buy happiness, but they would like to have just enough money to prove it. Reality is that such an amount of money does not exist. Money was never designed to purchase such life values. However, it can, and should purchase some pleasures, as well as the necessities of life. Wealth does provide protection in economically difficult times, something like a fortress.

Those to whom God has given special ability to get wealth, (Deuteronomy 8:18), should most certainly utilize that ability. Money-management is another issue. All of us, regardless of economic status, are equally required by God to be faithful with whatever has been placed in our care.

Perhaps more attention should be paid to provide advice and teaching to the not-so-wealthy. The "poor" many times are not so much in need of a hand-out as they are in need of money-management advice and teaching. Some people may be poor because of laziness; many more are poor because of poor money-management. In Jesus parable of the talents, the owner gave to each servant an amount *"according to their ability."* The one with the single talent was not judged for a lack of ability; he was judged for his lack of faithfulness. Some people are poor also because they live in a constant state of envy of those who have more, and so **"poverty is their ruin."**

"The wages of the righteous bring them life, but the income of the wicked brings them punishment."

This verse is a continuation of thought from the previous. It does seem to have a dual meaning or application. Yes, it does talk about financial income, but does not at all imply that it is the financial wages that bring life—especially eternal life. Nor is the word "wages" restricted to a financial application. The "righteous" earn wages other than, and in addition to, a financial paycheck. Such wages are paid out both in this lifetime, as well as in eternity. The financial wages earned here is perhaps not so much a matter of amount, but more a matter of how these earnings are spent and invested. Additionally, by their deeds, by their attitudes, by their kind concern for others etc., the righteous earn "wages" independent of finances, that bring them joy and fulfillment and therefore a life worth living.

According to the words of Jesus in Matthew 6:20, such earning and investing of wages, both financial and are practical, are for the benefits of self and others, is actually laying up treasures in heaven. The righteous person earns "wages" that bless the wage-earner both in this life and in the next.

In our text, the righteous and the wicked are the wise and the fool. The wicked includes the greedy, the selfish, the dishonest, the unkind, the dishonorable and the like. Those traits will not necessarily result in physical punishment or imprisonment; it may only result in a loss of trust and respect among peers, but even if not, such a person is robbed of the joy and fulfillment that was available. If so, that alone constitutes punishment in this life, to say nothing of the life hereafter. The person who thinks he "got away with it," really never did. You can always be sure your sin will find you out.

Proverbs 10:17

"He who heeds discipline shows the way to life, but whoever ignores correction leads others astray."

When children are small, we can "make them" do or say certain things. However, even then we cannot "make them" choose or reject specific attitudes and beliefs. Now consider adult children or grand-children. They definitely are beyond the reach of our control. For those who have chosen the "way to life" we need to give much thanks, while continuing to pray for them. For those who are in process of making life choices we can of course give "asked for" advice, and also to be much in prayer. For those who may have made wrong choices, too much advice may simply harden them to remain on their chosen path. So, what, if anything, can we do?

People are wont to say "all we can do now is pray." There may be a sense in which that is true, but it is not fully true. It is not absolutely true. We can do more. We must do more. No, we must not preach at them, but look at the first part of our text. *"He who heeds discipline **shows** the way to life."* (emphasis added) We, you and I, must by our own life choices, SHOW the way to life. The word discipline in our context has primary reference to the Lord's discipline. However, it has specific application to self-discipline. It is not enough to simply avoid specific obvious sins. Some people make excuse for some things by saying "that (whatever *that* refers to) is my one remaining vice." We must learn, and then demonstrate quietly, to live a disciplined life. But if we ignore correction, we actually lead people astray.

So, we can show the way to life, or else we actually lead people astray. We can never pray too much, but we absolutely must, by the grace of God, bring discipline to our own lives, in matters observable and otherwise. God always looks at the heart, and He also sees the external.

"He who conceals his hatred has lying lips, and whoever spreads slander is a fool. When words are many, sin is not absent, but he who holds his tongue is wise." Here's how it reads in the King James. *"Whoever conceals hatred with lying lips and spreads slander is a fool. Sin is not ended by multiplying words, but the prudent hold their tongues."*

This section speaks first to the foolish and then secondly to the wise. Have you ever been with someone who obviously hated (disliked) you, and then verbally denied it? Perhaps he even tried to appear friendly? That is so pathetic. Of course, some might be so good at the deception that you didn't even notice. It could also be that we, at times, are just not perceptive enough. The issue is not whether or not we perceive deception, but whether or not there is deception. God knows. And the perpetrator knows.

And then there is the matter of slander. It is almost certain that the one who conceals and lies about it, will then also take someone into his confidence and slander about it. The slander will quickly spread far and wide as rumor. Both translations above agree that such a person is a fool.

This is not just third person; you and I may be guilty of doing that very thing at times. That is never wise. It is always foolish. It is always sin. We, who are in the category of the righteous, the blood-bought children of God, also behave foolishly at times. We are not exempt. We may then try to talk our way out of it by using many words.

The prudent, the wise, the righteous "hold their tongues." The wisest thing we can do sometimes is to keep our mouth shut. My experience, and perhaps yours, would testify to the truth of that. But we may still need frequent reminders.

PROVERBS TO LIVE BY

Proverbs 10:20-21

"The tongue of the righteous is choice silver, but the heart of the wicked is of little value. The lips of the righteous nourish many, but fools die for lack of judgment."

Each of these verses has a compare and contrast component. In verse 20 I would probably have reversed the two; the heart of the righteous, and the tongue of the wicked. But God didn't. The "tongue of the righteous" speaks what the heart is full of. We remember the words of Jesus: out of the abundance of the heart the mouth speaks. True righteousness is God's gift to us if and when our heart trusts in God for the salvation He provides. So, Philippians 3:9 speaks of being in Christ "not having a righteousness of my own . . . but that which comes through faith in Christ . . . that comes from God and is by faith." Consider Abraham. Our own "righteousness" is described in Isaiah 64:6 as "filthy rags." Our text indicates that such true righteousness of heart will be reflected in our speech, and compares to "choice silver."

The heart of the wicked is of little value. That is insofar as having any lasting value. Such a person may be of "good moral character," and may give sound practical advice on some matters, but have minimal lasting value. One sage has advised that since coffee really isn't very good for you, you need to drink a lot of it to get more of what little good it has. If given and taken seriously, that advice would fit into the "of little value" category. Verse 21 is pretty much a restatement of verse 20.

Second Corinthians 13:5 instructs us to "examine yourselves." We can do that in relation to our righteousness, by paying attention to what we say. The mouth will speak out of the fullness of the heart. While none of us is perfect, our speech pattern will display righteousness if indeed it is there.

PROVERBS TO LIVE BY

Proverbs 10:22

"The blessing of the Lord brings wealth, and he adds no trouble to it."

Since Proverbs is written to teach wisdom for living in this world, there is no need to spiritualize this. Yes, Jesus talked about laying up treasures in heaven, and that true riches are eternal. And we should never forget that. It is also true that not everyone can acquire great riches here in this life. But many can, and should. What this verse is dealing with however, is that the ultimate source of wealth is the Lord Himself.

God told His people in Deuteronomy 8:18 that it is God "who gives you the ability to produce wealth." The dictionary is the only place where wealth comes before work. Yet many people to whom God has given the ability to produce wealth, nevertheless fail to produce it. In some cases, it may be that they were never really willing to work for it, and there may be other reasons. But for those who have it, whether little or much, just remember the Lord, and thank Him for His blessings. (Read the rest of Deuteronomy 8.)

A client asked for some "stewardship" advice, which I was able to provide. Had he asked for advice on increasing his wealth, I could not have helped him much since he was already making a million dollars a day. Not without smart and hard work, I might add. As far as I was able to determine however, he still did not have real financial freedom. More work and smarter advice may add to the wealth pool, but it does not add to the blessings of the Lord.

Real financial freedom comes only when 100% of one's money and asset management is submitted to the Lordship of Jesus Christ. And you can "take that to the bank." If He's not Lord of all, He isn't Lord at all."

Proverbs 10:23-25

"A fool finds pleasure in evil conduct, but a man of understanding delights in wisdom. What the wicked dreads will overtake him; what the righteous desire will be granted. When the storm has swept by, the wicked are gone, but the righteous stand firm forever."

Have you ever met a person who just seemed to delight in being mean and hurting others, whether physically or otherwise? No matter what age they happen to be, they are the man this text is referring to. Or, have you met some who talked real mean and tough, but they don't actually walk their talk. They are probably on their way, but this verse talks about people who take pleasure in evil *conduct*. And some of these people get elected and re-elected to positions of authority. You and I don't need to call them fools, but God does.

Now let me go to a little meddling; have we ever thought or said "I'd like to give him a taste of his own medicine." Let's leave the final judgment up to God, but in the meantime, Fools will get the reward for their deeds even in this life—at least to a degree. The text says what they dread will overtake them.

On the other hand, the people of understanding, the righteous, delight in wisdom. Therefore, what they in wisdom desire, will be granted. That may well include material benefits, but not because they were selfishly desired. I find no biblical support for the "name it and claim it" theology. The Bible does teach, however, "delight yourself in the Lord and he will give you the desires of your heart." Psalm 37:4 The more we delight in Him, the more He is able to give us the desires of our hearts. But God is not into magic formulas and tricky manipulation. He looks at the heart. And He sees our real motivations. Let's be wise.

"As vinegar to the teeth and smoke to the eyes, so is a sluggard to those who send him."

I am reminded again that "**all** Scripture is given by inspiration of God and is profitable for teaching . . ." and is therefore intended for us today. So, what can we learn here? Let's look first at the obvious. It is a warning against laziness by showing the potential and maybe inevitable consequences of laziness in business or work. If you have ever worked alongside a lazy person you know how irritating that can be. Being a "workaholic" however is not the antidote to laziness.

There is another look we can take, and this applies to the work of the ministry, and not only or even especially to "professional" ministers. It has been stated that 80% of the work in church is being done by 20% of the people. (It may well be more like 90/10 in many churches.) If that indeed is true, the question is: Why? Many people simply say "I work all week; Sunday is my day off." Retirees often use another line, and say "been there, done that." A pastor's job of course includes motivating, encouraging and helping. In the process it may become evident that some people are just not suited for certain jobs or aspects of ministry. But with proper help, an unsuited person may often become very well suited—if he/she is willing.

But now let's look at it from the perspective of the Lord of the harvest as He is sending out workers. As vinegar to His teeth, and smoke to His eyes is – not an unqualified worker, but one who is too lazy or is too careless to give it an honest effort. Not everyone is capable of doing everything, but each of us is capable of doing something. Let's not try to blow smoke into His eyes.

PROVERBS TO LIVE BY

Proverbs 10:27-28

*"The fear of the Lord adds length to life, but the years of
the wicked are cut short. The prospect of the righteous
is joy, but the hopes of the wicked come to nothing."*

These, and the following verses deal with the future of both the righteous and the wicked in this life. Eternity is not in view here. It may be time to be reminded that the Proverbs do not declare unconditional laws of the universe, but rather they are general indicators. So, we could say that the fear of the Lord, generally speaking, adds length to life. This would be true partially because the righteous, as they are called in the next verse, generally lead healthier, safer lives. The wicked tend more to go to extremes and excesses. In our current culture, the wicked would be more likely than the God-fearing, to use alcohol' drugs and other unhealthy practices to excess; they would therefore also be more likely to have and to cause more accidents. Clean living in all respects is healthier than non-clean living. One Thesaurus has 41 synonyms and 42 antonyms for clean living.

The next verse claims that the prospect of the righteous is a joy that only God can provide, while the hopes of the wicked come to ruin. By their lifestyles and personal choices, they do not open themselves up to what God in love would like to do for them. Medical science has long known that a joyful, happy outlook on life is healthier, and therefore tends to extend life from a purely medical perspective. The wicked may hope for a winning finish and a promising future, but their lifestyle prohibits it.

The enemy of our souls is of course constantly seeking to tempt us and trick us into choosing the wrong path, and often with some short-term successes. However, the One who promised never to leave us will not allow us to be tempted beyond our ability to endure. (1Corinthians 10:13)

PROVERBS TO LIVE BY

Proverbs 10:29-30

"The way of the Lord is a refuge for the righteous, but it is the ruin of those who do evil. The righteous will never be uprooted, but the wicked will not remain in the land."

The "fear of the Lord," as found in verse 27, speaks of our attitude toward Him. The "way of the Lord" here in verse 29 probably has in mind God's standards of wisdom, morality and righteousness for all mankind. As such it truly is a path and a place of refuge for us. Everyone should live by God's standards, but so often we run into a dead-end. We just don't know which way to turn or how to go on until we turn back to God's standards of right and wrong. Then, there it is.

Interestingly, the King James version has "the way of the Lord is strength to the upright." Probably more often than we realize, even on the right way we lack the strength to go on, but if it is indeed the way of the Lord for us at that point in our lives, it is our refuge, but it is also our strength. God's call and His command has in it the needed strength to go on to completion. And when we are battered and bruised in the battle, it has also the refuge for rest and recovery along with it. When Jesus said "without me you can do nothing" in John 15:5, He knew what He was talking about.

The last half of the verse could read "the way of the Lord is the ruin of those who do evil." Saying it that way does not change the truth, but it may help to get our attention. We would not know that doing evil is evil if there were no standard, but since God is God, the righteous standard is there. To violate that standard, therefore, is ruinous even in this life, how much more so in the next. The righteous, however, though they may at times stumble and fall, will never be uprooted and cast aside. Under His wings is a refuge in all the storms of life. PTL.

PROVERBS TO LIVE BY

"The mouth of the righteous brings forth wisdom, but a perverse tongue will be cut out. The lips of the righteous know what is fitting, but the mouth of the wicked only what is perverse."

I wonder if Jesus had these verses in mind when He spoke the words of Matthew 12:36-37: *But I tell you that men will have to give account on the day of judgment for every careless word they have spoken. For by your words you will be acquitted, and by your words you will be condemned.*

Our text says the mouth brings forth wisdom, and it also says the lips know what is fitting. But that is not to suggest a very wise and intelligent mouth and lips. Actually, this is just another way of saying our speech will reveal what is in the heart. The mouth "brings forth," but does not produce what it brings forth. It simply brings forth what was already produced inwardly. This is the idea of fruit-bearing. I have several fruit trees, from a lemon, to several different kinds of oranges to grapefruit. Each tree produces its own kind of fruit, but in every case, the fruit comes out and is seen on the branches.

What is evident in the use of wise and fitting speech is also true in the use of the speech of the wicked. The mouth and lips of the wicked simply reveal what has already been produced on the inside. When our politicians and public figures lie and cheat and steal and deceive, our culture seems to think that a simple apology will make it alright. The problem is not the words; the problem is the heart. An apology may be in order, but a change is needed.

So, when Jesus said "by your words you will be acquitted and/or condemned," He was really talking about what those words reveal about us. We need to change, and He is waiting to do the changing for us, if we let Him.

Proverbs 11:1

"The Lord abhors dishonest scales, but accurate weights are his delight."

The Book of Proverbs is so practical, isn't it? I mean it even looks into the minutia of business transactions. Is God really that concerned about a few cents per pound discrepancy of some commodity? I don't think so, but what He is very concerned about is the person who is causing the discrepancy. Jesus did not die to pay for the redemption of commerce, He died to purchase redemption of the people carrying on commerce. He died for you and me. Redemption is not merely a ticket to heaven, it is aimed at regenerating and transforming the whole person. The Moody Bible Commentary says about this verse that "God is profoundly concerned about ethics in business." Private **or** corporate, I might add.

It is true that some sins carry much bigger consequences than others. Maybe for that reason we tend to categorize sins as big or little. Honesty is compromised whether by two cents, two dollars or any amount you can think of by adding extra zeroes. God can "afford" any sum as well as any other sum, but that is never the issue. Dishonesty is dishonesty no matter what is involved. Again, the commentary says: "Dishonesty is serious because it is in the same category as other abominations including sexual immorality, idolatry, occult practices, child sacrifice, and lying." Wow!!

So then, sin is a matter of the heart, not just a ledger entry. And to paraphrase Jeremiah, the heart is incorrigible, we don't know how bad it is. But the redeemed of the Lord are being conformed and transformed into the image of Jesus Christ. I, for one, am still in process, so please be patient with me, God is at work.

"When pride comes, then comes disgrace, but with humility comes wisdom."

Over and over again, we find in Proverbs that the truly wise are teachable. So, what is it in a person that will cause him to reject or ignore teaching? Why will they so often not really listen to any viewpoint other than their own? Most often it is just a matter of pride; they think themselves too wise to need any further enlightening on anything. They may not really believe themselves to be all wise, or a "know it all," yet their personal pride, their deep inner need to be seen as superior, keeps them from acknowledging anything else. This text claims that when pride comes, so does disgrace. It is worth thinking about, after all, God said it (through His servant).

At this point, many of us can say (very quietly, of course) "been there, done that." How often have we taken an inflexible position on an issue, only later to be proven wrong? And the more adamant we've been, the more public the disgrace. If and when we've been more open to listen and to see the other side of the matter, we've been able to learn something. Humility does that. Nobody knows all there is to know about any matter, so we can always learn something, even if it is to broaden our understanding of the correctness of our initial position.

So, with humility comes wisdom. God has never designated me general manager or CEO of the universe—not even of my little universe. I will be wise then to not act as if He did. Among the benefits of humility, aside from gaining wisdom, is that everyday living will be much more stress-free, enjoyable and satisfying, and my relationship with the Lord will get "sweeter as the years go by."

PROVERBS TO LIVE BY

Proverbs 11:3

"The integrity of the upright guides them, but the unfaithful are destroyed by duplicity."

Have you ever been to a point in your life where you have said something like, "Well, all I can do now is pray?" Hopefully you have been praying, even while you tried everything else you could think to do, and not just tried everything else before praying. That may also be true for some. But reality is that even those who have been praying all along, still want to do everything they can to resolve the issue. There is not a medical issue of any kind that God cannot heal instantly, but most often He seems to use the medical profession to bring us to a point of healing. Early in his medical training, my son saw clearly that while a doctor may set a bone, or prescribe an anti-biotic, the healing itself is God's doing. For the Christian, prayer fits in before, during and after whatever is going on.

Our text is not a teaching on healing. However, it very clearly applies in that it teaches us that as Christians seeking to walk with the Lord and do the right thing, our integrity will guide us in what to do and what not to do. This will be true in all the affairs of life. The more honesty becomes our modus operandi in our dealings with both God and man, the more clearly our integrity will guide us in all things. People have experienced this to be true in secular employment situations, in ministry, in family and social matters and in the decision-making process.

In following this guidance, I have frequently made correct decisions and have taken appropriate action when I had neither the insights nor the knowledge or experience to figure it out for myself. *The integrity,* not the intelligence, *of the upright guides them.*

"Wealth is worthless in the day of wrath, but righteousness delivers from death."

I wish to add another Scripture to this before we consider this teaching: "The love of money is a root of all kinds of evil." 1 Timothy 6:10. Our text opens with "wealth is worthless," which is not the way we tend to view it, so let's take another look.

Neither money nor wealth is intrinsically evil. But in the cosmic scheme of things, money is rather limited in what it can do. Oh yes, it can buy a lot of stuff, including stuff that is actually needed for daily living. It can pay medical bills, but not buy health; it can buy fun, but not happiness, it can buy some friends, but not one meaningful relationship, it can provide for this life, but not for the next, and it cannot even make a dent in the judgment in the day of wrath.

The text continues: "righteousness delivers from death." The day of wrath in Scripture refers to the great and final judgment of God that ends in eternal death for all but those who have been given the righteousness of God as a gift of grace. Righteousness, God's imputed righteousness, absolutely delivers from eternal death. At times it also delivers from earthly death, or rather at least postpones it, in many instances.

Righteous living is much safer than wicked living by its lifestyle alone, and thus it has application for the here and now. Statistics show that in recent years the rate of Christian persecution and martyrdom has increased to the highest level in human history. Even so, many "righteous" have been delivered from death even there. It was not their money that did it. Money has its rewards for this life, but righteousness has rewards both for this life and for all eternity.

"The righteousness of the blameless makes a straight way for them, but the wicked are brought down by their own wickedness."

Again, as often in Proverbs, our attention is drawn to the paths of the righteous and blameless, versus the paths of the wicked. Instead of "straight" as in NIV and some others, the NASB has righteousness (of the blameless) will smooth his way. At times the path may include some difficult, steep grades and some unexpected curves so we can't see what lies ahead. That is because the path leads through enemy territory in this sin infested earth. But the righteousness of the blameless, the righteousness of God in the believer, will always make the path navigable. That, of course, is the promise of 1 Corinthians 10:13. He, the righteous God, will not allow the enemy to make the way impassable, but will always smooth it out so we can bear up under it.

Not so the path of the wicked. Oh, the enemy may not always block the path with debris, in fact he may make it rather smooth at times, but not because he loves his followers. The devil has no love—for anybody, not even himself. He often treats his followers well so as to make it appear, they have God's blessing, but the long-term goal is to ensure their eventual demise. His goal is that unbelievers go along their merry way, unaware that they are sealing their own doom.

There is an old song that says in part: "It's not an easy road, we are traveling to heaven, for many are the thorns on the way. It's not an easy road, but the Savior is with us. His presence gives us joy very day. It's not an easy road, but Jesus walks beside us and brightens the way." His righteousness smooths out the path for us.

"The righteousness of the upright delivers them, but the unfaithful are trapped by evil desires."

The first question you might think of is: what will the upright be delivered from, and by what evil desires will the unfaithful be trapped? The text does not specify, so obviously it could happen in various scenarios. But for starters, maybe both are facing the same thing.

At a golf course near where I live, apparently some golfers had worked out a fairly smooth scam that reportedly seemed to work, at least some of the time. An "unfaithful" man will go into the clubhouse, pay his fees, rent a set of clubs and then join the others at the first tee. After the game they all plan to meet in the clubhouse for coffee, but the "unfaithful" man excuses himself to "put my clubs in the car first." The "upright" man has and faces the same temptation, but his "righteousness delivers him."

Even if the unfaithful man were never to get caught, he would still be trapped by his evil desires for the rest of his life—unless he repents. Giving in to evil desires can very quickly become a way-of-life. Many a young person who has seen such behavior in his father has gone down that same road. In fact, one man told me how he had taught his sons to do a similar thing in department stores.

The upright man who is clothed in the righteousness of God will be delivered from such unrighteousness. Again, and again, the upright will be delivered. No, Christians are not perfect, but we do have the Holy Spirit living within to provide the necessary strength to resist such temptations. The process of deliverance is given in Galatians 5:25 ***"Since we live by the Spirit, let us keep in step with the Spirit."***

Proverbs 11:7

"When a wicked man dies, his hope perishes; all he expected from his power comes to nothing."

Another translation says "hopes placed in mortals will die with them." No matter the translation used, the hope will die when the mortal who placed the hope dies, and/or when the mortal in whom the hope was placed dies.

The wicked man in our text has naturally placed his hope in mortals; he has nowhere else to place it, so of course such hope will perish. All he expected from his power comes to nothing. We can see how this applies to national and international affairs, but in principle, it is the same in local and personal affairs. A small start-up business may have a written "business continuation plan," providing for someone to carry on the business in the event of the principal's inability to continue. That is merely good, common sense planning—providing it takes into account the Lord's Sovereignty. Many people try to control family affairs from "beyond the grave" in making out their last will and testament. (Such planning is usually not permitted by law.)

Here my thoughts naturally turn to a corollary issue, what about the plans of the righteous. Insofar as our ultimate hope in the Lord is concerned, that will not die or perish; it will be realized in glory. But what about our hopes for events related to this life? Don't we also have such plans and hopes? Of course, we do, and we should, but they must submit to the Lord's sovereignty. But those hopes and plans will most certainly involve and include "mortals", so will those hopes also perish? Not necessarily. However, we must make and place those hopes with the guidance of the Holy Spirit. The Apostle James in 4:15 advises: "you ought to say, if it is the Lord's will, we will live and do this or that." So, we need to follow the Lord's guidance throughout the process.

PROVERBS TO LIVE BY

"The righteous man is rescued from trouble, and it comes on the wicked instead."

At first reading, this indicates that the righteous never have trouble. So, when trouble does come, it must mean that the righteous are spared. And that in fact, seems to be what some are teaching in their "Health & Wealth" gospel. Such reasoning would imply that if and when a born-again believer does have trouble, it is because of a lack of faith or disobedience. But that would be no Gospel at all. The Gospel of Jesus Christ can also be called a gospel of truth, because Jesus Himself IS truth. In real life there is a big difference between faith and fantasy. A righteous person, as Proverbs often calls us, is righteous only because and through faith in Jesus Christ, and one's righteous is an imputed righteousness.

In Job 5:7 we read that man is born to trouble as surely as sparks fly upwards. Man, here refers to all mankind, both the believers and the unbelievers. Job's friends may have been the forerunners of the present day "Health & Wealth" preaching. Their claim was that Job must have been a "closet sinner" right along, and God finally caught up with him. God's reply to those friends is given in Job 42:8: *"You have not spoken of me what is right as my servant Job has."*

Now back to our text. When you are in trouble, be of good courage: you will be rescued from your trouble. Your trouble will not be victorious. The wicked have no such promise. Even though God blessed Job more after his time of trouble, he never did know why his trouble came, or, perhaps, where it came from. Nor did Job have Romans 8:28, at least not in written from. But we do. Before, during and after trouble, God is working in all things to conform us into the image of Jesus Christ. *"Though he slay me, yet will I trust in Him."*

"With his mouth the godless destroys his neighbor, but through knowledge the righteous escape."

As in Luke 10, the neighbor is not necessarily the one who lives next door, or even someone you know personally. Read the verse again, leaving out the words "his neighbor." With his mouth, the godless destroys. No, I'm not trying to delete anything out of the Scriptures, I just want us to place the emphasis where Scripture places it. What the godless do with their slanderous speech is to destroy. The fact that this evil must of necessity have an object, is almost incidental—except to the one who receives the brunt of this evil.

It seems to me that in our culture, this destructive behavior comes from many segments of society, including the major media, academia, politics and etc., as well as from individuals.

The promise to believers is that "through knowledge the righteous escape." OK, what kind of knowledge would that take? Thanks for asking. In Proverbs 9:10 we learn that "*knowledge of the Holy One is understanding.*" That is where it begins. We need to know Him personally and more and more intimately. As with the trouble in the previous verse, human nature wants: #1 to escape, and if that is not to be, then #2 to be delivered from. But through knowing the Lord we know that destructive, slanderous speech will happen, and we will be the target of some of it from time to time. So where is our escape? First, it cannot separate us from the love of God, so we can remain joyful and hopeful. Our reputation may be impinged and maybe even destroyed in the minds of people, but NEVER WHERE IT COUNTS.

Please read Psalm 37:3-6 for your personal assurance and encouragement. ***He will*** do what He said He would do.

PROVERBS TO LIVE BY

"When the righteous prosper, the city rejoices; when the wicked perish, there are shouts of joy. Through the blessing of the upright a city is exalted, but by the mouth of the wicked it is destroyed."

In this proverb, the issue is given in verse 11. Two things make a city (or country) rejoice: the prosperity of the righteous, or the perishing of the wicked. The next verse gives the explanation, or the reasons why this is so. The city, or country rejoices, or does well when the righteous prosper.

First let's take this prosperity as economic. The reason for the city rejoicing would be that the prosperity of the righteous is that they will pay the taxes, they will acquire their wealth honestly, and they will enforce the laws, thus bringing crime down. But consider also their spiritual prosperity. The righteous will be involved in civic affairs, thus influencing the kinds of laws that will be enacted, they will have a righteous impact on the lives of all, and will be a means of turning some of the wicked from their evil ways. More could be said.

There will also be rejoicing when the wicked will perish, either from the area or from life itself. This is not to say that we should individually rejoice over the downfall of the wicked, but the city, the community, and the country will be relieved of evil influence. Unfortunately, right now in the US, and in other Western countries, it is often the wicked who wield the political power.

However, God's word is still true. To find relief from regional or national disaster, it is the "righteous," God's people, who are called by His Name who need to humble themselves, to pray, and to seek His face, in other words to repent, so that God can hear and forgive and heal the city, the region, the community. Being a child of God is an immeasurable blessing, that carried individual responsibilities.

PROVERBS TO LIVE BY

Proverbs 11:12

"A man who lacks judgment derides his neighbor, but a man of understanding holds his tongue."

This proverb has a very simple, common sense message; yet it is greatly ignored and disobeyed by so many. (of us?) It is clear that there is no quarter here for judgmentalism. How often have you been talking with someone when another person enters the room and you quickly have to change the subject. That may be OK if you were planning a surprise birthday party or something, but that is not what this proverb is talking about. Notice the word "derides." Now be honest with yourself, are you ever guilty? Or more often than you care to admit? As redeemed people in a fallen world, we are all susceptible, and probably at least tempted in this arena. As one who is still in process of being conformed to the image of Jesus Christ, and not making any public confession at this time, I will say that I have far too often observed this type of thing going on. In fact, there are people for whom this seems to be a lifestyle. Judgmentalism and derisive speech to and about others is much too common among Christians.

Our text says people who speak that way lack judgment. In other words, they are not wise, but foolish. And I would venture to say many are not at all aware of the damage this does to their own testimony and to the lives of those who are victims of such derision. BUT, a man of understanding "hold his tongue." You know the old saying, *it is better to hold your tongue and be thought a fool, than to speak and remove all doubt.* In fact, there is great wisdom in keeping quiet at certain times. That is why the Apostle James (1:19) says *"Everyone should be quick to listen, slow to speak and slow to become angry."*

If none of this applies to you, see if you can un-read it.

Proverbs 11:13

"A gossip betrays a confidence, but a trustworthy man keeps a secret."

So many of the proverbs are just plain common sense, and should hardly need to be mentioned—except that by and large, we are not a terribly common-sense people. More importantly, God is concerned about every detail of the lives of people He loves. We have probably all had someone betray our confidence, at least as far back as the school playground. It's just that as we got older, the betrayals became more serious.

OK, we can't control what other people do, whether they prove trustworthy or not. But we can control whom we trust, and we can control how easily we trust them, and to what degree we trust them. Some of us are far too quick to share a confidence with someone who has not been "proven" expecting them to keep a confidence. Not too long ago I shared a miner confidence with a Christian brother from another church, whom I had gotten to know, and, I believed, to understand a little. We shared a number of values and similar experiences, so I shared a personal matter with him. I don't believe he ever mentioned it to anyone else, but he did some time later mention it to me in the hearing of a few others.

The lesson to me was to be more careful with what I share about myself, but more than that, to be very careful never to make any reference to anything another person may have shared with me. If it was shared as a prayer request, of course you will want to enquire how the matter is working out, but NEVER in the hearing of anyone else. Only with the one who shared the confidence with you in the first place. Let us strive to be the "trustworthy" person who will keep a secret. So, help me God! That is a part of wisdom; that is a part of godliness.

"For lack of guidance a nation falls, but many advisers make victory sure."

This proverb obviously is aimed at a nation, and therefore relates to national matters, particularly as they might apply to a war. Every nation has its own "intelligence gathering" operations and methods as needed just to conduct business, let alone a war. The immediate context of this verse with its reference to "victory" indicates military advisers. A national leader however, also needs advisers representing different political perspectives to adequately assess issues and needs. But most of us don't move in those circles. So, what, if anything, does this text have for run-of-the-mill Christian pilgrims?

As a minister and pastor, I have frequently been asked for advice by young men regarding the advisability of pursuing a career in ministry. I have always willingly given my advice (and it's not always the same) but then encouraged them to get advice from others as well. Ultimately, God is the only One who can give accurate guidance, but He often uses other people as His mouthpiece. Our text says "many advisers make victory sure." Some translations use the word "multitude." In other words, get all the advice you can.

But national leaders and ministers are not the only ones who need advice and guidance. As a matter of fact, everyone needs guidance when making any major decision. We cannot be too informed on any matter before making a decision. If we are listening, we may hear someone even unintentionally make a comment that raises a red flag, or that serves to confirm our own direction of thinking. God definitely has a plan for each one of us, and He is always speaking to us, but we are sometimes far from listening. Advisers can help.

PROVERBS TO LIVE BY

Proverbs 11:15

"He who puts up security for another will surely suffer,
but whoever refuses to strike hands in pledge is safe."

We might currently say it another way: it is not wise to co-sign a note for just anyone, or you may get stuck having to pay it off when the principle can't or won't. It has been suggested this "someone" could be a casual acquaintance. That would be in sync with the tone of the verse. But then someone might argue, it's OK, I can afford it. If I lose it, then it was just a bad investment.

But I believe there is a deeper principle involved here, and that is ultimate Ownership. Psalm 24:1 says it fairly clearly, as do numerous other Scriptures. "The earth is the Lord's and everything in it, the world and all who live in it." Psalm 50:10 lets us know that the Lord owns the cattle on a thousand hills, and in Haggai 2:8 He tells us He owns all the silver and the gold. God has entrusted us with a stewardship of His assets, but everything in our possession is still His. Therefore, to put up security for another without the Owner's consent is a violation of the trust.

I heard a speaker at a financial conference say that he had made it a practice to give away $500 each day to total strangers. This is fine, provided the Owner has so directed, and has entrusted you with the wherewithal to do it. The speaker did not mention those provisos, and if that, or any other acts of kindness and generosity are meant to purchase favor with God, that won't do it. The money you have at your disposal is not actually yours. The money I have at my disposal is ultimately not mine.

"Now it is required that those who have been given a trust must prove faithful." 1 Corinthians 4:2. That is the key to all money management.

PROVERBS TO LIVE BY

Proverbs 11:16-17

"A kindhearted woman gains respect, but ruthless men gain only wealth. A kind man benefits himself, but a cruel man brings trouble on himself."

The kindhearted woman in the proverb could be considered wisdom herself, as it is in chapter 8, and it could also be pointing us to the industrious woman of chapter 31. Or both! Obviously, respect is gained by being "kindhearted." That is not the same as **appearing** to be kindhearted. One can **do** a kindness without **being** kindhearted. But there are other qualities required to gain respect, and I would place integrity right up there along with kindness. Respect indicates a level of trust, or trustworthiness. Between Bible College years I got a job for which I was unqualified and inexperienced, because of the respect the business owner had for my father. I guess they figured "like father, like son." (They were not disappointed.)

Ruthless men could be those who operate a business, even within the confines of the law, but are unconcerned about people, focusing only on the bottom line. They are cruel taskmasters. All they can possibly hope to gain is wealth, but at what cost to themselves! Any so-called friends they may have, do not respect them either. They are not real friends. What a price to pay for mere wealth! No respect and no friends.

"A kind man benefits himself." This kindness is not self-seeking but rather self-giving. Yet such a person greatly benefits himself, as well as others. This benefit may well include financial gain, because such a person is a candidate for the Lord's special blessing. And the glorious thing is, we can become more kindhearted on into old age. Those who do, will continue to increase in respect and in personal benefit. You can sign up today; it is private between you and the Lord.

PROVERBS TO LIVE BY

Proverbs 11:18-19

"The wicked man earns deceptive wages, but he who sows righteousness reaps a sure reward. The truly righteous man attains life, but he who pursues evil goes to his death,"

The whole Book of Proverbs presents the contrast between wisdom and folly to show the benefit of the one over the other. This proverb really deals with values, more than with mere money. When we think of earning wages, we naturally think of monetary returns for our labor. Money itself is neutral, it is a commodity that is intrinsically neither good nor evil.

The word "deceptive" here does not indicate wages earned by deceit, although that would be included. Rather it refers to the deceitfulness of thinking and anticipating that those wages will bring true, satisfying and gratifying rewards, once accumulated in a sufficient amount. Intellectually we all know that "money does not buy happiness," but often at our faith level we are like the one who said "I know that, but I'd like to have just enough money to prove it to myself." This foolish man is wicked because he is investing his whole life in that which is temporary and has no lasting value. His work ethic may be commendable, but his values are out of sync.

"The wise person who sows righteousness, reaps a reward." He, like the foolish man, is also earning monetary wages to provide for his family, etc., but he has a longer-range perspective. Therefore, his reward is sure; he "attains life"—eternal life. The Gospel of salvation by grace through faith is New Testament, although much of the Old Testament points to it. But Proverbs deals with life down here, life that is designed to prepare us for life to come. Proverbs deals in part with that preparation. My question is: how are we doing with our preparation? Are we packed and ready to go? Ready or not, when we get to the end of the road, we're gone.

PROVERBS TO LIVE BY

"The Lord detests men of perverse heart, but he delights in those whose ways are blameless. Be sure of this: the wicked will not go unpunished, but those who are righteous will go free."

This is a very sobering concept revealed here. It does not say God detests the perverseness in a man's heart, it says God detests the man of perverse heart. That sounds very stern, because it is. My first thought when reading this proverb was "it must mean God detests the sin, but He still loves the sinner. But the Holy Spirit immediately drew me back to the text before I could finish the thought. **God detests men of perverse heart.** So, what is a perverse heart? The Moody Bible Commentary came to my rescue; it says: "One who is perverse 'is set against God and community to serve self.'" That serves to clarify, but who is it that has a perverse heart? One who is set to serve self, is set against God. Is it just the criminals, the "down and outers" the druggies, the adulterers? Sadly, that would be *plus* you and me—at times. (Jesus told Peter "Get behind me, Satan." What can we do when we become aware that we have become self-serving? What must we do? Very simple, if not easy; we must repent, confess and forsake. It has always been relatively easy to confess; it is the repent and forsake where we have trouble.

He delights in those whose ways are blameless. (It is OK to say Hallelujah at this point.) Those who are righteous will go free. It is not that we are intrinsically better than others, but the moment we placed our faith In Jesus Christ for salvation, He wrapped us in a garment of His own righteousness. Those in this category will not remain perverse toward God. If/when they fall into this trap, they will repent, confess and forsake.

So, while these verses give stern warning, they also provide blessed assurance.

PROVERBS TO LIVE BY

Proverbs 11:22

"Like a gold ring in a pig's snout is a beautiful woman who shows no discretion."

Physical beauty can be held in too high esteem, both by those who have it in abundance and by those (men) who admire it. I never knew them, but the Bible says Job's three daughters were the most beautiful women "in all the land." Had they not also been women of wisdom and discretion, I doubt the Bible would have mentioned their beauty.

This proverb pulls no punches; a most beautiful woman who lacks discretion is likened to a pig with a gold ring in its snout. I sometimes wonder if perhaps Hollywood is trying to prove this proverb wrong. Good luck! And men, just because women are more beautiful than we are doesn't leave us off the hook. Lack of discretion is equally odious in all of us, men and women alike. We've all seen it, we've all encountered it, and dare I say, we've all exhibited it. I heard one man say of another "at the very least, you used incredibly poor judgment." What is that if not lack of discretion.

It is interesting that God (through Solomon) would use this analogy. The pig was the most detestable creature in ancient Israel, and pork was the most UN-kosher food. If beauty without discretion is so ugly, that places discretion on a very high plain. Both beauty and discretion are God-given, but discretion has to be developed, it has to be exercised. And the more discretion is exercised, the more natural beauty will shine forth. Have you ever met a rather ordinary person, male or female, and the better you got to know them, the more beautiful they appeared to become? What happened? The character of Jesus was being displayed. You found them to be a person of unusually good discretion. If you find you are not attracting friends, it may be time for a personal inventory of your use of discretion, especially in speech.

PROVERBS TO LIVE BY

"The desire of the righteous ends only in good, but the hope of the wicked only in wrath."

This proverb may well have some of the idea of discretion still in mind. If so, the desire of the righteous would include a careful follow-through of the desire with action. In other words, the righteous person will follow through on their desire with action, working to help make it happen.

The righteous person may have some desires that are neither good nor right, but being righteous, he will bring those desires to the Lord for confirmation or rejection or perhaps correction. This is in part what James 4:15 is about: "If it is the Lord's will . . ." I frequently find myself praying, Lord, if this is not good or right for me, please help me to see that. I tell the Lord that my over-riding desire is for His will to be accomplished in any given situation. I'd rather have that than the specific thing I'm pursuing.

So, if our desires are submitted to the Lordship of Jesus Christ, then those desires will only end in good. If that is not the case, then at that point we are not being righteous, and therefore we cannot claim this promise.

If the "hope of the wicked" were only hopes for evil things, this half of the proverb would be redundant. The wicked, in fact, may often hope for good things, such as a happy life. He may even achieve it in measure and for a time, but it will only end in wrath, says our text. He may even hope for heaven, as many do, but a good moral life will not cut it. Without the Lord, no one can achieve the ultimate good either in this life, or certainly not in the next.

In the end, this proverb is a reminder of God's Sovereignty and his righteous judgment.

Proverbs 11:24-25

"One man gives freely, yet gains even more, another withholds unduly, but comes to poverty. A generous man will prosper; he who refreshes others will himself be refreshed."

Wise people are generous people. Generosity is not a spiritual gift that some have and others do not. Nor is it specifically a fruit of the Spirit. Generosity is wisdom in action. At this point, true wisdom and worldly wisdom part company.

The fear of the Lord is the beginning of wisdom—in us as individuals. Wisdom itself has no beginning, as God has no beginning. But as the people of God, the Holy Spirit, who is God, resides in us. That does not automatically make us wise, it merely assures us that wisdom is available, and when implemented and exercised, it will grow—or we will grow in it. As the boy Jesus grew in stature, He also grew in wisdom, Luke 2:52. As we grow in understanding, knowledge of the Word of God, and obedience, we will also grow in wisdom.

In the natural course of life, who could ever even suspect that by being generous and giving to others, one would experience an increase? The laws of mathematics are clear, if one has X amount of whatever, and he gives a portion of that away, he will have something less than the original amount. The laws of God are also clear, "give, and it will be given to you." Jesus proved that dramatically many times, but look at the feeding of the 5000. How did the increase happen?

He also demonstrated that in a less dramatic, but equally miraculous, way in my life. When in faith and obedience to a direct "call" from the Lord I increased our giving beyond the tithe, the Lord enabled us to pay off a significant amount of debt in 12 months without any increase in income. Mathematically it could not have happened, so therefore I cannot explain it. Some people do not believe me, and I don't blame them, but God nevertheless did it, because He is God.

Proverbs 11:26-27

"People curse the man who hoards grain, but blessing crowns him who is willing to sell. He who seeks good finds goodwill, but evil comes to him who searches for it."

In James chapter five we read about hoarding, and about wealth gained by oppression and dishonesty. In the immediate context it does not talk about immediate judgment of such actions, but judgment will come. Verse 3 states that "your gold and silver are corroded. Their corrosion will testify against you and eat you flesh like fire." We see this concept in our current stock market. Both individuals and corporations are guilty of manipulation for personal gain. Verse 26 of our text describes this principal in agrarian terms, namely the acquiring of personal gain, no matter the hurt or cost to anyone else. The Sovereign God is keeping records.

So now let's look at verse 27. What you seek for in others you will get yourself, is the principle here. The one who seeks to bless others by making a fair deal, will himself be blessed. The one who seeks to impoverish others for his own gain will harvest the evil he sought to bring onto others. This proverb is talking about and dealing with financial matters. Those are the easiest to understand. It is easy to calculate the bottom line, even when we can't control it.

But now take it to relational matters. The one who seeks to exalt and bless others, will be exalted and blessed; the one who seeks to manipulate others and blame them will himself be manipulated and blamed. The one who is always looking for faults in others will himself be found guilty of those and other faults. The one who seeks to minimize and overlook the faults of others will have his own faults minimized and overlooked and forgiven. Jesus taught "forgive and you will be forgiven." If you have to look back into the past to remember the faults of others, you have not yet forgiven.

Proverbs 11:28

"Whoever trusts in his riches will fall, but the righteous will thrive like a green leaf."

Whoever would be foolish enough to trust in riches? Doesn't everyone know that money and riches are totally unreliable? Well, the "whoever" is people of all stripes and colors and stations of life, Jews and all types of gentiles. Even some Christians, who have trusted the Lord for salvation from sin, tend to trust in wealth for living. It is a human malady. Money we can see and touch, and we have already seen some things money can buy, and that can be very appealing. We can easily anticipate what things money could provide us personally, if only we had more of it.

I have known some very wealthy people who use money and trust in the Lord. I've also seen some who try to use the Lord, but really trust money for everyday living. I have not yet seen how some of them have ended up, but God has. So, I'd rather just take His word for it. He says those who "trust in riches will fall." They will! May not have fallen yet, but they will. I have already fallen more than once, so I don't want to take a chance of falling in this critical area of life, especially if that fall were to be at my last and final exit.

Then comes that crucial word, but. But the righteous will thrive like a green leaf. None of us, depending on the analogy we use, are the whole tree (or the whole enchilada) but we can be a green leaf on the tree. Most of us may never own a yacht, many of us can't even afford to fly first class, but our day is coming. We will thrive like a green leaf. A green leaf has everything provided for it. Check! A green leaf can serve its whole purpose for its life. Check! A green leaf can hang out with others of its same kind and purpose. Check! A green leaf can provide protection for those seeking a safe, shady place to be. Check! Let's hear it for the green leaf.

Proverbs 11:29

"He who brings trouble on his family will inherit only wind, and the fool will be servant to the wise."

Some scholars have said that this is probably referring to a foolish or wayward son. Is so, it could possibly be that Jesus was referring to this situation when He told the story about the prodigal son in Luke 15. That son certainly brought trouble on his family, and although he repented and returned home, and was restored as the younger son, his inheritance was gone. Since he repented, does that indicate he could have gone to heaven? Absolutely yes! Could his inheritance be restored as well? No. The Father had one estate, which he divided between his sons, and that was it. Proverbs deals with what is *wise for this life*, and "wasting" his inheritance was not it.

Bringing trouble to a family can also be done by a wayward daughter, a foolish husband or wife. Many a man has brought trouble to his wife and children and lived to see everything disappear, blown away as if by a wind. Here today, gone tomorrow. Because of the grace of God, anyone can repent and put his trust in Jesus Christ for forgiveness, and end up with a glorious future in heaven. But the wasted years cannot be restored. They are gone with the wind. One cannot UN read a book, nor can anyone UN live a wasted life. And regretting the past does not change the past.

The fool will be servant to the wise. In Jesus' story, the older son was wiser with his inheritance, even though he left some things to be desired— as we all do. The one who brought trouble came asking to be hired on as a servant. Since he could no longer claim a share in the family farm, we can assume that he was indeed hired, (we don't know) and so for his foolishness he now served the wise.

Actions, ALL actions have consequences.

Proverbs 11:30

"The fruit of the righteous is a tree of life, and he who wins souls is wise."

Two verses back we learned that the righteous will thrive like a green leaf. Now we take it a step further, the righteous will not only thrive like a green leaf, which gets its nutrition from the tree, now the fruit of that righteousness "is a tree of life" which will now give life and sustenance to other leaves and branches, even to the point of producing fruit, i.e. grapes. However, to use Jesus' analogy of the vine and the branches, we must remain attached to the vine, for "apart from me, you can do nothing." The wise, or the righteous, are now in a position to give life to others, such as the grapes in John 15.

Keeping in mind that Proverbs reveals benefits of wisdom and righteousness for this life, and yes, ultimately for the next, we can look to some significant "now" benefits. Since verse 29 shows tragic results of bringing trouble on one's family, let us not forget the flip side. To not bring trouble, but rather to contribute toward a good family life, will result in life-long good family relationships. Both family and community life will be its own reward for righteous living.

"He who wins souls is wise." That is not confined to the Billy Grahams of the world. Solomon had never heard of Billy Graham when he penned these words under the inspiration of Holy Spirit. These words, therefore, are meant for you and me. Are we helping others make wise choices and decisions? What personal effort, what money, what prayers, what of life-style are we investing in seeking to win souls to Kingdom living now? Do our lives attract or repel people in our families and communities, to or away from trusting the Lord?

Just asking!

Proverbs 11:31

"If the righteous receive their due on earth, how much more the ungodly and sinner."

This is an interesting proverb. It states very clearly that it is talking about this life, and not eternity. The phrase "receive their due" is variously translated in different versions. The NKJV says "will be recompensed," the ESV, "is repaid," the NASB, "will be rewarded," but they all agree that it is "on earth." Since eternal life is a gift of grace, and our faithfulness will be rewarded in heaven, then the righteous can only be rewarded or repaid on earth for their misdeeds. This has to be what Paul in Galatians 6:7 calls reaping what we sow. A man reaps what he has sown. That is a sobering thought. Our text talks first about the righteous; we will be repaid for our misdeeds here on earth. Consider first that not one of us is righteous in himself; we are only righteous in the righteousness of Christ. Oh, we are totally forgiven in Christ. No sin is so great as to keep us out of heaven; all are covered by the blood of Christ Jesus. For that matter, no sin is so great as to keep the UN righteous out of heaven—provided he accepts God's provision of salvation. Here on earth, actions have consequences, **all** actions have consequences.

That being so, "how much more the ungodly and sinner. Why "so much more?" Consider this, when a Christian sins and then goes to the Lord to confess, repent, and obtain eternal forgiveness, he still faces the consequences of his sin. He is still responsible for his actions. But when an unbeliever sins, he has no place to go for refuge, for forgiveness, for help with the consequences. He does not have the Holy Spirit within. Even though his "reward" may not be quick in coming, it is coming. He will suffer the consequences in this life—and in the next.

Proverbs 12:1

"Whoever loves discipline loves knowledge, but he who hates correction is stupid."

The old Geneva Bible says foolish instead of stupid, and the King James says brutish, so the newer translations are on the right track with stupid. But to actually <u>love</u> discipline — isn't that stretching it a little? First of all, remember that discipline is not the same as punishment, although at times discipline may include punishment. Primarily it is a training exercise. It is getting the object of the discipline or training going in the right direction.

The Moody Bible Commentary assumes "we all make mistakes" to which we would readily agree. Those mistakes have consequences, but if we accept the consequences as discipline, and avoid repeating the same mistakes, we will gradually overcome them. If you continue to live in the past, even though God has forgiven your past and has blotted it out of existence, you may still hate yourself for some "stupid mistakes" you have made and continue to reap what you have sown. Wouldn't you love to be freed of that irritation? Well you can, but you must accept the Lord's discipline and gain deliverance through the knowledge and application of His provision. I don't know that one has to necessarily love the process of discipline; it can at times be painful, but accept it gladly, and yes love it, knowing the end result will be freedom and deliverance.

Those who hate correction to the point of refusing it are "stupid." Hebrews 12:6 reminds us that the Lord disciplines those He loves and He chastens or corrects each of His redeemed children. If I consistently exceed the speed limit, sooner or later I will be "corrected." I know from experience. (Not lately) Then the issue becomes "how will I accept the correction?" I know one thing, I like not having tickets, and I also like not having to hit the brakes when I see a cop. And there are issues that are much more eternally consequential than traffic laws. Think about it. We can be wise, or we can be stupid, (foolish) our choice.

Proverbs 12:2-3

"A good man obtains favor from the Lord, but the Lord condemns a crafty man. A man cannot be established through wickedness, but the righteous cannot be uprooted."

Not to tamper with the translation from the Hebrew here, but think of the "good man" as the "wise man." The wise man is able to see the moral implication of things and thereby choose that which is better and pleasing to the Lord. The not-so-wise might say "let's just try it and see what happens." A wise man obtains favor from the Lord, not because he is smarter or better, but because he chooses smarter and better. Realistically, this begins in ones thought processes. A wise man will shy away from negative and degrading thought patterns, leading him to make better choices and take actions. This pleases the Lord, and thus he obtains favor from the Lord. After all, as a man thinks, so is he.

A crafty man is one who is skillful in scheming and deceit. Have you ever met someone like that? Was it a Christian or a non-Christian? Well, it could be either one. Just because we know we should never **be** like that, doesn't mean we never **are**. Whenever we read a text like ours today, it would be a good idea to take inventory. Praise God for the wonderful grace of Jesus.

"A man cannot be established through wickedness," any man. That is, a crafty man will never have an unmovable, solid foundation. He is always hiding something, always covering up, always having to explain things away. Righteousness is much more stable; his foundation, the Word of God, is always solid, even when he himself has slipped and even fallen. He can get up again and the foundation is still firm. He just needs to go to the "cleansing fountain," and God's favor continues to be his portion.

Proverbs 12:5-6

"The plans of the righteous are just, but the advice of the wicked is deceitful. The words of the wicked lie in wait for blood, but the speech of the upright rescues them."

Let me remind us again that the proverbs are not absolutes; they are not "thus saith the Lord," and therefore that is the way it is 100% of the time. No, they are rather words of wisdom that speak in generalities. The righteous, much more often than not, will make plans that are right and just. If the advice is deceitful, it is most likely to have come from the wicked. If you know that to be true, and it is, then you know what to look out for. To pay heed at this point is wise.

The wicked, most often, will seek first and foremost to advance themselves and their own agenda. General "wisdom" says to look out for number one. Well, one might ask "shouldn't we look out for our own family first? Absolutely! In 1 Timothy 5:8 (God speaking) says "If anyone does not provide for his relatives, and especially for his immediate family, he has denied the faith and is worse than an unbeliever." That is pretty straight forward, but it clearly requires that this "provide for" is done honestly and justly. The "righteous" can best be expected to meet those requirements.

The phrase "lie in wait for blood" is not restricted to murder or attempted murder; rather the focus is on deceptive words being used to entrap someone else, perhaps for reasons of personal gain or maybe revenge. This could be done attempting to make a business deal, or maybe to diminish someone's reputation in the eyes of the public. This part of the verse could well be intended to apply first to the deceiver himself. Either way, "the speech of the upright rescues them." Some of us might do well to re-evaluate our speech in light of those words.

PROVERBS TO LIVE BY

Proverbs 12:11-12

"He who works his land will have abundant food, but he who chases fantasies lacks judgment. The wicked desire the plunder of evil men, but the root of the righteous flourishes."

In Solomon's day, abundant food did not refer to food stamps or welfare checks. It had to be earned by what the land and the livestock produced, and that depended a lot on the farmer's hard work. One commentator says: "frivolity fills no cupboards." In our high-tech society, the majority of employees in one particular company were counting on winning the lottery as their "retirement plan." Talk about chasing fantasies! However, intellectually that is just about on par with counting on welfare. God's plan has always been for mankind to work for a living. So much so that 2 Thessalonians 3:10 states that "if a man will not work, he shall not eat." Notice it does not say if he cannot work; there is a difference. As with so much of our "progressive" thinking, it is progressing in the wrong direction.

The issue in our text here is not so much physical labor on the land, although that often is the healthiest and most satisfying labor, rather, the point is that we should earn our keep by honest work, of whatever type it is—even writing. But you may ask, what about retirement? Yes, what about it? Some have said that the word retire is not in the Bible. Sorry to burst your bubble. In Numbers 8:25 the priests were required to retire at age fifty. However, according to the context, they only retired from active duty, but continued to assist the younger priests. When we no longer need to work in order to earn a living, we can call it retirement, it really means we are now free, and available to do what we like, and serve the Lord and/or His people. This can most certainly be the most fulfilling work we've ever done.

Proverbs 12:13-14

"An evil man is trapped by his sinful talk, but a righteous man escapes trouble. From the fruit of his lips a man is filled with good things as surely as the work of his hands rewards him."

As you read that opening phrase, you may have thought about some people with very sinful talk, but they were never been trapped by it. Maybe not yet! I know of quite a few politicians like that. But God never said they would be entrapped right away. Their time is coming. We have never been put in charge of God's time table; we are not even privy to it. Trust God, His word is sure.

In Matthew 12:37 Jesus said "by your words you will be acquitted and by your words you will be condemned. Our text does not say that others will be entrapped by his sinful talk, although that too is often the case, but sooner or later, the evil man will himself be entrapped. And it is not so much the words themselves, but more the intent and purpose of those words. "If our hearts do not condemn us, we have confidence before God." I John 3:21. So we are talking about self-condemnation, and self-acquittal before God.

The righteous man escapes trouble. Specifically, he escapes **that** trouble. He does not need to worry that his words will entrap him, because he speaks truth, kindness and goodwill. The text continues with "from the fruit of his lips a man is filled with good things." Ultimately, these good things come from God, but in the immediate they can also come via human response to the righteous one's words and actions. The text refers to the immediate, as indicated by reference to the rewards of honest work and labor. For the farmer, his works are rewarded annually at harvest—or sooner. Relational rewards do not follow a precise cycle of seed-time and harvest, but they are nonetheless certain.

Proverbs 12:15-16

"The way of a fool seems right to him, but a wise man listens to advice. A fool shows his annoyance at once, but a prudent man overlooks an insult."

There may be more to this first phrase than we immediately perceive. Essentially this phrase tells us what it is that makes the man a fool in the first place. He is a fool because he thinks he is always right; he always knows best. His way "seems right to him." Why in the world would he want to waste his time to listen to another viewpoint, or to any advice, when the only correct solution is already clear? His rule of life is to do that which is right in his own eyes, to walk in the way of his heart. This is very reminiscent of the condition of Israel in the time of the Judges. That book ends with the words "everyone did as he saw fit." And that is still the human tendency. The law of God, given by the grace of God points to the right, the wise way to go.

If not seeing the need for advice is what makes one a fool, then conversely, looking for and listening to advice makes one wise. Or look at it this way, listening to advice keeps the wise man from becoming a fool. Here is where I become "preachy," can a wise person at times act foolishly? I can. By the grace of God, I trust never to degenerate into adopting a fool's lifestyle. But let us be on guard, only the grace of God can keep us safe and secure.

With that clear in our thinking, the next verse is comparatively easy to understand. The fool can't even remain civil in light of another viewpoint, and has no intention of sitting by quietly while another viewpoint is mentioned. He underscores his annoyance by insults. The wise man, here called prudent, knows what would ensue if he answered this fool "according to his folly," and so he overlooks it. Of these two options, let us prudently choose the way of wisdom.

Proverbs 12:17-18

"A truthful witness gives honest testimony, but a false witness tells lies. Reckless words pierce like a sword, but the tongue of the wise brings healing."

Verse 17 conjures up a court scene where the witness is required to take an oath to speak the truth. Perjury has serious consequences, and so serves as a further inducement to be truthful. However, for the righteous person, this should be fairly inconsequential. Since he is imbued by, and answerable to a higher Power, and truth is his lifestyle. However, even among believers who are indwelt by the Holy Spirit, there are those to whom speaking the truth is more of a problem than it is for others. Just as we have different spiritual gifts and talents, so we also have different weaknesses and frailties. It behooves all of us therefore, to be alert and hold to the truth, not only in court and in legal matters, but also in ordinary communications with all others. A literal translation here might read "he who breathes truth reveals righteousness." How is that for motivation to truthfulness?

A person who is skilled in lying can speak words that in a court of law would be deemed truth, and yet the communication is definitely untruthful. We hear that all the time.

The next verse shows the practical results of both truthful and lying speech. Reckless words pierce like a sword. The playground ditty about "sticks and stones" is wrong. Words can and do hurt—very deeply sometimes. Words can be purposely intended to hurt, and we've all been recipients. But the tongue of the wise brings healing. One of the greatest privileges and blessings is to bring words of healing and encouragement to one who has been so hurt. I can only imagine how a medical doctor feels when he is able to bring healing to someone. We can all do it when the wounds are verbally inflicted. Let's ask God to make us "healers of the heart."

Proverbs 12:19-20

"Truthful lips endure forever, but a lying tongue lasts only a moment. There is deceit in the hearts of those who plot evil, but joy for those who promote peace."

Since the Proverbs provide "lessons for living," this proverb is for our learning and use today. Truthful lips" indicate that the point here is our truthful speech. But with Pilate, we might ask "what is truth". Jesus answered that in John 14:6 when He said "I am the truth." The essence of all truth is God. Truthful speech, therefore, is anchored in God. Truth is truth, whether spoken by a believer or a non-believer; the speaker does not make it true or untrue. Truthful lips merely mean the truth itself, as spoken by a righteous person.

But the lying tongue is the lying speech of a "wicked" person. In our 21st century, that speech seems to be increasing exponentially. It may well outlast the career of the wicked person, but that is "only a moment" in the greater scheme of things. Lies may well eclipse truth for a time—even a long time by our standards, just as cloudy skies may eclipse the sun for days on end. (Those living in the Pacific Northwest know that.) However, the sun is still shining; just ascend about 30,000 feet and you'll see. Lies are spoken for the purpose of deceiving and plotting self-interest. Lies, being evil, thus promote strife and division.

There is however joy *in the hearts* of those who promote peace. This is not a negotiated peace where one party overlooks one specific lie, providing the other person agree to not pursue another one. Real peace can only be had when it is based on truth. One person may stop swinging verbal fists because the other person has a bigger arsenal, but that is not peace. Peace and truth are a matter of the heart, and that is the center of joy.

Proverbs 12:21

"No harm befalls the righteous, but the wicked have their fill of trouble."

This seems to be a very broad statement, for both sides of the issue. No harm befalls the righteous? Really? And the wicked have their fill of trouble. Always? We know otherwise. The righteous have been persecuted to the death in every era since Stephen was stoned to death. Some of the wicked have seemed more trouble-free since the time of Job's friends. The Psalmist, a righteous man, said *"All day long I have been plagued; I have been punished every morning"* Psalm 73:14. A few verses earlier, verse 4, he says *"They have no struggles; their bodies are healthy and strong."* God's word will remain true for time and eternity, so how do we reconcile these seeming contradictions?

To begin with, we must accept by faith that God's word is true whether we understand it or not, and there are no contradictions, even when there seem to be. Once our faith is firmly anchored in God, we can proceed to seek understanding. However, we must keep in mind that God said *"As the heavens are higher than the earth, so are my ways higher than your ways and my thoughts than your thoughts."* So, there are some things we just will never understand. Nevertheless, "All Scripture is given by inspiration of God and is profitable . . . for instruction . . . that the man of God may be (complete), thoroughly furnished unto all good works." KJV 2 Timothy 3:16.

Proverbs are given to help us live our daily life successfully, growing in godliness and Christ-likeness. Knowing that the benefits stated in this text will generally be true in this life, and absolutely in the next, should help us on a daily basis to "shun the wrong and do the right."

"The Lord detests lying lips, but he delights in men who are truthful. A prudent man keeps his knowledge to himself, but the heart of fools blurts out folly.

Verse 22 continues the theme of honesty from the previous verses, really just adding further motivation. And what great motivation for absolute honesty it is! Honesty delights Him, whereas He detests dishonesty. What more could be needed? Yet, how little we often focus on delighting and pleasing the Lord! Too often we just go along non-chalantly, merely focusing on life issues as they arise without giving much, if any, thought to pleasing the One who controls all the circumstances of life. We are familiar with the cliché "if the wife ain't happy, ain't nobody happy." Well, what about the Lord? If a man's happiness is linked to the wife's happiness, -and it is, how much more true is that in relation to the Lord. If we are not pleasing Him, we surely are a long way from experiencing the joy and happiness that could be ours.

Verse 23 provides a new lesson that could fall under the heading of learning to live wisely with others. A prudent man is a wise man, and if you are wise you won't be a "motor-mouth." We've all met people who seem to believe they must have the final word on everything. There is no need to tell everything you know in any discussion or conversation. If you know what you are talking about, share only as much as is pertinent at any given stage of the conversation. People can always ask for further insights, and if they don't, then don't give it. Only a fool thinks he knows everything, and he proves that by blurting out all he knows, or thinks he knows. The one who knows when to keep quiet will gain friends and influence people. But more importantly, he will enjoy the personal satisfaction of his good relationships with other people.

Proverbs 12:24

"Diligent hands will rule, but laziness ends in slave labor."

The word "diligent" is defined as "characterized by steady, earnest, and energetic application and effort." As an employer or supervisor, one would look for those characteristics in employees. However, that should describe the person, and not just his work ethic. The immediate application of this text would be to workers and laborers in the marketplace. However, one who is diligent in character and not only in activities on the job will be the one to advance. In Luke 16:10 (NASB) Jesus said "He who is faithful in a very little thing is faithful also in much." The concept of diligence fits right into that verse.

God chose David on that basis, taking him from the sheep pens to become king of Israel; David chose Solomon for those same qualities. Both sacred and secular history is replete with instances of people who were advanced, based on their diligence. And that does not end at age 65, or whenever people retire. Ecclesiastes 9:10 says whatever your hand finds to do, do it with all your might," or with diligence. Let's rephrase those first four words: "diligence will pay off." It works on the job, it works in church, it works in the community, it works in school, it works in developing relationships. In other words, it works. It has to, it is God's design. It is not only too soon to quit it is also too soon to slack off.

Our text says "laziness ends in slave labor," and by that time the person is already defeated. So, let's not go there. For the believer, it is never too late to repent and obtain forgiveness, but it may be too late to regain lost ground. But it is never too late to be faithful and diligent in your walk with the Lord.

"An anxious heart weighs a man down, but a kind word cheers him up."

This proverb has no comparison or contrast between the righteous and the wicked, nor between the wise and the foolish. Rather it is a word to the depressed or anxious and of heavy heart, which can happen to anyone and probably does, at least at times. So, let's look for a moment at what might cause this. In the parable of the sower, Jesus refers to the "cares of this world." Considering world conditions for a day or two, can produce enough "cares" to last a life time. But we had fair warning. In John 16:23:33 Jesus told us "In this world you will have trouble." How right He was! Raising children in a permissive and promiscuous society, concern for grandchildren, tension on the job, financial difficulties and many more, are all causes for depression and heaviness of heart. Each of us has our own unique, and yet similar issues that can weigh us down.

The "kind" or good word from the Lord is enough to cheer us up, to give us fresh hope. That word, uniquely tailored by the Holy Spirit for our situation, will lift the load that is weighing the heart down. Jesus said "My yoke is easy and my burden is light." In I Peter 5:7, a verse we all need to know, says "Cast all your anxiety on him because he cares for you." The problem is, however, that when we are depressed, heavy laden and anxious about our situation, we don't feel like turning to the Scriptures. In extreme cases, one might even feel he cannot pray or read the Bible. That may be when the Lord wants to deliver that kind word with you as the courier. Galatians 6:2 "Carry each other's burdens, and in this way, you will fulfill the law of Christ." Do you know anyone right now who needs to hear a kind word from you?

Proverbs 12:26

"A righteous man is cautious in friendship, but the way of the wicked leads them astray."

That is an interesting concept, a righteous man is cautious in friendships. That can be very good, practical advice. Moving into a close friendship with a relative stranger is dangerous and potentially disastrous. Friendship requires a measure of self-disclosure, and a "wise" person will be a little cautious in that regard. Don't open yourself up too completely too quickly. Yet this is merely a caution.

The NASB however, translates the first line of this proverb as ***"The righteous is a guide to his neighbor."*** That would make the next line a contrast to the first, which is very typical in Proverbs. Assuming this to be the better translation, let's take a look at it. A guide in what way? Probably not having anything to do with home maintenance projects, although that could open the door to do what is really intended here. A righteous person will guide his neighbor in matters of righteousness, first by his conduct and then potentially with verbal advice. Imagine a neighbor who is pleasant and just a good neighbor. He does not attend any church and shows no interest in spiritual matters. You talk about church one day and he tells you he went once, and decided it was not for him. To try to persuade him would probably be counter-productive. What he needs is not so much church; he just needs to meet Jesus. As one of the righteous, you need to let him/them see Jesus in you, guiding them to the Savior. There are enough "others" who want to lead them astray.

To somewhat loosely paraphrase Jesus, when I am exalted, I will draw all kinds of people to myself. By our lives, (and words) let us exalt the Lord Jesus Christ.

Proverbs 12:28

In the way of righteousness there is life; along that path is immortality."

What a marvelous verse of encouragement and warning to keep us from falling. There is life at the end of the tunnel and that life is immortal. The history of Old Testament Israel is one of calling and falling. Once Israel was on their way to the Promised Land, they developed a pattern of forgetting God and falling away, and then coming back to Him, only to forget and drift away again. That pattern repeats all the way through Malachi. The trouble is we are not too different. I trust this verse finds you in very close fellowship with the Lord after whenever your last drifting away may have happened. The grace of God is strong enough to bring us back, and the blood of Christ is sufficient to keep on cleansing us from all sin. So, let's look at the text.

"In the way of righteousness," means our daily walk in the routines of life throughout the week. In **that** walk, there is life. Jesus said that He had come to give us life in fullest measure, my paraphrase of John 10:10. So what we have is not only life at the end of the tunnel, we have enjoyable, wonderful, exciting, fulfilling life all along the journey. We used to sing "Sweeter as The Years Go By." I learned the words of that song before I learned the truth of it, but the truth is there for each of us in full measure every day, in our righteous walk.

And then it says along that path is immortality. So, we won't get our immortal bodies until the resurrection, but the immortal life is ours on that path along the way. Are you blessed? Christianity is a **now** relationship with Jesus Christ. He is always with us in the present moment. Oh, what joy to walk with Him each day!

Proverbs 13:1-2

"A wise son heeds his father's instruction, but a mocker does not listen to rebuke. From the fruit of his lips a man enjoys good things, but the unfaithful have a craving for violence."

For the son to heed the father's instructions, the father must communicate clearly and consistently. The son's ability to understand will change with maturity, but the consistency is a constant. A thing cannot be right and good one day, but wrong or inconsequential the next. Furthermore, not all children have equal capacity and/or "style" of learning. If properly and clearly presented, the wise son will heed the instructions. But wisdom itself has to be taught by life and word in order to be learned. But not all children are wise. As a matter of fact, all children (and adults) are "mockers" to a degree some of the time, some more than others. Since everyone begins life with a sin nature already in place, we cannot guarantee the final outcome. As always, this proverb is "generally" true.

Moving on to verse two, I take it that the man in verse two is the wise son of verse one, thereby making him now a wise adult. While he may no longer have an earthly father to give instruction or advice, this man has transferred the habit of "heeding" from an earthly father to the authorities in his life and principally to the Heavenly Father. I remember very few of the details of my father's instructions to me, but I remember the principles he taught by his life and word—especially the instructions that pointed me to godly living. So, my heeding and learning continues.

For those of us who are well past the child-rearing age, it may be that our take-away is the challenge to continue heeding the Father's instructions, written for us in His "instruction manual."

Proverbs 13:3

"He who guards his lips guards his life, but he who speaks rashly will come to ruin."

The operative word here seems to be "guard." The one who guards his lips or his speech, also thereby guards his life. It is easy to understand that we need to guard our steps when walking on uneven terrain, but how do we guard our lips or our speech? For some insight on that, let's add to our text Philippians 4:7 *'the peace of God which transcends all understanding will guard your hearts and your minds in Christ Jesus."* If we put those two together, it seems the best way to allow the peace of God to guard our hearts. Great, but how do we do that? For the Bible's answer to that, we just back up another verse in Philippians: *"Do not be anxious about anything, but in everything by prayer and petition, with thanksgiving, present your requests to God."* Whoa! That is enough information for a full- length sermon or more. But essentially, keep in very close communication with the Lord, bringing all our concerns to Him, and then learn to trust Him implicitly. So, guard what you say and don't say, to other people and to God.

In true Proverbs style, this verse talks to us about what is good for us in our everyday living. Guarding our lips is for our own good, and for our enjoyment of this life while we prepare for the next. Sure, others will be blessed as well, and we want that, but this will greatly enhance our own lives, regardless of what benefit accrues to others. In verse 1 we learned to heed instructions. Now need to heed this instruction to "guard our lips" as well.

The last part of the verse adds a little additional motivation, as if the benefits were not enough. He who speaks rashly—who does not guard his lips, will come to ruin. So, there is also the avoidance of the negative. The one who speaks rashly will come to ruin. Maybe not within minutes, and maybe not within years, but the verse is very definite; he "will come to ruin." If the blessing side of the proverb is for us, then so is the negative. We guard or protect our lives by guarding our speech, and just as surely, we will come to ruin if we speak unadvisedly.

Proverbs 13:4-5

"The sluggard craves and gets nothing, but the desires of the diligent are fully satisfied. The righteous hate what is false, but the wicked bring shame and disgrace."

You are probably familiar with the saying, the only place where success comes before work is in the dictionary. Well, we could add that the mind or imagination of the sluggard is another exception. Work is not a curse it is a blessing. When Adam & Eve sinned, God did not curse work, He cursed the ground which made the work harder, requiring sweat and toil. Genesis 3:18-19. But work itself is a blessing. The idea of the "Welfare State" is the devil's attempt to upend God's design. In 2 Thessalonians 3:10 God said "If a man will not work, neither shall he eat."

Our text says he "craves." To me that indicates a very strong, desire, almost like a compulsion. Yet he does nothing constructive to obtain, though he probably tries dishonesty, as implied in the next verse. The diligent, on the other had does not *crave*, but he *desires*. Desire is good. This desire compels him to work to obtain what he desires. It motivates him to discover what it will take to obtain what he desires; it may not mean greater effort, but perhaps wiser effort, all within the bounds of what is honest and honorable. If the desire is for a relationship with a particular person, he may have to learn something about this person and then seek to provide whatever it is that pleases him or her. The effort put in will be proportionate to the strength of the desire.

Now, how strongly do we desire a closer relationship with the Lord? Is it a true desire, or just a passing fantasy? In Ephesians 5:10 we are instructed to "find out what pleases the Lord." Not so we will know that information, but rather so that we may do those things and be "fully satisfied."

Proverbs 13:6

"Righteousness guards the man of integrity, but wickedness overthrows the sinner."

Here, as in verse 5, the righteous person is a wise person. Dishonesty is never wise. In this text however, it is the righteousness of the wise person that "guards the man of integrity." His own righteousness guards or keeps him from lying or cheating, and so to remain a person of integrity. His righteousness has enabled him to make a firm commitment to integrity.

Since the devil is, and has been, a liar from the beginning, there is not a person on earth whose integrity he has not challenged, including that of the Lord Jesus Christ. Nor is there a person on earth *except* the Lord Jesus who has not compromised his integrity at one time or another. For the believer who has the Holy Spirit, who is the power of God, there is an adequate resource. The Holy Spirit *can* keep us, and He *wants* to keep us from sinning. Yet I do not believe He *will* keep us unless we have an *a priori* commitment to integrity, and are specifically trusting Him to guard and keep us.

A favorite verse for many in this context is 1 Corinthians 10:13: "When you are tempted, he (the Holy Spirit) will also provide a way out so that you can stand up under it." "He will provide a way out" applies to every individual temptation or test. So just because you maintained your integrity yesterday is in itself no guarantee for today; we must trust Him each time, and He will provide each time.

The flip side is "wickedness will overthrow the sinner," who is basically left to his own resources. One might ask "can't God also help the sinner?" and the answer is yes, but the sinner does not have the indwelling Holy Spirit, so the 10:13 promise is not for him.

Our text simply tells us what will generally happen.

Proverbs 13:7-8

"One man pretends to be rich, yet has nothing; another pretends to be poor, yet has great wealth. A man's riches may ransom his life, but a poor man hears no threat."

This section again deals with the matter of integrity. There are so many ways a person can be something other than fully honest. Here we have two men pretending to be something they are not. Since no reasons are given for the pretense, we can only guess. Why would anyone who is poor pretend to be rich? To me an obvious reason would be to try to enhance his perceived status or importance. That would be unwarranted pride. 1 John 2:15 tells us that "everything that is in the world, the cravings of sinful man, the lust of the eyes and the boasting of what he has and does—comes not from the Father but from the world." The poor man pretending to be rich would fit all three of those classifications.

Now for some meddling! Have you ever received praise for something you did not deserve? Perhaps you received credit for doing something that in reality was done by someone else and you knew it. Was it a struggle to let them know you were not the one? Or did you simply let it go. After all, you made no claim to have done it, they just credited you. Or did you ever receive praise for a job well done, but instead of receiving it graciously, you tried (maybe half-heartedly) to say "Ah it was nothing." Now you can get praise for your humility as well, so you've been doubly exalted. No matter how you try to explain it to yourself, it was deception. You pretended to be something you are not, and the motive was selfishness. And God calls that sin.

The last part of our text shows there are benefits as well as problems with both riches and poverty, and blessed is the one who can maintain their integrity through it all.

"The light of the righteous shines brightly, but the lamp of the wicked is snuffed out."

This text uses the words "light" and "lamp" as metaphors of "life." Both the righteous and the wicked have life, though earthly life is temporary for both. I find it interesting that the "lamp" of the wicked will be snuffed out, even though it may never have been lit. In other words, when their life runs out, that is it. However, the "light" of the righteous continues to shine brightly. However, before we jump into eternity with this, lets again be reminded that Proverbs deals with issues of this present life. Yes, eternity is awaiting us, but it is how we live this life that needs to concern us now, providing we have the other assured.

In His Sermon on the Mount, Matthew 5:14, Jesus said "You are the light of the world." Then He went on to say "let your light so shine before men . . ." In other words, even though we have the light, it is possible for us to conceal the light. Actually, Jesus **IS** the light, John 9:5, but we have the light when we have Jesus. We are the light only in the sense that we are reflectors of His light within. You can let your light shine only where you are. We are only responsible to clear away the debris so the light can shine. Hence, we have cute sayings like "bloom where you are planted." Why not? You can't bloom anywhere else. Our lives must reveal Jesus where we are, to those who can see us.

The lamp of the wicked, their lives, will be snuffed out. After that they will be in eternal death—separation from God. The life of the righteous will then shine more brightly than ever. But for now, are there clouds of complacency, carelessness, selfishness, doubt or sin concealing your light? Get rid of them by faith, through confession and repentance, and let's "let it shine."

Proverbs 13:10

"Pride only breeds quarrels, but wisdom is found in those who take advice."

We have all seen pride and arrogance on display, and it is disgusting. It looks bad, it sounds bad, and it smells bad. You want to avoid seeing it at all costs—especially in yourself. Our text says it only breeds quarrels, (often accompanied by mistrust and other negative reactions and results.) We could say it "always" as well as "only" breeds quarrels and troubles of many kinds. The end result is never good. We often see it among Christians as well as unbelievers. Why is that? Well, there is this thing called our "sin nature." Pride was the original sin that caused Satan's downfall, and he has inflicted it upon all mankind ever since.

As redeemed children of God, however, we have the power to overcome pride through the indwelling Holy Spirit. But **we** have to overcome; we have to exercise wisdom in making our choices about attitudes and reactions. Wisdom grows and increases as we heed good advice. We have already learned that if "if any of you lacks wisdom, let him ask of God who gives generously," James 1:5. However, He does not randomly pour it on us while we sleep. He generally gives wisdom through the Scriptures and through advice from others and through experience. We do not gain it automatically, even with our head in the Bible.

We begin by asking God for it, and then we need to look diligently for it, first in the Bible, but also in all of our life experiences. Often, we will gain wisdom by observing it in the actions of others; we may gain it while in general discussion with others, and that could be on any subject. If Jesus Christ is sovereign of life, wisdom will not come only in discussing "spiritual" matters. Ask, seek, knock, and search diligently; trust and obey, and wisdom will come to you.

Proverbs 13:10

"Dishonest money dwindles away, but he who gathers money little by little makes it grow."

This may not be true in every single situation, but numerous studies confirm it to be true in general. The AMPC translation reads: *"Wealth [not earned but] won in haste or unjustly . . . will dwindle away.* Estate planning in the 1980s had an IRS statistic that said "an inheritance, regardless of size, will be gone in six months." I've seen that happen over and over. One exception was a young man's $7 million-dollar inheritance which lasted just a few years.

Every family should teach their young children certain money management principles, including earning, saving, spending and investing. There is wisdom in that. Young children cannot learn that on their own, and waiting for them to grow up may prove financially disastrous. That is why this proverb gives the warning first to catch our attention, and then gives the solution next. For adults who have not yet learned this, and there are many we need to begin with the foundational truth stated in Psalm 24:1. *The earth is the Lord's, and everything in it, the world and all who live in it.* 1 Corinthians 4:2 teaches that as stewards of God's property, we are required to be faithful, and Jesus taught in Matthew 25 that He entrusts different servants with differing amounts to manage, "each according to their ability."

As "stewards" of His property, we are accountable to the Owner for how we earn or gather, spend, save and invest those assets. Details are found in a study of both Old and New Testaments. Today's proverb deals with the investment part, and advises to "gather little by little." No get rich quick schemes! Concepts like "dollar-cost-averaging" are taught in Ecclesiastes 11. Let's be faithful to do what we know to do as in Matthew 25:27.

Proverbs 13:13

"He who scorns instruction will pay for it, but he who respects a command is rewarded."

This proverb is not specifically addressed to the righteous, or to the wicked. It is like one of the whosoever's of the Bible. Whoever reads this or hears it, yes, our final payday is still future for all those living, but the results indicated in this text are to be applied to this life.

He who scorns instruction will pay for it. He will pay, not necessarily or even primarily with money, but much more importantly, he will pay with life consequences. If you try to pick up a live rattle snake with your bare hands, you will pay for it. That is all there is to it. So, the wise thing is, don't! It is very possible to read this text and automatically apply it to "the younger generation." And yes, it does apply there, nearly as much as it does to those of the "older generation" who should know better by now. Granted, the younger generation will have a different set of circumstance and therefore make different excuses for scorning, rather than heeding instructions. But so does everyone else in every generation. God says in effect you can ignore me if you want, you can scorn my instructions if you want, but there will be consequences. The blood of Jesus Christ bought redemption to remove the penalty for our sin, but not to remove all the consequences. Rattle snakes do not ask whether you are a believer or not before they decide to strike.

"But he who respects a command is rewarded."

HALLELUJAH!

This person will be rewarded. God said so. Final reward for obedience comes at the Judgment Seat of Christ, but the reward in this life too is assured. The biggest reward I can envision on this matter is and will be peace of heart and mind. No regrets!

Proverbs 13:14-15

"The teaching of the wise is a fountain of life, turning a man from snares of death. Good understanding wins favor, but the way of the unfaithful is hard."

Of course, the only One fully, totally and completely wise is God, the source of all wisdom. Solomon was next in line as far as wisdom goes. In his day, he was the wisest man living, and it is his writings, directed by the Holy Spirit, that we are considering. Later in life however, he too made some very unwise decisions for himself and his nation. In the writings of Proverbs, however, we have the writings of the wisest of men, directed by the all wise Creator God.

"The teaching of the wise is a fountain of life" is a true statement. Yet it has a qualifier. The teaching by itself is pretty much useless unless it is accepted and followed by the recipients of the teaching. If those teachings are accepted, they will indeed turn a person away from the snares of death. The student must have enough wisdom to discern which teaching is wise, and which is merely information. Information alone, no matter how potentially valuable and accurate it may be, can never turn a person "from the snares of death." Those "snares" are deliberately designed to "kill, steal and destroy," John 10:10, both for the duration of this life and the next.

Good understanding comes from absorbing and practicing wise teaching. The better our understanding, the more we will win favor with our fellow earth travelers. Life here and now is good, and can be enjoyable even in the midst of difficulties. We can rejoice in the Lord always. But the way of the unfaithful is hard. So many of this world's promises are for fun and joyful entertainment, but they turn out to be hard and bitter disappointments. It takes wisdom to discern which promises are for long-term good, and which are short-term only, bringing on a "hard life" in the end.

"Every prudent man acts out of knowledge but a fool exposes his folly. A wicked messenger falls into trouble, but a trustworthy envoy brings healing."

The prudent man is a wise man, and because he is wise, he is also a righteous man. The verse says nothing about his speech, although that can be taken for granted to be included. A prudent man will of course speak out of wisdom because he is wise. The point I see in this choice of words is that a person may *sound* wise in his speech if he is careful enough. However, if he is truly wise and prudent in character, it will be evident in his conduct with or without words. The foolish man may not always *sound* foolish, but his true character will be exposed one way or another. Remember the old saying: *You can fool all of the people, some of the time, you can fool some of the people all of the time, but you can never fool all of the people all of the time.* And of course, you can never fool God. The Moody Bible Commentary says of this verse One's character is "written all over one's conduct." A foolish person seems not to ever understand that.

The contrast between these verses is between the prudent (or wise) man and the wicked (or foolish) person. There was no texting or even email in those days, so messages were sent by human carriers. In high level international negotiations, that is still the way it works. The wicked messenger was evidently sent with a communication and he got into trouble—possibly because he messed up in some way. Maybe he changed the message to suit his own purposes, we don't know. At least he proved unreliable in some way. The trustworthy envoy gets the job done and smoothes over any friction or difficulty. He represents his superiors well. He brings healing and peace and calm to a tricky situation. He is wise.

PROVERBS TO LIVE BY

Proverbs 13:18

"He who ignores discipline comes to poverty and shame, but whoever heeds correction is honored."

Those who are accustomed to think in terms of all discipline consisting of punishment for misdeeds and stupid mistakes will need to correct their own thinking before this proverb can be understood and appreciated. So, look at it. First of all, discipline is correction as evidenced in the use of words. The foolish man ignores discipline when it is offered and suffers for it. The wise person accepts the discipline and is thereby corrected. Consider 2 Timothy 3:16 as discipline. *"All Scripture is given by inspiration of God and is useful for teaching, rebuking, correcting and training in righteousness."* God disciplines those whom He loves, Hebrews 12:6, by teaching them what they do not know, rebuking those who have strayed, correcting those who have erred and training those who walk with Him in obedience. He does whatever is needed to make His children righteous.

Our text says that whoever ignores discipline, whoever decides to "go it alone" or to do "my way," will come to poverty and shame. The shame is not in receiving discipline, the shame is in ignoring discipline. Poverty, financial or otherwise, may not come immediately to the one who refuses or ignores advice and warnings, but it will come at or before a final reckoning. Along with the poverty will come shame and embarrassment. Whoever heeds correction, however, will not be shamed but honored.

It takes humility to accept rebuke or correction, but true humility is pleasing to both God and man. Pride and arrogance and self-righteousness is detestable. The humble person will learn from his mistakes and not repeat them. The one who is humble enough to mend his ways when he is disciplined/corrected, will be honored.

*"Every prudent man acts out of knowledge but a fool
exposes his folly. A wicked messenger falls into trouble,
but a trustworthy envoy brings healing."*

The prudent man is a wise man, and because he is wise, he is also a
righteous man. The verse says nothing about his speech, although that can
be taken for granted to be included. A prudent man will of course speak
out of wisdom because he is wise. The point I see in this choice of words
is that a person may **sound** wise in his speech if he is careful enough.
However, if he is truly wise and prudent in character, it will be evident
in his conduct with or without words. The foolish man may not always
sound foolish, but his true character will be exposed one way or another.
Remember the old saying: *You can fool all of the people, some of the time,
you can fool some of the people all of the time, but you can never fool all of the
people all of the time.* And of course, you can never fool God. The Moody
Bible Commentary says of this verse One's character is "written all over
one's conduct." A foolish person seems not to ever understand that.

The contrast between these verses is between the prudent (or wise)
man and the wicked (or foolish) person. There was no texting or even
email in those days, so messages were sent by human carriers. In high
level international negotiations, that is still the way it works. The wicked
messenger was evidently sent with a communication and he got into
trouble—possibly because he messed up in some way. Maybe he changed
the message to suit his own purposes, we don't know. At least he proved
unreliable in some way. The trustworthy envoy gets the job done and
smoothes over any friction or difficulty. He represents his superiors well.
He brings healing and peace and calm to a tricky situation. He is wise.

Proverbs 13:18

"He who ignores discipline comes to poverty and shame, but whoever heeds correction is honored."

Those who are accustomed to think in terms of all discipline consisting of punishment for misdeeds and stupid mistakes will need to correct their own thinking before this proverb can be understood and appreciated. So, look at it. First of all, discipline is correction as evidenced in the use of words. The foolish man ignores discipline when it is offered and suffers for it. The wise person accepts the discipline and is thereby corrected. Consider 2 Timothy 3:16 as discipline. *"All Scripture is given by inspiration of God and is useful for teaching, rebuking, correcting and training in righteousness."* God disciplines those whom He loves, Hebrews 12:6, by teaching them what they do not know, rebuking those who have strayed, correcting those who have erred and training those who walk with Him in obedience. He does whatever is needed to make His children righteous.

Our text says that whoever ignores discipline, whoever decides to "go it alone" or to do it "my way," will come to poverty and shame. The shame is not in receiving discipline, the shame is in ignoring discipline. Poverty, financial or otherwise, may not come immediately to the one who refuses or ignores advice and warnings, but it will come at or before a final reckoning. Along with the poverty will come shame and embarrassment. Whoever heeds correction, however, will not be shamed but honored.

It takes humility to accept rebuke or correction, but true humility is pleasing to both God and man. Pride and arrogance and self-righteousness is detestable. The humble person will learn from his mistakes and not repeat them. The one who is humble enough to mend his ways when he is disciplined/corrected, will be honored.

Proverbs 13:19

"A longing fulfilled is sweet to the soul, but fools detest turning from evil."

This verse is tied to the previous one, and continues the idea of the discipline required to accomplish worthwhile goals and desires. God has built into every human a desire for happiness and joy, and were it not for sin, everyone would look for that fulfillment in God. As it is, we naturally seek to find joy and happiness on our own—and fail. The best we can do is to perhaps achieve some fun and temporary release from certain stressful life situations. Fulfillment to capacity or completeness can only be had if, 1. It is a God ordained desire and 2. If it is achieved within the framework of a life lived in fellowship with Him and following His guidance. Such fulfillment is indeed "sweet to the soul" now in this life. If there will be added sweetness as a result of this fulfillment in the next life as well, that is just an added bonus. Proverbs teaches us how to live in this life.

The fool wants the same sense of fulfillment and sweetness of soul for his desires as well. And many of those desires could well be wholesome and good, but he insists on working toward that fulfillment in his own way. He wants to be the captain of his soul and the master of his fate. Whether or not he knows the song, or has ever even heard it, he wants to finish his life and get to heaven with his life theme having been "I did it may way." And that is natural, and quite understandable—but it is not super-natural and it must be. Our text says the fool detests turning from evil. Sure, because that is all he knows, and can know. The King James tells us in 1Corinthians 2:14 in *"the natural man receiveth not the things of God; for they are foolishness to him: neither can he know them."* So, he does what comes naturally; we can do and be what comes super-naturally.

Proverbs 13:20

"He who walks with the wise grows wise, but a companion of fools suffers harm."

The Proverbs of Solomon are a collection of wise sayings to help guide readers (and heeders) in navigating the vicissitudes of life successfully. No one single proverb will necessarily be applicable 100 percent of the time to every individual. They are generally true most of the time.

This could be summarized by the old saying: "a person is known by the company he keeps." Immediately you can think of situations, real or imagined, where this is true. But there are exceptions. Jesus was known as a friend of sinners because He "hung-out" with them, but He never became like them. So, we need to look carefully at this one. Not only is one known by the company he keeps, one is also shaped by the company one keeps.

He who "walks with the wise" does not become wise just by walking around the lake with a wise person; one becomes wise by spending time with and emulating a wise person over time. His wisdom can, and needs to be, studied and learned and copied. Notice it says such a person will "grow" wise. It will take time, because while wisdom in action can be observed, it has to be implemented in personalized circumstances. The same "saying" that is wise and right in one situation may be completely out-of-place and destructive in another.

A companion of fools suffers harm. We can and should be the kind of friend of sinners that Jesus was, if we want to win them over to Christ. Being a companion however, suggests more of the idea of enjoying and sharing in the same kinds of life activities and values. In wisdom one would encourage a fool away from his folly; being his companion would be to follow his foolish enticement into folly.

"Misfortune pursues the sinner, but prosperity is the reward of righteousness."

One commentator suggests that the "misfortune" that pursues the sinner is really "the wrath of God" that is pursuing them. If that is the meaning, then it shows the love of God, because He is pursuing them in order to turn them around before it is too late. God hates evil, and since the evil has already been atoned for in the blood of Christ, God is now pursuing the evil doer in order that He might show mercy. This would then equally apply to believers like you and me who also commit evil at times, and God loves us too much to let us get away with it.

However, there is another aspect to this and that is that the evil itself will create and produce the misfortune that will pursue the sinner. Numbers 32:23 puts it this way: "Be sure you sin will find you out." That is an eternal principle of God, and the sooner we acknowledge that, the better off we will be. It would pay us in this life alone to avoid being pursued by misfortune. On top of that, heaven will provide eternal rewards and benefits.

And then there is the promise that "prosperity is the reward of righteousness." Especially in our Western culture we are so prone to equate prosperity with economic success that we may totally miss the prosperity that comes our way. Consider this: God Himself promises this prosperity to accrue in this life. If we take Him at His word, we can begin to look for its fulfillment in this life. We need to constantly look forward to the eternal glories yet to be revealed, and doing so will serve to give value and prosperity along the way. "Everyone who has this hope in him purifies himself," 1 John 3:3.

"Misfortune pursues the sinner, but prosperity is the reward of righteousness." The choice is ours.

"A good man leaves an inheritance to his children's children, but a sinner's wealth is stored up for the righteous."

The "good man" in this proverb is the one who has frequently been called "righteous" in Proverbs. We would refer to the good man as a godly man, a Christian. The context of the verse makes it plain that the inheritance here refers to material assets. So, the God who owns everything has something to say about our estate distribution plan. So, to paraphrase our text, it says we should leave an inheritance to our children and to our grandchildren. If you want to know how to apportion it, you will need to ask the Owner of all you have. You are, after all, His "steward."

I recall meeting with a wealthy businessman to discuss his estate plan, and he began by saying "I don't want to make my children rich." So, while he was leaving them a financial inheritance, their biggest material inheritance would be his work-ethic, not any specific amount of money. Their primary overall inheritance would be spiritual in nature consisting of biblical values which he and his wife had sought to inculcate in their children's lives. I believe he had it right.

Throughout history, even prior to Luke 15, there have been those who squandered inheritances and opportunities, and so while we may seek to minimize that outcome, we cannot control it. We do what we can, while we can, and then we must leave the results with God. However, our text cautions that "the sinner's wealth is stored up for the righteous." That is not to say that God will take the wealth of the sinner and re-distribute it among the righteous. However, the sinner will not live to see the full potential benefit of the inheritance, whereas God will more than make it up to the righteous. I have seen God bless and multiply faithfulness beyond any explanation, and that is His promise.

Proverbs 13:23

"A poor man's field may produce abundant food, but injustice sweeps it away."

This "poor man" could equally well be a righteous man as a wicked or foolish man. None of us have been promised immunity from evil and injustice in this world. The abundance of food in the first part of the text is the result of hard work and diligence. True, at times poverty comes as a result of laziness, and sometimes as a result of unwise choices and actions. Most "get-rich-quick schemes" end in poverty for all but the scam artists who promote them. In cases like that the poor man has no one to blame for his poverty but himself."

To those who have become poor because of self-inflicted attempts at "short-cuts," and that may include more of us than we would care to admit, Isaiah has a wonderful promise in 30:15: "in repentance and rest (in the Lord) is your salvation, in quietness and trust is your strength." The word "repentance" of course means to turn around; in other words, don't make the same stupid mistakes over and over again. But our text speaks of those who have become poor because of some injustice inflicted on them. Most of us have experienced some losses (not necessarily to the point of poverty) because of injustices inflicted on us. So, where do we turn?

Both Old and New Testaments are replete with promises of God's care and provision. God always has done, and is doing His part; we don't need to worry about that. Too often our problem is that we expect God to replace whatever we have lost through injustice, while God is concerned to build the character that has been damaged in the process. He will take care of the wrong-doer in His own time. Right now, He wants to make a godly man or woman out of you. "In quietness and trust" is our strength too.

"He who spares the rod hates his son, but he who loves him is careful to discipline him."

The message is simple; the application not so much. Parents who love their children will indeed discipline them. That is what parents do—if they love their children. Whether we care to admit it or not, and many do not, all parents learn very quickly the truth of 22:15 that "folly is bound up in the heart of a child." In other words, we are all born with a sin nature, and so "all have sinned." Therefore, discipline is necessary. Where the difficulty comes in is that babies do not come with an instruction manual for "this particular model." So, while all children need discipline, not all children respond to or learn equally to each type of discipline. Most young couples and singles seem to know pretty well what form of discipline someone else's misbehaving child needs—until they have their own.

Our text uses the word "rod' as do several other Scriptures, see 22:15 for example. Neither these nor any other Scripture references ever condone nor advocate any form of child abuse. But neither do they exclude physical punishment as an effective mode of discipline to be used lovingly and wisely in times when other modes of discipline have failed to produce corrective behavior. Parents love their children too much to allow them to wander off into danger unchecked. In many instances verbal instructions and warnings are sufficient to ward off moral, physical or spiritual destructive behaviors. When parents "have tried everything," professional counseling can be helpful. But keep in mind that the most Wonderful Counselor in the world is always available, and He does not charge $150.00 per hour.

So, love your children enough to correct them. Their future, and all eternity is at stake.

Proverbs 14:1

"The wise woman builds her house, but with her own hands the foolish one tears hers down."

This verse is not talking about a wise woman being a good carpenter, although some may very well be that. I have seen some very enviable crafts produced by women in our local woodworking club. Solomon was not concerned about that here.

In our American parlance we would call this wise woman a homemaker as opposed to a home-breaker. It has nothing to do with whether or not she also brings in any earned income. The point is by her attitude, actions and speech she builds up, while the foolish one tears down. She may be a gourmet chef and keep a meticulously clean house, but that is irrelevant to the issue at hand. In Proverbs 31 she is described as a woman of noble character who brings good and not harm to her household. The familiar pithy saying that "the hand that rocks the cradle rules the world" is referencing the wise woman.

What we are saying here about the wise versus the foolish woman would applly equally to men. We already know too much about "deadbeat" husbands. In this text, the woman is in view. The foolish woman may be the one who too much of the time has a negative outlook on life, and that negativity is expressed in criticizing and complaining to and about her husband and perhaps also her children. The wise woman on the other hand maintains a positive outlook, and she reserves her constructive criticism for a private, appropriate time. Just as a wise husband loves his wife, so a wise woman honors her husband and her children.

"He whose walk is upright fears the LORD, but he whose ways are devious despises him."

This proverb provides us a "self-evaluation" tool that will hold true before God; it is a tool He has provided for our use. It does not measure four or more personality traits, just the fear of the Lord versus a hateful disregard for the Lord. The "fear of the Lord" is seen in an upright lifestyle, and "despising" the Lord is seen in a devious or deceptive lifestyle. This in no way suggests our own self-evaluation will be the final standard of life. It merely enables us to see with our own eyes, (providing we actually look) the direction or the bent of our lives.

By itself, our self-evaluation is prone to be too subjective; we may tend to be too hard on ourselves, or more likely, too forgiving of ourselves. Self-evaluation therefore needs to be based on the standards of the Word of God.

We begin therefore with a look at phrase "he whose walk is upright." The day will come when we, the children of God will be perfectly sinless in our walk—but not in this life. In our self-evaluation therefore, we are not so much looking for a single unconfessed sin in our lives, as in our lifestyle. In our "walk," our attitudes, our actions and our words, is our tendency to be upright and obedient to God's word, or is there a pattern of ignoring certain things we'd rather not deal with. Do we, as a lifestyle, confess and forsake or turn away from things that would dishonor the Lord.

The other side of the coin is the devious walk. Do we pretend that certain attitudes and actions really don't matter that much? Our excuse may be "it's just the way I am; I didn't mean anything by it"?

Is this a time for your own personal self-evaluation?

PROVERBS TO LIVE BY

Proverbs 14:3

"A fool's talk brings a rod to his back, but the lips of the wise protect them."

Some scholars claim the first part of this verse is somewhat difficult to translate. A very literal translation could read "a rod of pride." The 1984 NIV is quoted above, whereas the newer NIV has "A fool's mouth lashes out with pride." The older English translation used by Commentator Matthew Henry has it "in the mouth of the foolish is a rod of pride." No matter how it is translated, the problem is with the talk or speech of the fool. That would be true of the one who speaks factually of things he does not know or understand. Such speech could be costly in the loss of friends, reputation and perhaps position. We've all heard someone challenged with the words "Ah, you don't know what you're talking about." It seems that foolish talk may well ostracize a person. No one wants to be constantly subjected to such drivel. But where does the idea of pride come into this picture? It could be egotistically claiming the credit belonging to someone else. This could be plagiarism, or outright stealing. When you move on to combine such egotism with ignorant and foolish speech, you can see a mountain of trouble piling up. Here our text goes one step further; such foolishness can merit and bring on punishment, as indicated by the rod on the back. We probably all have a measure of experience with such talk.

The lips of wise people protect them from such problems. Some times the better part of wisdom is to remain silent in a given situation. You are probably familiar with the old saying: "better to remain silent and thought a fool than to speak up and remove all doubt." Wise people learn when to keep silent as well as when and how to speak for the benefit of others. And it is a matter of learning, because none of us are all-wise in ourselves.

Proverbs 14:4

*"Where there are no oxen, the manger is empty, but
from the strength of an ox comes an abundant harvest."*

This proverb uses an agricultural illustration to make a point. To increase production a farmer must invest a lot of hard work and money in proper equipment. Dreams and wishes alone often turn to nightmares.

Some years ago, it was my blessed privilege to pastor a rural church where practically the whole congregation were. Each year I spent at least some days driving a tractor or a combine; not enough to turn me into a farmer, but enough to give me a sense of appreciation for their lifestyle. Thinking back from that to my early childhood, I remember one farmer switching from working with a team of horses only, to working with a small tractor. I believe he was able to do at least twice the amount of work in about half the time. I'm guessing at that ratio, but this proved a good investment.

The principle at stake here would apply in very other type of endeavor as well. The old adage says "it takes money to make money." Jesus seemed to agree with that, judging by His use of the parable of the talents in Matthew 25:14-30. In the fourth chapter of his book, the apostle James basically tells the entrepreneur to put his trust in God and then proceed to open a branch operation in another city to expand his holdings. This is the exact opposite of the theology of our day called. "Name it and Claim it." Our text basically teaches us to trust, plan, venture and work. He concludes that section with "anyone who knows the good he ought to do and does not do it, sins."

It seems that some of us who were maybe not-so-wise, got too soon old and too late smart. We should never be afraid to take God at His word, nor should we enact our own plans and wishes, and then ask God to prosper our efforts.

"A truthful witness does not deceive, but a false witness pours out lies. The mocker seeks wisdom and finds none, but knowledge comes easily to the discerning."

Taking these two verses together, we again see that it is character that counts. Of course, words are important—very important, but a person's character guides in the purpose of what he is saying, and therefore also in the choice of the words themselves.

A wise person, one who is truthful to the core, does not merely use truthful words which can be interpreted to deceive and present a different message. His character is not geared to deception, it is geared to transparent honesty. A false witness, on the other hand "pours out lies." The ESV reads he "breathes out lies." It just comes naturally to him, as natural as breathing. Even when using truthful words, the false witness seeks to use them in such a way as to deceive. These verses do not imply that the false witness never tells the truth or that a truthful witness never tries to deceive. Rather, they show the ultimate condition of truthful or deceptive characters.

In the last part of this proverb, the false witness of the first part is called a mocker, and the truthful witness is called discerning. The mocker apparently has no desire to change his ways or his character; he merely wants wisdom to deceive more effectively. That would be a little like asking God to help you sin without getting caught. That is mockery, and wisdom therefore eludes him.

Knowledge, however comes easily to the person of truthful character, because his aim in life is to be a true child of God. He seeks to understand the implications of possible actions, enabling him to make wise choices. God therefore gives him discernment.

"Stay away from a foolish man, for you will not find knowledge on his lips."

I wonder if perhaps Solomon had his devotions in Psalm 1, the day he wrote this proverb. To paraphrase part of the Psalm, blessed is the one who does not "hang out" with a foolish person, because he will perish. Our text says to "stay away" from such a person. Some translations suggest that we "go away from" such people. One may inadvertently find himself in the presence of foolish people; if so, leave! They have nothing of value to impart, and they might possibly draw you in if you remain. So, stay away from foolish, wicked people if you can, and go away if you must. Just don't get involved with them; their foolishness just might rub off on you.

I can hear the argument coming from certain faithful church people already; how are you going to win them if you avoid them? What about "friendship evangelism?" Didn't Jesus hang out with sinners? Usually those are insincere question, asked mostly by those looking for an excuse to not take a clear stand because they want to keep company with the wrong people. If these are sincere questions, you have missed the point of the proverb. Yes, we are supposed to present the love of Jesus to lost sinners; no one is better than anyone else. We are all undeserving sinners, and God so loved the world, including you and me. But you cannot win a bank robber to Jesus by joining him in his next heist.

The point in this proverb, and in Psalm 1, is that it is foolish to desire the company of fools and wicked people for some strange personal satisfaction or gratification. We can gain nothing of value from such association, and we place ourselves in grave danger by going that way, and spending time there.

Proverbs 14:8

"The wisdom of the prudent is to give thought to their ways, but the folly of fools is deception."

The opening words of this proverb would seem to indicate that there is also a wisdom other than, or different from that of the prudent. I suppose that would depend on the definition of wisdom. The Apostle James speaks of two kinds of wisdom, so let's see how he differentiates. First, he speaks of a wisdom that is not the true wisdom from heaven, and then defines the wisdom that does come down from heaven. The first could be called the wisdom of this world. Included in that would be the intellectual wisdom which could more accurately be called knowledge. It is academic. It is theoretic. It comes from book-learning and does not necessarily involve any practical application. The Book of Proverbs does not advocate or deal with that kind of so-called wisdom. The wisdom in our text is that which James called the "wisdom from heaven."

The possessor of this true wisdom "gives thought to his ways." He is aware of himself and of his surroundings. He does not take everything at face value. He is not so easily deceived. He understands that often "there is more to it than meets the eye." In other words, he is prudent—not gullible.

The folly of fools is deception. They seem to firmly believe they can "get away with it." They have no concept of what God was talking about when He said "be sure your sin will find you out" in Numbers 32:23. That is as foolish as the little boy with cookie crumbs all over his face saying "I did not eat that cookie."

Those of us who believe we have the wisdom of the prudent, don't we at times fit the description of the folly of the foolish? And that before God!

Proverbs 14:9

"Fools mock at making amends for sin, but goodwill is found among the upright."

Other translations may say "mock at sin" itself which might mean they even try to deny any existence of sin. Several translations indicate they mock guilt, or the guilt offering required under Old Testament law. The fact remains that sin produces guilt, and the only provision for fully removing the guilt is the blood of Jesus Christ. Denial won't do it, laughing about it won't, adjusting one's personal value system won't, passing a federal law to legalize it won't, and even popularizing the sin won't remove its guilt. These attempts may enable one to harden his heart and conscience sufficiently so he can live in relative ease about it; maybe even forget about it entirely. Yet the guilt remains.

Our text in the NIV says "fools mock at making amends for sin," so let's take a look at that. The first step in making amends would be to admit the sin. You cannot confess it, nor can you make amends for it until you recognize its existence. To confess means to say the same thing. If God calls it sin, I too must call it sin so He and I can work on it. Depending on what the specific sin is or was, making amends could require making monetary repayment or restitution of some kind. It could require a *sincere* apology, which carries with it the idea of repentance; that is renouncing and forsaking the offense. Sincere public apologies are virtually unknown in our cultural and political environment; all that is required are the words 'I apologize." Thus, the guilt remains.

Goodwill is found among the upright. The upright, the wise, the prudent, the honest, the righteous desire and seek to retain or reestablish goodwill, beginning with making amends when needed.

PROVERBS TO LIVE BY

Proverbs 14:12

"There is a way that seems right to a man, but in the end it leads to death."

As we make our way through life, we are constantly making choices between two or more options. Most often those choices are made based on our desires and goals. For younger people those choices often relate to a desired career or perhaps a lifestyle, or even family issues. Certainly, some choices relate to religious and/or moral issues. Whatever the subject matter of the choice, or the stage of life when the choice is made, ALL CHOICES HAVE CONSEQUENCES. All of those consequences relate to this life, be they short term or long, but many of them also have eternal consequences.

Complications arise when a choice is made in all earnestness and best intentions proves to be counter-productive. The choice made does not provide what was promised or anticipated. Perhaps the basic structure has been compromised by termites—literal or figurative. The wrong choice may have been made because of failure to seek advice or to investigate the issue adequately. Often the wrong choice has been made because of not taking time to "seek the Lord" on the matter. Our text says the choice "seems right," but in fact proves to not "be" right.

Though a wrong choice may be made deliberately by the fool," that would likely not be true of a child of God. However, because some choices or ways seem right and yet end up in death, it is vital for the believer to keep in close communication with the Lord, both before, during and after the initial choice is made. Consequences may not be removed, even for the believer, but they can be redeemed. By His grace, God is at work "in all things" to work for our good, Romans 8:28. So, also be His grace, may we seek to avoid those wrong ways.

Proverbs 14:14

"The faithless will be fully repaid for their ways, and the good man rewarded for his."

This couplet again relates to this life. There will indeed be implications for life after death, but Solomon's concern here is with the present and the immediate future. What can the faithless, as well as the good man, expect to receive immediately, or in the foreseeable future, as a result of his actions? In keeping with the style of Proverbs, this message is to the foolish and to the wise. Here the foolish, perhaps backsliders, are called faithless, and the wise the good man.

The message is clear and unambiguous. First, the faithless will be fully repaid in this lifetime, for their ways. Most people seem to think they can "get away with it," whatever the "it" is. Whenever we have been wronged, we want and expect immediate resolution of issues, but that does not seem to happen. In fact, often it seems they do "get away with it," and they won't ever need to "face the music." But look again at the text; it does not promise that **WE** will be repaid for what others may have done to us, they will be fully repaid. Nor does it say that our legal system will "get them." God says they will be fully repaid in this life, and just how He will see to that is really none of our business. We have instead, an opportunity to trust God.

Secondly, the good man (the one who is wise) will be rewarded for his ways. Many of us have been conditioned to think in terms of a "pie in the sky" type of Christianity. Our reward comes when we go to heaven, and that is correct—sort of. Heaven and eternal rewards for faithfulness and crowns etc. are promised "in the sweet by and by." But there are tremendous rewards that come to us for faithfulness now. These we should pursue because they pay double dividends. Rewarded in full here, and rewarded again in eternity.

Proverbs 14:15

"A simple man believes anything, but a prudent man gives thought to his steps."

Like the previous verse and the next two, these comparisons may well be between careless and wise or prudent Christians. We have the Source of wisdom and truth residing within, but that does not automatically make us immune to deception. Most of us know that from experience; we have both deceived and been deceived. And if we are generally very careful to be truthful, we may easily believe that of others as well, and thus at times become very gullible. This proverb tells us it is foolish to "believe everything you hear." Do you remember Y2K? Were you one who believed—at least in part, that indeed beginning at 12:01am, January1, 2000, power-grids around the country would cease to function correctly?

As I am writing this, we have just passed the 3rd or 4th deadline date this year (that I heard) when banks would confiscate our money. The proposed solution was to take our money out of the banks and buy gold or silver. This last date when this disaster was certain to occur was just 2 weeks ago. Only the bank of heaven is absolutely fail-proof, but it would be foolish to believe every doomsday prediction. It is a foolish man, a simple man, a gullible man who believes everything he hears, because much of what we hear is intended to deceive, and some is just simply wrong.

A sensible man, a wise man, a prudent man "give thought to his steps." Only Jesus is the Truth, and the Bible is the written truth. Therefore, our ultimate trust must be in the God of the Bible. By trusting Him for wisdom and guidance, we can avoid many pitfalls of everyday life. In 1 John 4:1 we are taught not to believe every spirit, but to "test the spirits." That is being prudent, sensible, safe and wise.

Proverbs 14:16

"A wise man fears the Lord and shuns evil, but a fool is hotheaded and reckless."

This verse reminds me of Proverbs 9:10: "the fear of the Lord is the beginning of wisdom." We want the wisdom, but how desperately do we want the Lord Himself? There is so much more to the fear of the Lord than simply knowing a definition of what the term means. As we suggested when we looked at that particular Proverb back in March, it involves truly knowing Him. Knowing Him so well and so intimately that we actually "hunger and thirst" to be righteous. Too many Christians are still looking to see what they can get away with—or should that be all Christians from time to time. Sometimes we may shun evil (and even the "appearance" of evil) because we want to appear to be righteous. But do we really desire to be righteous because of our love for Him? Yet sin still has its allure. Not all sins, but just certain sins still look very desirable. How intimately do we know Him? Or even want to know Him?

We know that we will not achieve sinless perfection in this life, but the more consistently we wisely shun evil, the less that evil will appear desirable and alluring. The better we get to know Him, the more we will want to shun evil. Wisdom comes not only from asking, but also from acting on the wisdom we have already acquired. It is a growth process. Even Jesus "grew in wisdom and stature, and in favor with God and man." Luke 2:52.

Now let's finish the proverb: "a fool is hotheaded and reckless." I certainly do not like the idea of being thought a fool, and hotheaded really is not appealing either, but reckless, well, keep in mind that I am a type A personality. True! But above all, I am a child of God, indwelt by the Holy Spirit.

PROVERBS TO LIVE BY

Proverbs 14:17-18

"A quick-tempered man does foolish things, and a crafty man is hated. The simple inherit folly, but the prudent are crowned with knowledge."

A quick-tempered, or hotheaded man often does foolish things because he does not take time to think about what he is doing, nor about the probable consequences. Probably most of us fall into that category from time to time—or at least we used to. We sometimes act or speak foolishly because we did not take time to think. With maturity and wisdom that should be occurring less and less frequently. You have heard the saying "from bad to worse," and that is what's going on here. It is bad enough to do foolish things because one is hotheaded and quick-tempered; it is much worse to do foolish or stupid things by intent or design.

The next word to look at is "crafty." The crafty man intentionally plots evil. That is the bent of his character, it is almost like "a way of life" for him. If there is both an honest and a deceptive way to do "it," the crafty man will choose the dishonest way. I well remember trying that kind of deception against a 4th grade classmate. It backfired. Between my dad and the Lord, I was taught not to pursue such a lifestyle. Had I succeeded, who knows what the outcome might have been. But our text anticipates a next step. "The simple inherit folly." Those who are naïve and continue along that way "inherit" foolishness. Whatever a person inherits become his permanent possession—unless he gets rid of it somehow.

However, the prudent, the wise, are crowned with knowledge. The fear of the Lord is not only the beginning of wisdom, Proverbs 9:10, it is also the beginning of knowledge, Proverbs 1:3. Not bad, by a deliberate choice, (the fear of the Lord) and the lifetime pursuit of that choice, we can be crowned with both wisdom and knowledge.

Proverbs 14:22

"Do not those who plot evil go astray? But those who plan what is good find love and faithfulness."

One commentator said of this verse that both those who plan evil and those who plan good "will be paid in their own coin." Galatians 6:7 teaches that we reap what we sow." Since God established that as a divine principle, it applies equally to the wise and the foolish, to the good and the evil, the believer and the unbeliever.

I have talked with some people who seemed absolutely convinced that with better planning and plotting, they could carry out their evil plans without bearing any consequences. And just where did I talk with them? In prison. Their bravado and confidence seemed to come from the fact that some of their other misdeeds had never been discovered or landed them in prison. Therefore, this prison sentence was evidence of a flaw in their "plotting." Nothing more. They did not accept that this prison term was only the initial consequence; that ultimate accounting for both their public and secret deeds was still future.

Now let's look at the positive half of the proverb. Those who plan what is good find love and faithfulness. In his commentary Matthew Henry said of this text: "How wisely those consult their own interest who not only do good but devise it.

Sometimes we have a spur-of-the-moment opportunity to do good to someone, and how blessed we are if we do it. But this proverb speaks specifically to the matter of planning by design to do good. Isaiah 32:8 comments "the noble man makes noble plans, and by noble deeds he stands." Such a person finds love and faithfulness, not as payment-in-full, but as a gift of divine mercy. Hmmm, maybe a good investment for us would be to search for opportunities to do good, then make careful plans, and then just do it.

Proverbs 14:26-27

"He who fears the Lord has a secure fortress, and for his children it will be a refuge." The fear of the Lord is a fountain of life, turning a man from the snares of death."

The person who does not fear the Lord, be he a carnal Christian or a non-believer, has only his own wisdom and skill and provision as his fortress. That is not very secure at all. That is a little like trusting in a tent for protection during a tornado. Yet that is also the only security he is teaching his children, so they too have no fortress to go to in the storm. Many people live by the old adage "the Lord helps those who help themselves." Our text (supported by all of Scripture) tells us the Lord helps those who trust in him; those who "fear the Lord."

The text continues with "the fear of the Lord is a fountain of life." We have already learned that the fear of the Lord is both knowledge and wisdom, but how is this true of life? In several ways. He is the source of knowledge, wisdom, life and more, but this verse talks about life. All physical life has its source or beginning in Him, and He is the source of spiritual life. He gave us life when we were born, and new life when we were born again. But I don't think either of those are in focus in the context here. In this text the fear of the Lord proves to be a fountain of life by turning a man from the snares of death. Remember what Jesus said as recorded in John 10:10, the thief (the devil) comes only to kill, steal and destroy. The "fountain of life" comes into play when by the fear of the Lord, we avoid getting caught in those snares of death, and so physical life is extended. By this same fear of the Lord our children too can be delivered from these snares of death, as can others in whose lives we may have an influence. Think of it, by the fear of the Lord we can bring both physical life (extension) and spiritual life to others.

PROVERBS TO LIVE BY

Proverbs 14:29-30

"A patient man has great understanding, but a quick-tempered man displays folly. A heart at peace gives life to the body, but envy rots the bones."

One reason a patient person has greater understanding than others is that he takes time to listen and consider before jumping to conclusions. Jumping to conclusions is a very common, but profitless exercise. You don't lose any weight by doing it but you do lose understanding, and probably friends. The issue is very practical, and also very important, and Solomon comes back to it again in 29:20 "Do you see a man who speaks in haste? There is more hope for a fool than for him."

Think back to a time when you spoke in haste, without listening carefully for the purpose of understanding. We've all done it. What did you actually gain, if instead of listening you mentally prepared your response? What did you lose? Whatever else, you probably totally lost the sense of divine peace of heart and mind. I have at times recognized, after the fact, that I actually displayed folly while attempting to display superior understanding.

Now think back again, and ask yourself why you felt you had to respond in haste. Wasn't there a certain amount of anger involved in the motivation? That would be called "quick-tempered." Was there perhaps a measure of envy because the other person was beginning to sound too wise and understanding, and you thought you were really the one with superior insight? I don't know, but these and other factors are included in this text.

The patient man gains personal understanding and thereby also gains wisdom, and as an added bonus, he also gains a heart of peace which makes life much more enjoyable. That is worth going for, especially if you consider the alternatives.

Proverbs 14:31

*"He who oppresses the poor shows contempt for their
Maker, but whoever is kind to the needy honors God."*

We know and understand that poverty is sometimes brought on by
a person's own evil or wickedness, and sometimes by misfortune or even
foolish mistakes or stupidity. But that is certainly not always the case. In
an agricultural society it could also be brought on by drought which man
cannot control. So, which of these, or other causes of poverty, did Solomon
have in mind when he said "don't oppress them"? He must have been
thinking of those who are poor through no fault of their own, because they
could not help it; so, they were not to blame. True! But he was thinking just
as much of those who became poor through laziness or other reasons that
could have been avoided. Poverty and neediness in this proverb are points
of application. The issue however is "do not oppress." To oppress anyone,
poor or not, is to show contempt for God. That is serious business! But!

This is another one of those conjunctive "but" proverbs. But, if we want
to honor God in this arena, we must learn how to show kindness to the
poor. It must not mean to lift them out of poverty, because comparatively
few of us could do that to even one person or family, let alone a whole
segment of society. But then again, charitable giving is only one of many
ways to show kindness, and is sometimes the wrong way. A better way
often is to help the poor work his own way out. Let God be the Guide,
since we are seeking to honor Him. In our efforts to show kindness we
may sometimes be taken advantage of, but how He uses our kindness is
His business. We may not see the benefits of our kindness to others in this
life—or we may, but that should not matter.

Our goal is to honor God.

Proverbs 14:32

"When calamity comes, the wicked are brought down,
but even in death the righteous have a refuge."

The book of Proverbs teaches wisdom with the primary view to living wisely in this life; eternity is nevertheless always kept in view. This proverb seems to focus more specifically on the eternal, keeping in mind that this life is preparation for the next.

One commentator says of the first part of our text that in his death the wicked are "driven away" in their wickedness. That would reinforce the fact there is no second chance after death. Many people are wise enough to know that they should turn away from their selfish wickedness, but seemingly not wise enough to know that "now is the accepted time, now is the day of salvation." Enough calamity comes in this life, enough difficulty, trials and temptation and failure, to realize we need "external" help. That help is found only in the Gospel of grace. Failure to act on the knowledge of need and to call upon that Help shows the depth of human folly. Indeed, Satan has blinded the eyes of those who do not believe.

But, "even in death the righteous have a refuge." Like the wicked, the righteous have enough calamities, trials and failures to know they need external help, but their help is always near. The more readily and regularly we call on that help, the more wise and prosperous we become. The Refuge and Hope applies very much to the here and now. Scriptures are replete with reminders to call upon the Lord in the day of trouble, and our praise and thanksgiving should reflect our dependence on Him. But our text focuses on the eternal; even in death the righteous have a refuge. We could add to the commentator and say we are "driven to" our refuge.

Hallelujah!!

Proverbs 14:34-35

*"Righteousness exalts a nation, but sin is a disgrace
to any people. A king delights in a wise servant, but a
shameful servant incurs his wrath."*

One might read this first verse, and conclude that the problem in our
nation is corrupt politicians. Surely, we see a lot of that. Others might
see it as a degraded immoral entertainment industry, or the media, or
the education system, or whatever. Certainly, sin abounds in all these,
and every other segment of society. Our text does not narrow it to any
specific element of the nation. Simply "righteousness exalts a nation, and
unrighteousness, or sin, is a disgrace to any people. But don't we need to
find someone to blame for the mess we're in? Maybe the problem is with
"all of the above" in combination. Surely there must be someone we can
blame!

It should not be too hard to figure out that if righteousness is the
solution and the blessing, then sin or unrighteousness is the problem.
Perhaps we have sought to fix the problem by choosing a more conservative
leadership, or if we are more liberal in our philosophy, to fix the problem
with more and better welfare programs. But, the solution is not to be found
in a reform of our institutions; that could come in due time, once we solve
the real problem, and return to righteousness. But how do we do that?

The same God who gave Solomon this text also gave him 2Chronicles
7:14. "If my People, who are called by me name, will humble themselves
and pray . . ." God will solve our problem when you and I return to
righteousness in our own personal lives. So, it is up to you and me. Perhaps
it would help if we take that verse, only instead of "my people," put our
own name there, and ask God to show me my own need to pray, and turn,
and seek. Righteousness exalts individuals as well as nations. It's worth
a try.

Proverbs 15:1-2

"A gentle answer turns sway wrath, but a harsh word stirs up anger. The tongue of the wise commends knowledge, but the mouth of the fool gushes folly."

How fitting that this text should follow the previous one. Most of our interpersonal problems do not begin with anything major. Slight disagreements would rarely escalate if we would faithfully heed the words of this text. Whenever a disagreement arises between two individuals, each one needs to avoid a harshness in attitude, because that can be detected even before it can be heard. "Of course, I tried to give a gentle answer, but that guy was so totally intransigent, "there was just no reasoning with him." You may have never used words like that, but have you ever thought that way? Have you ever tried to justify yourself with such reasoning? In so many arenas of life we all want to be first, but when it comes to resolving a disagreement with another, we tend to all want to be second. After all, "he started it. I'll apologize if he will."

Here we get right back into the matter of the wise versus the foolish. Wise persons can and will get into disagreements at times. But "the tongue of the wise (will) commend knowledge," thereby keeping the disagreement from escalating into a quarrel or worse. The mouth of the fool "gushes" folly, because the fool seeks primarily to prove himself right. He will have his say, and let the chips fall where they may. He can worry about the consequences later.

Look back at the last disagreement you had that ended with hurt or bitter feelings; were you wiser, or more foolish in the encounter? Now look back at the last disagreement that ended agreeably, and harmoniously; who was the first to speak and act wisely? By the power of the indwelling Holy Spirit, each of us can be wiser today than we were yesterday.

Proverbs 15:3

"The eyes of the Lord are everywhere, keeping watch on the wicked and the good."

What a powerful statement of both inexpressible encouragement while simultaneously producing a dreadful fear. For the believer, it is marvelous to know that one cannot go where God isn't or can't see. For the wicked "it is a fearful thing to fall into the hands of the living God." In Revelation 4:8 John saw that the angels had eyes all around, even under their wings, and none of them have macular degeneration or glaucoma, so they can see a lot. But "God is all eye," says commentator Matthew Henry, so He sees everything. He sees not only to perceive, but to appraise and evaluate motives in what He observes. One thing God cannot do is to overlook anything. I can ask my friend to "forget I just said that," but there is no point in trying that with God. If I said something wrong, I can only confess and repent, and when it is covered by the Blood, there is nothing charged to my account. I am then cleansed, forgiven, and delivered or redeemed of that wrong. That wrong is then not overlooked, but removed. Such intimate, absolute and complete knowledge of us by a righteous and perfectly just God is a frightful thing to any unbeliever.

But our God also sees the good we do or even attempt to do as well, even to the point of a kind word, or a cup of water to one in need. He sees worship and obedience, and love and kindness, and furthermore, He does not just see from a distance because He is also everywhere present. He is always "a very present help in times of need." He is a strong Tower and our Refuge. Whenever we are in danger of stumbling or straying, He is there as our protector and Guide. Aren't you glad "the eyes of the Lord are everywhere, keeping watch"?

PROVERBS TO LIVE BY

"The tongue that brings healing is a tree of life, but a deceitful tongue crushes the spirit."

We might well ask how our tongue, our speech, can be healing. Our speech is much more important and consequential than we can know or can even imagine. Remember Matthew 12:37 where Jesus said "By your words you will be acquitted and by your words you will be condemned."

I'm sure few, if any of us, are really aware how many daily opportunities we have to speak "healing words." Nor are we aware of how many times we actually speak hurtful, rather than healing words. I do know however, that the indwelling Holy Spirit is very much aware, and He is waiting and longing to help us "shun the wrong and speak the right words" at the right times. So why does He not prompt us to speak healing words at the right time, and stop us from speaking hurtful words? Well, I believe He does in fact prompt us, but too often we simply are not listening—at least not to Him. He does not, and will not force us, because we are created with a never-ending freedom of choice, and He will not violate our freedom. We choose whether or not to listen, and we choose whether or not to obey. Often, we make those decisions out of habit or lifestyle, rather than careful consideration.

So, what can we do about the dilemma? Let me suggest we begin by daily praying for wisdom and alertness in this matter. Now try to understand your past patterns, both your successes and your failures in speech. Then follow that up by anticipating and looking for new opportunities to come our way. Every time you do speak healing words, celebrate it with nobody at the party except the Lord and you. "Each victory will help you some other to win." In this process, "Christ is (being) formed in you," Galatians 4:19.

Proverbs 15:5

"A fool spurns his father's discipline, but whoever heeds correction shows prudence."

The words "discipline" and "correction" in this verse are pretty much synonymous, because the purpose of discipline is to either correct where one has gone wrong, or to keep one going on correctly when no wrongs are present. Furthermore, Solomon assumes that this will primarily happen in the home, and that it is the father's responsibility. Thus, a father's discipline ought to include encouragement and commendation. Countless testimonials and life experience show that this is precisely where many father's (and mothers) frequently fall short in their discipline. Our text tells us that he is a fool who spurns such discipline. But really, where is the teenager who does not at times think that the father, or whoever is doing the discipline, is the one who is foolish. Parents just don't understand. They are so old fashioned. We've probably all been through that, regardless of what we did physically. So, what does that prove? That we were normal, or that God via Solomon was right? We were fools to spurn discipline.

Now, lest we think that at age 50, or 80, or whatever age we are, we are past all that, consider the wisdom side of this equation. "Whoever!" So long as we work under the supervision of bosses and superiors, we need discipline/correction, and when we are "the boss," we may need it more than ever. OK, so we'll wait for retirement. Nope! Still need it. In fact, from our youth onward, we need to learn more and more to take our discipline directly from the Word of God. We simply graduate from our father's discipline to **The** Father's discipline. He is working within us to make us more like Jesus Christ, Galatians 4:19. That process is called "sanctification." So, how are we doing?

PROVERBS TO LIVE BY

"The house of the righteous contains great treasure, but the income of the wicked brings them trouble."

This proverb seems to be a companion to the one in 10:22, which says *the blessing of the Lord brings wealth, and he adds no sorrow to it.* Today's proverb is not saying that every righteous person has great material wealth, and therefore anyone who does not have great wealth cannot be a righteous person. That may be the teaching of some in what is called The Prosperity Gospel, or Health and Wealth Gospel, or Name it and Claim it, etc. I do not believe Scripture supports that view. So, what does this Proverb teach?

I believe the "great treasure" includes material wealth, but is not restricted to that alone. Genuine Christians may be impoverished for many reasons, quite apart from what is God's desire for them; ignorance of financial principles, greed (or the love of money), disobedience, becoming victims of fraud, to name just a few. But even in this life, financial prosperity is never the greatest treasure. Our God is Sovereign, and He knows what is best for each one of us, and is fully able to provide whatever that is. He is much more interested in what we are, than in what we have. The same amount of wealth that blesses one person, might destroy another; God knows. "No good thing does He withhold from those whose walk is blameless" Psalm 84:11.

Think of the greatness of treasure to be found in a healthy, happy family, where everyone knows and loves the Lord, and is living with the hope of eternity. Some of the most miserable people on earth may well include those who count their wealth in the multiplied billions. Their income brings them only trouble. No matter how much one has or thinks he does not have, God says "godliness with contentment is great gain." We could say it is "great treasure."

Proverbs 15:7

"The lips of the wise spread knowledge; not so the hearts of fools."

We have seen that wisdom and knowledge are not the same thing; that wisdom comes from God; that wisdom is honed or cultivated through its pursuit, and that we can choose wise versus foolish thoughts, words, and actions. Here we notice the lips of the wise and the hearts of fools both express what we **are**. That reminds us of the words of Jesus in Luke 6:45: *"The good man brings good things out of the good stored up in his heart, and the evil man brings evil out of the evil stored up in his heart. Out of the abundance of his heart his mouth speaks."*

There will probably always be times and occasions when we will need to, by deliberate choice, determine to speak wisely while our whole being wants to expose and rebuke some stupidity. That is called resisting temptation. But that is not what this proverb is all about. The "lips of the wise spread knowledge" is not so much planning and choosing to wisely say the right thing, or disperse knowledge; rather it is a matter of allowing the "wise fullness" of the heart to bubble over. We do that, whether we plan it or not. For example, if or when our heart is full of anger, we cannot communicate love, no matter what words we use. When the heart is full of God's wisdom, that communicates; when the heart is full of foolishness (or evil), that too communicates.

What fills our hearts is determined by what we feed it; in that sense, it is our choice. Since none of us have yet achieved our goal, let me simply ask: do our "lips" (words, actions, thoughts, and actions) more consistently "spread knowledge" than a year or two ago?

Proverbs 15:8-9

"The Lord detests the sacrifice of the wicked, but the prayer of the upright pleases him. The Lord detests the way of the wicked, but he loves those who pursue righteousness,"

A casual reading could make one think that the Lord detests wicked people. From there it would be an easy step to conclude that being good and doing good are required for God to love us. From there the logical conclusion would be that salvation is by good works, or at least aided by works, plus Christ's death on the cross. Either way, they consider works to be a vital ingredient in salvation. Fortunately, that is not what the text says.

Verse 8 plainly says it is the "sacrifice" of the wicked that God detests, and verse 9 adds it is the "way" of the wicked that He detests. I take the sacrifice of the wicked to be their own effort at earning merit with God, and/or earning their own salvation. Such sacrifice in our day often consists of being honest, being generous, being charitable, being faithful to family, etc., etc. All good and proper in their time and place, but that runs cross-grain to God's gracious provision. In fact, it seeks to negate God's sacrificial gift. The way of the wicked would include all forms of such sacrifice, and refers to the general lifestyle of the wicked, whether moral or not.

Who then are the "upright"? First of all, they are the ones who have received God's sacrificial payment for their sins, and are therefore declared righteous, or "upright" by God. Therefore, they now "pursue" righteousness, not as payment or re-payment for our sins, but as expression of love to the God who so loved that He gave. The Proverbs often call these people the "righteous," but never the sinless. They are declared righteous, and will one day be sinless. In the meantime, they **pursue** righteousness because they want to please Him who has declared them righteous.

"Stern discipline awaits him who leaves the path, he who hates correction will die."

This verse is primarily directed to believers, because unbelievers are not on "the path" to begin with. It is however also for unbelievers, because they are moving away from the path that they know is right. The stern discipline is for both groups.

The previous verses showed us that the Lord detests both the sacrifice and the way of the wicked. However, He loves the persons so much that He is willing to administer "stern discipline" to cause them to repent and return. Since He loves wicked, rebellious people that much, He certainly loves His own enough to discipline them equally. We must always remember that the Lord's discipline is designed to correct us, restore us, and bring us back to "the path." Sin's punishment has been paid. Hebrews 12:11 confirms what we already know, that "no discipline seems pleasant at the time, but painful. Later on, however, it produces a harvest of righteousness and peace for those who have been trained by it." Since discipline is not pleasant but painful, we may dread it, we may endure it, and we may even hate it. That is our choice, but for those who hate correction, there is a strong warning, namely an untimely death. That's what it says, "he who hates correction will die."

According to Moody Bible Commentary, another translation of this verse suggests: "Discipline is evil to those who abandon the way." If that is correct, there is no wonder they "hate it." God detests their way, and so He brings stern discipline and so they in turn hate His discipline. Such a direction of life will bring death. In light of that Ezekiel implored his people in 18:31 "Why will you die, O house of Israel?" or selfish Christian or rebellious unbeliever.

"Death and destruction lie open before the Lord—how much more the hearts of men."

The first part of this verse deals with the all-seeing eye of God, His omnipotence, His omni-presence, and His sovereignty. The American Standard has "Sheol" and "Abaddon" in place of death and destruction. Nevertheless, together they refer to the realm of death.

If we take death or Sheol as referring only to the grave, we are too restrictive, because among the dead are those whose bodies were never discovered to mankind so there was no grave. Those too "lie open before the Lord. Come resurrection time, God knows precisely where every atom and molecule is. He will not need to search or even to consult the record books. According to Revelation 9:11, one of the names of Satan is Abaddon, so this would take in his person and his abode. That too "lies open before the Lord." All the devil's stealth and wizardry and deception also are an open book to God. We can be, and frequently are deceived about one thing or another, but God cannot be deceived. Ever! Hebrews 4:13 tells us that "Nothing in all creation is hidden from God's sight. Everything is uncovered and laid bare before the eyes of him to whom we must give account." Even hell and destruction are open before the Lord. That being so, we now proceed to the last part of the proverb.

If all evil, including the source of evil is open before the Lord, "how much more the hearts of men." To those who might be trying to hide thoughts and attitudes from the Lord, this may be a somewhat frightening thought, but to those who are seeking to be transparent before Him, this is reassuring to say the least. He already knows your mistakes and failures, so there is nothing to hide. He loves you just as if you had never sinned, and He is taking you toward sinlessness.

Proverbs 15:13, 14-15

"A happy heart makes the face cheerful, but heartache crushes the spirit. The discerning heart seeks knowledge, but the mouth of a fool feeds on folly. All the days of the oppressed are wretched, but the cheerful heart has a continual feast."

Obviously all three of these proverbs deal with the human heart. Obvious too is the fact that this does not refer to the heart that is the concern of the cardiologist. Rather, it has more to do with one's disposition and perspective on life. For today we'll look only at the first one.

In the first proverb, we notice that the heart warmed and made happy by the "Joy of the Lord" (generally) shows up as a cheerful face. The face, more than anything else, displays our emotional reality. When asked how you are, and you tell someone you are fine when really you are not, he probably knew that before he ever asked. You may not want to tell the person what concerns you, but generally your face is more honest than your words about such matters. Don't waste your time trying to refine your skill of speaking convincingly; work rather on keeping your heart "right with God." Your heart will tell your face. Your heart can be happy, even when circumstances are not.

But heartache, whether verbally announced or not, "crushes the spirit." Different circumstances cause heaviness of heart, such as physical health issues, economic issues, regret over errors made, strained relationships etc., and often times it may be helpful to talk about it with someone who understands. It might be a friend or family member, a pastor or counselor, but it must be someone you trust. The old song goes "no one understands like Jesus," and incidentally, no one can heal the heart like Jesus either, so let's begin there. Just remember, "A happy heart makes the face cheerful."

Proverbs 15:13, 14-15

*"A happy heart makes the face cheerful, but heartache crushes the spirit. **The discerning heart seeks knowledge, but the mouth of a fool feeds on folly. All the days of the oppressed are wretched, but the cheerful heart has a continual feast."***

Today we continue with the next two proverbs, beginning with the character of your heart. The discerning heart reveals wherein you find satisfaction and fulfillment. Bumper-sticker theology may claim fishing as the ultimate good. The discerning heart will examine the issue to determine its wisdom; it seeks knowledge. The discerning heart is always seeking knowledge in regard to whatever issues must be faced. It is too wise to accept everything at face value. The face will not reflect that seeking so much as your questions and pursuits will. Wisdom consists of both shunning and pursuing.

A fool "feeds on folly." He is satisfied with his folly and sees no need to seek for something better. In the days when in our part of the country, a good starting wage for common labor was $1.00 per hour, a friend was up to $1.15 because of good performance. His life goal was to get up to $1.25. But "Beyond the horizon there's more, there's more."

The Last of these three, the heart shapes one's outlook on circumstances. I spoke with a gentleman this morning who was told by his doctor that they did not know the problem, but "your organs are shutting down." He was dying. First reactions were natural, but then the heart reminded him "God is in control," and peace came. Now, several months later he is back at work, and he is no longer afraid to die. The cheerful heart has a continual feast. This is not "Pollyannaism." There may be full awareness of the severity of the situation or the finality of the diagnosis, still the heart can be cheerful. It is a God thing. If no one else comes to the feast, let it be just you and God.

Proverbs 15:16-17

"Better a little with the fear of the Lord than great wealth with turmoil. Better a meal of vegetables where there is love than a fattened calf with hatred."

Deep down, we all know there are things far more valuable than great wealth. Among these certainly are physical and relational health—especially in the family. Still in all, we generally tend to strive for more wealth, which is fine if the "striving" is kept in proper bounds. In these verses, we learn the secret to the "continual feast" of the previous verse. The key word here is "better."

There is nothing intrinsically wrong with great wealth, or with the proper pursuit of it. We could easily re-state verse 16 to say: *"Better great wealth with the fear of the Lord than a little with turmoil."* That would be true, but would not help the argument. That is precisely what too many people are attempting to accomplish already. This proverb is trying to tell us that the pursuit of righteousness is that which is "better." It is like Jesus said to Martha of Bethany, Mary has chosen the "better," and it will not be taken away from her. People often strive for the good life, but they focus on wealth instead of the fear of the Lord. It is the focus, the priority that is wrong. Neither wealth nor poverty lead to godliness, and genuine godliness does not necessarily lead to either wealth or poverty. The Apostle Paul said to Timothy—and to us, "godliness with contentment is great gain . . . (so) if we have food and clothing, we will be content." 1 Timothy 6;8-9.

Paul goes on to say, "the love of money is the root of all kinds of evil." It is in fact idolatry. Some people find neither wealth nor godliness because they are practicing this "American" form of idolatry, and God cannot bless our idolatry, even if we sincerely ask Him to. Maybe it is time to re-focus our values and priorities.

"A hot-tempered man stirs up dissension, but a patient man calms a quarrel."

Do you ever get angry when your computer does stuff on its own? When my computer does that, I'll sometimes call my son and explain what "the stupid computer" did this time. He listens and then calmly tells me "you obviously pressed something." So—it was not really the computer, (at least not this time) it was the operator.

This proverb teaches that dissensions, quarrels and fights are not caused by issues and subject matters; they are caused by people. I was guest speaker at a church in another state one time, and the pastor told me later that the church had had a serious "fight" over the selection of the color of the carpet. Whether or not we are personally involved in such a "fight," analysis will always tell us more about the people involved than about the matter being fought over. Nor is the dissension resolved by one party being proved more in the right than the other. Things happen; people react. In one of my visits to a Southern State, one of the locals informed me that the civil war was not yet over. He was not saying that combat was continuing; only that the issues were not resolved to everyone's satisfaction.

Our text says the hot-tempered man stirs up dissension. He may have kept the volume of his voice under control, but not the tone. Maybe he just stirred things up and then sat back to watch it unfold. The patient man, on the other hand (who incidentally is also the wise man) calms the quarrel. Dissensions and quarrels will happen, and the Bible never tells us which side of an issue to support. It simply tells us in Romans 12:18 "If it is possible, as far as it depends on you, live at peace with everyone." If that is not possible then at least be a patient, wise person who seeks to calm the quarrel.

"The way of the sluggard is blocked with thorns, but the path of the upright is a highway."

This is not saying that the way is blocked with **literal** thorns. If that were the case, he could simply find a better road to travel and remain a "sluggard" while he was at it. Rather, it is his mental outlook which makes every little obstacle seem insurmountable, so he gives up before he ever really gets started. The way **seems** like it is blocked with thorns. The Amplified puts it this way: "The way of the lazy is like a hedge of thorns [it pricks, lacerates, and entangles him]. This man needs an attitude adjustment. But it is not only attitude that is the problem.

Notice that the comparison is between the "sluggard" or lazy person, and the "upright." This tells us that it is primarily a spiritual matter. However, this problem may not be resolved by simply "asking Jesus to save him." To use contemporary jargon, this man may well be a Christian. Have you ever met a lazy Christian? Have you ever been one? Laziness is not confined to the realm of physical work or job-related issues; it can crop up in all arenas of life. Any time we fail to obey God in some matter, we are prone to make excuses like perhaps I was going to but "the way was blocked with thorns." Translation: it just seemed too hard.

Probably everyone reading this page really wants to be a godly man or woman, and we remember that Jesus said "My yoke is easy and My burden is light," but He must not have had my situation in mind. My way is anything but easy. Sure, I would like to be able to get up earlier for Bible reading and prayer, but I'm not getting enough sleep as it is.

OK. Is Jesus Christ Lord, or is He not Lord; is He sovereign or is He not Sovereign; am I a sluggard or am I upright. We must answer these matters for ourselves.

Proverbs 15:21-22

"Folly delights a man who lacks judgment, but a man of understanding keeps a straight course. Plans fail for lack of counsel, but with many advisers they succeed."

Why would folly delight one who lacks judgment? One reason might be that being a fool, he just doesn't know any better. He probably thinks "this is as good as it gets." When I was a kid on the farm, we had a saying: "happy as a pig in the mud." If there is no mud in the pig-pen, a pig will dig around in the dirt until it makes mud. When you realize that a pig has no sweat glands, this begins to make some sense. But why would a fool want to live that way? Because he lacks judgment, he can't figure it out for himself, and he is not wise enough to seek counsel.

Have you ever been foolish enough to not seek counsel, nor to heed it when given? I have. By just reading the first part of verse 22 one could think the counsel of just one person would suffice; and on some issues that might be true. "But with many advisers they (the plans) will succeed." One who is not wise enough to recognize the value of counsel may decide what he wants and how to obtain it without due consideration, and so he delights in pursuing his foolish way all the way to disaster.

Our text says "plans fail for lack of counsel." It doesn't say all plans, nor does it say bad plans or even good plans. It simply says plans, so it is not a 100% guarantee for all plans. A rule of thumb might be "if it merits planning, it deserves counsel." If a plan is bad it deserves to fail. However, that failure might have been avoided by seeking counsel. The more consequential the plan, the greater the need for diversity of counsel. Only God knows the end from the beginning. So, if we lack wisdom, we begin by asking God, and then by seeking the advice of others.

Proverbs 15:23-24

"A man finds joy in giving an apt reply—and how good
is a timely word! The path of life leads upward for the
wise to keep him from going down to the grave."

When we were kids, we learned an acronym for joy: Jesus first, others second, yourself last. True joy comes from Jesus, and putting the interests of others ahead of your own does indeed bring joy. The Incarnation, and all that pertains to it, was all in the interest of others, so for us to put others' interests ahead of our own is to a degree Christ-like.

Our text focusses specifically on our speech. Giving an apt reply or a timely word has the promise of bringing joy. Neither the "reply" nor the "timely word" need necessarily to be particularly pleasant. They are simply what is needed at the time, and will bring joy to the one who utters them and to the one who hears. I recall after hearing such a word at times thinking and/or saying, "I'm so glad you said that, because . . ." Such replies and timely words demonstrate wisdom, which is the theme of this Book. I may not be smart enough to figure out why a particular word is needed right now, and yet be wise enough to speak what the Holy Spirit is prompting me to say. This again shows the vast difference between wisdom and knowledge, though they may often run parallel and operate together. We may well need to grow in knowledge, but Oh how desperately we need to grow "in wisdom and in favor with God and man." Give an apt reply or speak a timely word, and I promise you on the authority of God's word that you will experience joy.

This section ends with reminder that the path of the wise leads upward, and the way of the foolish leads to death. Wisdom is beckoning you to pursue it, and it will reward you.

Proverbs 15:25-27

> *"The Lord tears down the proud man's house but he keeps the widow's boundaries intact. The Lord detests the thoughts of the wicked, but those of the pure are pleasing to him. A greedy man brings trouble to his family, but he who hates bribes will live."*

These three verses all deal with the same heart issue, but each from a somewhat different perspective. The proud man, the wicked man and the greedy man can be different people, or they can be the same person, but in heart attitude and life values, they are all the same. All of us, unless we are very careful, will fit each of those roles at one time or another. Not one of us is beyond the scope of any of the sins mentioned. Nor are we beyond the scope of the protection of the Holy Spirit. Therefore, Paul told the Corinthians (1Cor. 10:12) "If you think you are standing firm, be careful that you don't fall."

In the first scene, the powerful proud man in his greed is taking possession of the widow's property. He may even have some legal right, so he thinks he can get away with it, and he possibly will—in this life. But final accounting is still to come. In our case, while we would never even think of doing the exact, same thing, we might well be able to "justify" our own actions, but verse 26 deals with the thoughts of the man, as well as his deeds. Any "shading" of real motives is a "thought process," and the "Lord detests" the thoughts of the wicked. Finally, there is a consequence that our families will have to bear for our thoughts, attitudes and actions. It is not only a matter of facing God in judgment one day, we bring the "trouble" on ourselves and our families now, in this life.

"The thoughts of the pure are pleasing to him" and if we learn to "hate bribes" or other forms of evil, He promises "abundant" life now, and eternal life to come.

Proverbs 15:28

"The heart of the righteous weighs its answers, but the mouth of the wicked gushes evil."

The Moody Bible Commentary comments: "Prudent speech is a moral issue. . ." That being true, we can agree that we should be truthful, proper, and gracious in our speech. There is no place for crudeness or rudeness. Both the words we use, and the tone in which we use them, as well as timing of them, are of critical importance.

Often in the daily grind of living, we are required to give impromptu answers or comments, with really no opportunity to pre-think it. There is no time to "weigh the answer." What then! James 1:19 tells us to be "quick to listen and slow to speak," but how does that fit in? Jesus said: "out of the overflow of the heart, the mouth speaks." It would seem that at least the impromptu, un-premeditated speech comes from the "overflow" of the heart without considering or "weighing" the comment. OK, but you can't just say "I'll get back to you on that one." Besides, I'm not the only one. We all face the same issues on this. True, and James 3:2 does tell us that "we all stumble" in our speech. Wow, is he right there!

Let's get back to the words of Jesus; "out of the overflow of the heart. . ." Is there a way to control and determine what the overflow is, or will be? All of Scripture would answer a resounding Yes! We responsible for what fills our heart to overflowing. Colossians 3:16 teaches "Let the word of Christ dwell in you richly." That is full to overflowing. No, we cannot store up all the right answers and comments in advance with more Bible knowledge, but as we fill our hearts and minds with Scripture, the Holy Spirit will conform our lives to the image or likeness of Jesus Christ. In another context Jesus said "you will be given what to say, for it will be. . .the Spirit speaking through you." Let's be sure to fill our hearts correctly.

Proverbs 15:31-33

He who listens to a life-giving rebuke will be at home among the wise. He who ignores discipline despises himself, but whoever heeds correction gains understanding. The fear of the Lord teaches a man wisdom, and humility comes before honor."

The word "listens" here means more than simply hearing what is being said in the rebuke; it means heeding, it means acting on it. Just as "no discipline at the time is pleasant," (Hebrews 12:1) a rebuke will not be pleasant at the time. Once it is perceived, however, that the rebuke is "life-giving," whether literally or figuratively, it takes on a whole new dimension. Such rebukes are given by the wise and serve to teach wisdom to the one who will heed them. Therefore, those who wish to be wise will seek the company of those who are wise and will not allow us to go on with foolish decisions and actions.

The one who "ignores" the rebuke or the discipline has indeed heard it, but chooses not to act on it. While we are in the process of becoming wise, we have probably all been guilty of ignoring, but have hopefully then learned to "listen." The one who persists in ignoring the disciplinary rebuke, actually despises himself. One might think he merely despises the rebuke, or the one who gave it, but such a one deceives himself. To gain understanding we must heed the correction.

One who submissively worships the Lord in "reverential fear," learns the wisdom that the Lord is trying to teach through people and circumstances. All that however, requires true humility, and such humility precedes honor. Our world's system promotes "go for the honor, go for the big name, go for the recognition, go for the glory, and forget about humility." God says "those who hono fr me, I will honor." (1 Samuel 2:30) Let God be your "wisdom Teacher."

Proverbs 16:1-2

"To man belong the plans of the heart, but from the Lord comes the reply of the tongue. All a man's ways seem innocent to him, but motives are weighed by the Lord."

Being made in the image of God includes our ability to think, plan, and reason. However, He did not make us to be **like** God by giving us omniscience. Our thinking, planning and reasoning therefore need to remain submissive to **Him,** who is omniscient. He wants to give us guidance, direction, insight, and wisdom in our planning, but He will not do our thinking and planning for us. So, we need to go ahead and do our own planning, asking for His guidance along the way. This evidently includes our speech and our intended reply, because our text says "the reply of the tongue is of the Lord." but when our planning is done under His supervision, He will give us the reply, and it will be **from Him.**

That we do not achieve total perfection is evident from the wording in verse 2. Notice what the verse does not say. It does not say "sometimes a man's ways seem OK because he reached a pretty good conclusion." With careful planning one may perhaps be totally correct. Astute business people do this all the time, so from a common-sense business perspective, these ways may indeed be "innocent" or correct. Nor does our text say that such plans are never right. Some are, and some are not. Plans (or "ways") and planning are really not the issue here. It is a matter of motives. Even James in 4:13-17 never indicates that the man was wrong in his plans to open a "branch store" in another city. They were simply made in exclusion of Divine intervention. Motives in planning are bad when they are selfish by not being submissive to the Sovereignty of God. Our plans as well as our thoughts, words and deeds need to be subjected to the Lord's scrutiny. He weighs them all anyway.

Proverbs 16:3-4

"Commit to the Lord whatever you do, and your plans will succeed. The Lord works out everything for his own ends even— the wicked for a day of disaster."

In the previous set of verses we saw God's Sovereignty and human limitations in relation to our planning. With that in mind, we now look at the logical or wise conclusion. Since we are supposed to plan, even without omniscience, and the Sovereign God who knows the end from the beginning is in control, it is wise to submit both our planning and its outcome to the Lord. Then the promise is that those plans will succeed. This does not mean that we can make plans selfishly, and **then** commit them to the Lord to give His approval and grant "success." The planning **process** must also be submitted to the Lord so He can direct and supervise it, and then success is assured.

Finite humans cannot begin to comprehend infinity; we cannot comprehend the grace, the wisdom, the love, or any of God's attributes. The best we can do is to believe that He is who He said He is and does what He says He does.

Here He says He "works out everything for his own ends." How He can take my finite plans and work them out to accomplish His own ends is beyond me. And then comes this shocker: "even the wicked for a day of disaster." How can His holy purpose be achieved by the wicked? Don't ask me, but go with me to Romans 8:28. "We know (not understand) that *in all things* God works for the good of those who love him, who have been called according to his purpose." (emphasis added) But how? All I know is that He has done, is doing, and will do all that he has said. If that presents a problem to our understanding, it is no Problem to Him. "He that did not spare his own Son . . . how will he not . . . graciously give us all things." (Romans. 8:32)

"The Lord detests all the proud of heart. Be sure of this:
They will not go unpunished."

This proverb deals with the issue of being "proud of heart." Let us remember first of all that the God who looks at the heart 1 Samuel 16:9, sees and knows. Man can only look at the outward appearance, which may be the reason we may not see our own pride. Yet, pride will express itself, even when there is a valiant attempt to hide or camouflage it. Thus a keen observer will most often detect it. The more extreme the pride is, the more obvious it will be. But what really is pride?

My old Webster says it is first "inordinate self-esteem, conceit." Romans 12:3 says it is to "think of yourself more highly than you ought." However, as those created "in the image of God," we ought to think of ourselves too lowly. God did not make us junk; He made us only "a little lower than the angels." To put ourselves down may simply be a form false humility, a fishing for someone to tell us we are really great. So it is a good thing that God does look at the heart.

Pride can appear to be based on a lot of things, such as accomplishments, pride, material wealth, or good looks, or even their melodious voice, smart kids, their education, or their I.Q. The list could go on. But none of those types of things are fundamentally a basis for pride. **At its base, selfish pride is the result of an inadequate view of God.**

In 1 Corinthians 4:7 God asks "What do you have that you did not receive? And if you did receive it, why do you boast as though you did not?" Now then, when God looks at your heart and mine, what does He see in relation to pride? What do we see in ourselves when we ask God to search our hearts and show us what is really there? Christians have as much pride problem as non-Christians.

Proverbs 16:6-7

"Through love and faithfulness sin is atoned for; through the fear of the Lord a man avoids evil. When a man's ways are pleasing to the Lord, he makes even his enemies live at peace with him."

The opening phrase is interesting and perhaps a little disturbing to some. Does it refer to God's love and faithfulness to us, (God so loved that He gave) or does it perhaps refer to man's love and faithfulness to his fellow-man (do unto others as you would have them do to you)? Next question. Does it refer to man's love and faithfulness (obedience) to God? How about this: God so loved the world . . . and on the cross the whole sin question was atoned for. Then our love and faithfulness to God appropriates that atonement for anyone who so loves. The result of that combination would be a love and faithfulness for our fellow-man.

The next phrase is self-explanatory; "Through the fear of the Lord a man avoids evil." The fear of the Lord is, or includes, love and faithfulness. Our fear of the Lord, our love and faithfulness to Him, will enable us to avoid evil. Probably we have all tried to avoid evil—with only limited success, by sheer determination and/or mental calculations. We know a thing is wrong and we should not do it. Then we consider further, it seems inviting or enjoyable to do it, and there is very little chance of anyone ever knowing, or it could be very profitable. Then we sometimes do right and sometimes not. The only guaranteed way to avoid evil is a genuine "fear of the Lord" which, as we know, "is (also) the beginning of wisdom." Well, we know which pleases the Lord, so go ahead.

Now re-read verse 7. Proverbs teaches wisdom in general terms. Not everyone in every circumstance will at all times be at peace with us, but generally yes, when our ways please the Lord He will make even our enemies to be at peace with us. Romans 12:18 gives some clarification, but not an excuse: "If it is possible, as far as it depends on you, live at peace with everyone." The key is "the fear of the Lord."

"Better a little with righteousness than much gain with injustice."

We are all familiar with the cliché "money can't buy happiness" and the smart aleck-y addendum:" but I'd like to have just enough to prove it." This proverb makes it clear that the issue is not little or much, but rather justice or injustice on both the accumulation and the administration.

I well remember the time I went to a Home Depot to buy a few spikes of a particular size and type, and found only one. I picked it up to show an attendant what I wanted. I pocketed the spike and followed him as he went and found them for me. When I got to my car, I felt the extra spike in my pocket—not paid for, so I went back in and explained to the check-out lady what had happened. She did not want to re-open the sale for an 8 cent item, so she said "forget it, I'll take care of it." I thanked her, promised to pay her back next time I came in since J had no change on me at the moment. Weeks later I came back to the store on another quest, and totally forgot my "debt." Once I got home and realized my carelessness, I had to make an extra trip back to the store. Sure enough, she was there and she remembered. I doubt she had lost any sleep over 8 cents, and the amount had very little impact on her personal budget, or the store's bottom line, but it was a matter of personal integrity. It is equally important to be honest, whether the amount is little or much.

In Luke 15:10 Jesus teaches: "Whoever can be trusted with very little can also be trusted with much, and whoever is dishonest with very little will also be dishonest with much." And as 1 Samuel 16:9 constantly reminds us, "God looks on the heart." He never says "Ah, forget it, it was only eight cents." It is only the selfish heart that can "just forget it."

Proverbs 16:9

"In his heart a man plans his course, but the Lord determines his steps."

Some people are great planners. They set a goal, whether it be short term or long, and then they carefully plan how to achieve that goal. This is very commendable, and I dare say, many of us would do well to learn from their example. To paraphrase the Apostle James, "we ought to make plans," but to do so in submission to the Lord's Sovereignty. (James 4:13-15.) Our text is not so much challenging us to make plans, as it is to caution us how we make those plans. So, let us consider the last few words: "the Lord determines his steps." This is not saying that since the Lord determines our steps, why waste your time planning. It is saying that in our planning we need to seek the Lord's His will in the matter.

To be perfectly honest, none of us have achieved perfection in this matter. At times we all make plans without truly sensing, or even seeking, the Lord's direction. Does He then still "determine our steps?" What about the times when we think we are following His direction, only to find that we missed it? What about the times we deliberately plan a direction that we know deep down is wrong? It is just something we desperately want, and so we follow our own way. How can God be directing those steps!

First of all, God desires to direct your steps during the planning process. He wants to keep you from taking those steps in the wrong direction. Then, if your planning was done in the realm of His direction, then He wants to and will direct your steps in carrying out your plans. If, and when your plans were made contrary to His will, He will then take those failures and direct them for your good—providing you are a child of God. He will "in all things" work for the good of His own.

PROVERBS TO LIVE BY
Proverbs 16:11

"Honest scales and balances are from the Lord; all the weights in the bag are of his making."

The concern here is not whether the scales register ounces and pound versus grams and kilos. The concern is absolute and total honesty. A few chapters later (20:10) we read that the Lord literally detests "differing weights and measures." Even justice is often pictured as a balancing scale. God is absolutely true and righteous, honest and just, and that is what He expects of us, whether in commerce, legal matters or general speech.

The once all too common cliché used to excuse exaggeration was "evangelistically speaking." This was in reference to the habit of some speakers to grossly exaggerate attendance at their meetings. I too used that phrase occasionally when I was young and naïve, until a Youth for Christ speaker drew my attention to the fact that there is no such thing as "evangelistically speaking." Something is either true, or it is untrue. If I am verbally reporting that our attendance was approximately XX number, that is acceptable—if true. But to throw out a larger than accurate or estimated number, just to impress is being dishonest. This would fall under the category of differing measures, and God does not merely disapprove, He detests such dishonesty.

The administration of governmental authority and justice is established by God. We are therefore to submit to it, according to Romans 13:1. In the same vein, our exchange between people, whether in commerce or any other interchange, comes under the jurisdiction of God, even when there has been little or no legal wrong done. In other words, we can be legally right but morally wrong. God still looks at the heart.

PROVERBS TO LIVE BY

Proverbs 16:16-17

"How much better to get wisdom rather than gold, to choose understanding rather than silver. The highway of the upright avoids evil, he who guards his way guards his life."

The first verse here declares how inestimably better wisdom and understanding are than gold and silver. It is not only "better," but "how much better." Those words do not denote measurement, like 25% better, but express disproportionate superiority. The value of gold and silver is that, if you have enough of it, it can pay a doctor's bill, but it can't buy your health; it can pay for a funeral, but it can't extend your life. The superiority of wisdom and understanding is measureless, and to see that we must go to the next verse.

Those who choose wisdom and understanding are here, as so often in the Proverbs, called the upright or the righteous, because of what wisdom and understanding accomplish or produce; because of what it is that makes wisdom superior. It is the wise, the upright who desire to avoid evil—even if we don't always succeed. The foolish seem to want to flirt with evil, and they mostly desire not to get caught in their foolishness. Being foolish, however, they generally fail to look far enough ahead and even brag about their foolish deeds for which there have yet been no adverse consequences. They look for immediate gratification and thrills, regardless of longer-term consequences, so their priorities are aligned accordingly.

The highway, or lifestyle of the upright avoids evil. Sin may seem alluring at times, but the wise understand enough to consider the end results. Thus, by choosing the way that avoids evil as much as possible, they are actually "guarding their life." By avoiding the evil and guarding their lives, the righteous may very possibly accumulate gold and silver along the way as well, by the grace and blessing of God.

Proverbs 16:18-19

"Pride goes before destruction, a haughty spirit before a fall. Better to be lowly is spirit and among the oppressed than to share plunder with the proud."

Again, the first verse sets out the problem, and the second expands on it and reveals the consequences of it. Pride goes before destruction is given as an absolute, although destruction may not absolutely depend on pride. A haughty spirit can fully expect to be followed by a fall. The Bible is replete with examples that show this to be true, and a careful examination of more current history also confirms it. Among the most public people to demonstrate this are politicians—of both parties. It occurs to me therefore, that perhaps politics is a most precarious calling for a Christian. (And I believe without a Divine calling, a Christian ought not to pursue it.)

Daniel 4:30 shows the pride of Nebuchadnezzar and then verse 31 says while "the (proud) words were still on his lips" the fall came. Was there no possible escape? Only one. Just a few verses earlier Daniel asked the king to repent, but he was too proud. Way back in Job 40:11-12 God said in effect: "if you won't humble yourself, I'll do it for you."

Our text says it is better to be lowly in spirit, even if it requires submission to abject poverty, than to persist in an attitude of pride, even if that should bring you power, prestige and plunder or wealth. There is nothing here to imply that humility of spirit leads to poverty or obscurity; only that even if that should occur, you would still be better off in the long term than to persist in pride. One of the well-known politicians in America today has, in my opinion, also been one of the most conceited, and he seems now to be caught in a downward spiral. Is it too late to repent? It is never too late to repent. Nor is it too late for you and me to repent if/when we are found to have a "proud spirit."

"Whoever gives heed to instruction prospers, and blessed is he who trusts in the Lord."

After the caution of the previous verse about being lowly in spirit, even if that results in "oppression" or abject poverty, we need this verse to give us balance. Prosperity and blessing **will** come to those who "give heed to instruction"—and that sometimes includes material prosperity and blessing. The next question then would be "what instruction" must one heed.

Ultimately, wisdom comes from God, so the primary object of this reference to "instruction" must be the instruction of the Word of God. However, God also instructs us through other means. Very often godly instruction comes through godly people, and sometimes also through experiences of life. Often God allows things and events to touch us so that through them He can teach us wisdom, and teach us to trust Him. God allowed Paul's "thorn in the flesh" to remain, so that Paul might not only hear, but learn to know that "my grace is sufficient." Learning that His grace is sufficient is just another way of saying "learning to trust Him."

The last part of the verse guarantees God's blessing to the one who "trust in the Lord." Romans 10:17 tells us "faith comes from hearing." That "hearing" is not just what happens via our ears at church on Sunday morning. Hearing is also all intake of the Word of God. All too often we may hear audibly, and read visually without ever really taking it in. Our text begins with "giving heed." That is what builds the trust which brings the blessing.

God wants to bless us. He wants to prosper us. He wants to bring us into greater Christ-likeness. He is only limited by our level of submission and surrender, our measure of heeding His instruction, and then trusting Him more fully.

Proverbs 16:21-22

"The wise in heart are called discerning, and pleasant words promote instruction. Understanding is a fountain of life to those who have it, but folly brings punishment to fools."

The wise in heart in verse 21 are the same ones who have understanding in verse 22. Wisdom and understanding are pretty much synonymous; the "wise" have good understanding, and those who are able to "understand" are wise.

Therefore, it seems that wise people tend to associate with each other. In the process of socializing, one wise man sharpens another wise man. Thus, a wise person sharing an insight is recognized by the others as "discerning." In this atmosphere of mutual interchange, there is also mutual pleasure, and all the while instruction is being promoted. I have had the pleasure of sharing Scriptural insights with another, and then in the pleasant conversation which ensued we were both instructed. We both gained further insight. Iron was sharpening iron, Proverbs 27:19. Wisdom may sometimes be imparted along with knowledge in a formal "instructor/student setting." Informally, the truly wise are continually promoting instruction by their wise words and insights and understanding.

Understanding, or wisdom, "is a fountain of life to those who have it." Notice it does not say it is a fountain of life **by or from** those who have it, although that will also be true, but it is first a fountain of life **to** those who have it. Those who have wisdom will find their measure of wisdom to be a fountain of life, an encouragement, a motivation, a source of obtaining more and greater wisdom. What a blessing in disguise!!

Conversely, the fool exudes folly; he has no wisdom to impart, and his folly brings its own reward—punishment.

PROVERBS TO LIVE BY

Proverbs 16:23-24

"A wise man's heart guides his mouth, and his lips promote instruction. Pleasant words are a honeycomb, sweet to the soul and healing to the bones."

In our current culture, there is a lot of advice to "just follow your heart." Often this may imply "don't do too much thinking, (empty your mind) and don't worry about the consequences. If you like it and want it, do it." In other words, let your fleshly, even immoral and selfish desires determine your actions. That is opposite of what this proverb is teaching.

A wise man's heart here means his whole character. Based on who you are in Christ, consider carefully what you say and how you say it. Probably we have all said things that were definitely true, but they were said in a cutting, maybe even in a vindictive way. That was unwise. Forgiveness and restoration may be possible, but not without a change of heart. So, think before you speak; speak so you won't need to apologize. When we let the character of Christ guide what we say, then our words will promote instruction. Such words will be prudent and even persuasive and very compelling.

Our text defines such words as "pleasant." People will love to be where such a wise person is, they will enjoy listening and will want to be friends. Furthermore, those words "are a honeycomb." They are sweet to the soul, and healing to the bones. Whose soul and whose bones? I believe the text implies the sweetness and healing is for the hearers of such speech. But I think they apply also, and maybe even primarily to the speaker. The wise person who speaks pleasant, sweet, healing words will himself be blessed even before those words reach the hearer. So, if your "bones" your insides, your emotions need some sweetness and healing, impart that sweetness to someone else, and reap the benefits yourself.

PROVERBS TO LIVE BY
Proverbs 16:27-28 (27-30)

"A scoundrel plots evil, and his speech is like a scorching fire. A perverse man stirs up dissension, and a gossip separates close friends."

Some dictionary definitions of "scoundrel" are: mean, worthless, cruel, dishonest, unprincipled, dishonorable, deliberately evil. Scripture talks about such a person more than once, but I know of no other Scripture where the word "scoundrel" is used. Though the writer takes four verses to describe the scoundrel, it is not meant as an exhaustive description. It does, however, giver significant insights.

I'm sure we have all met, or known of someone who fits aspects of this person. Should you ever meet one when you look in the mirror, then know that it is time to repent. We are all equally sinners, even though we do not all sin in the exact same way. The hymn writer says we are sinners by choice, and aliens by birth. Let's look at a few of the descriptive characteristics of a scoundrel listed in this passage.

1) He plots evil. The first clear memory I have of plotting evil was in 4th grade, when I sought to discredit a fellow student. I don't know what anyone else's is, but if that is still a part of anyone's life, that person is biblically a "scoundrel." 2) A perverse man. This is a person who has "turned away from what is right." Our text says he "stirs up dissension," and Prov. 6:19 tells us God "hates" that. 3) A gossip. If you thought gossip was not all that bad, think again. Gossip "separates close friends," which is the opposite of love—God's greatest command. "Everyone will know that you are my disciples, if you love one another." John 13:35. 4) A violent man. This does not mean toting a knife or a gun. It includes enticing a neighbor off the right path of life, 5) A deceiver. He "winks" to plot perversity, and evil. (verse 30)

"But for the grace of God," that describes you and me.

Proverbs 16:32

"Better a patient man than a warrior, a man who controls his temper than one who takes a city."

Patient!! Who has time to be patient in this day and age! I have sometimes said most of my patience is **im**patience, and I'm sure many would admit to the same malady. But think about it, isn't that a sad commentary on ourselves? What has impatience ever accomplished, besides issues like heart disease.

This proverb ties patience and a controlled temper together. Indeed, they are probably often two sides of the same coin. Temper itself is not a sin, providing it is kept under control. There are things that should and do stir us to anger as soon as we learn of them; it is the instant reaction that can lead us into sin. I have often marveled at Jesus' temper control. The Gospel of Mark is very "time conscious." In Chapter 11 we have a record of Jesus arriving in Jerusalem for the last time. He immediately went to the temple and "looked around", vs 11, and then went to Bethany, where He had just come from. What did He see when He looked around? He saw the "mess" of commercialism, and while it ignited His anger, He did not "blow up." He did not say, as I might have, "This stops NOW! The next day He went back to the Temple, and with full control of His temper, "cleaned up the mess."

It is unimaginable, just how much trouble we could sometimes save ourselves, by just stepping away from the problem for a while before jumping in and taking action. We were taught to count to 10 before responding in anger. Jesus took overnight, so it is OK to sleep on it, at least.

It is better to be patient than to barge in and take control, especially when it is none of your business. It is better to control your temper than to conquer a project.

"Better a dry crust with peace and quiet than a house full of feasting with strife."

This theme is repeated several times in the Proverbs, as well as other places in both Old and New Testaments. It is not that Solomon simply forgot he had already said this, nor that he needed to fill the page. Rather, it is because God knows this needed repeating for our good. That applies to all repetitions in the Bible.

We do not need things repeated because we have entirely forgotten that we have read it before, although at times that may be true. We need it repeated because we have neglected to obey it. We need it repeated because we have just let it slip. We need it repeated because we have not made it a high enough priority in our lives. We need it repeated because it is just not that important to us. We need it repeated because we need to see how important this is to God. We need it repeated because we need to see it for our good.

Solomon is saying that if it is a choice between working overtime to add to your investment portfolio or to add to a bond of family love and peace, you had better choose family. Neglecting the family is a sign of having already neglected the Lord—even if we are born-again Christians. Under the inspiration of the Holy Spirit, Paul wrote to Timothy (6:6) that "godliness with contentment is great gain." In the opinion of this preacher, *without contentment, godliness is impossible.* See if you do not agree. God said: "he who does not love his brother . . . cannot love God." 1 John 4:20. I believe that whoever is not content, is not trusting God to provide and care for us as He promised. Philippians 4:19: "My god will meet all your needs according to his glorious riches in Christ Jesus.

PROVERBS TO LIVE BY

Proverbs 17:3

"The crucible for silver and the furnace for gold, but the Lord tests the heart."

Taken in its most literal sense, the first part of this proverb can be statistically verified. How much heat, for how long, and how frequently applied to obtain the purest silver and gold are all factors. I don't fully understand all about that, but I have a general idea of what is involved. When we apply that concept to the purification of life, it gets a lot more complex. And yes, the Lord does that purifying in our lives when He deems it necessary. But many times, when we find the "heat" is on, it may not be the Lord at all. It may be other people or even self-criticism and second guessing.

In the course of life, each of us will be misunderstood at times, each will at one time or another be falsely accused, each will make honest mistakes – stupid, at times, but nevertheless honest mistakes, and not intentional wrongdoing. All of that can be very "trying." But the last part of the verse is for us today: "the Lord tests the heart." No matter what is going on outwardly, God looks at the heart, and if everything is OK there, then just relax. Not only is our eternal destiny assured, so is our day-to-day well-being. I John 3:21 puts it this way: "if our hearts do not condemn us, we have confidence before God." And that is better than any approval by men can ever be.

When the Lord "tests the heart," it is not to find out about us; He already knows what is in our heart. He knows what we are, but more than that, He knows what we **can** be. He knows all about us—every detail, past, present and future. He tests us so that WE can know where we have come from, where we are, what we are, and what we can be. He never tests us so that the Holy Spirit can find something wrong in order to condemn us or make us feel guilty; but so that we can come to Him for cleansing, yes, but so that He can change us. We need never fear or shrink from His testing, even though some tests hurt. Rather, let's pray Psalm 139:23-24 for ourselves. Search me, Oh God, try me, test me, find the "offensiveness" in me, and then "lead me in the way everlasting."

Proverbs 17:4-5

"A wicked man listens to evil lips; a liar pays attention to a malicious tongue. He who mocks the poor shows contempt for their Maker; whoever gloats over disaster will not go unpunished."

The first verse of this proverb is separated by a semi-colon, not by the contrasting conjunction to show what the wise or the righteous do. If no righteous people ever behaved like the evil ones in this regard, we would not need to address it here. After the election of 2016, some of the media definitely displayed a "malicious tongue," and some people of all political and religious persuasions seemed to have "gobbled it up." Knowing what we know, why would anyone listen to evil lips? Granted, we may not always be sheltered from hearing the evil, but why listen to it! Why pay attention to it and perhaps even spread it! The answer is simply that we have not yet fully overcome sin's allure; the sinful nature is still with us. Let's not be too quick to say: "I'm not like that, it doesn't apply to me." Let's take time to check up on ourselves, or better yet, ask God to check up on us.

The second verse deals with the same problem with a different focus. Have you ever "mocked" the poor, or perhaps showed disdain for the poor? Maybe not *because* they are poor, but because of our assumed reason *why* they are poor.

Sometimes we hear expressions like "It's his own fault." Our text says when we say that, we show contempt for their Maker. That is a very serious charge. And then the last portion, "Whoever gloats over disaster will not go unpunished." Expressions like it serves him right, or that will teach him, or variations thereof fit this category. God still looks on the heart, and He says such actions and attitudes will not go unpunished. Thank God, His grace is greater than all our sin, so may His grace rest on you in abundance today.

Proverbs 17:6

"Children's children are a crown to the aged, and parents are the pride of their children."

Some of the readers of Proverbs to Live By are grandparents—as is the author of these miniature life lessons. Many of us agree with the sentiment of the cliché, "if we had known that grandchildren would be so much fun, we would have had them first." And then there is reality. Not everyone is equally blessed in regard to family relationships, though we all love our children and our grand-children. In his 3rd Epistle, John writes: I have no greater joy than to hear that my children are walking in the truth." He was of course referring to his spiritual children and probably grand-children. However, that is certainly true of our physical children and grandchildren.

Matthew Henry comments on this proverb, saying "They are so, that is, they should be so, and, they will be if they conduct themselves worthily, they are so." As a pastor, I fully agree with John's statement. There is no greater joy for me either, except that joy is multiplied when your children and grandchildren are both my flesh and blood, as well as my spiritual children.

Apparently, our text assumes that the children have been taught the wisdom and righteousness that Solomon has been proclaiming, and they are walking in that way. However, our children, even those who have received the Lord, have to make their personal decisions about values and obedience to the Lord. Having raised our children with a goal to instilling biblical values into their lives, and seen them raise theirs, we get to learn how to release them into the Lord's capable hands. What is left for us is to keep setting the example, committing them into the Lord's care, and trusting Him with whatever concerns come up.

Proverbs 17:9

"He who covers over an offense promotes love, but whoever repeats the matter separates close friends."

The Love Chapter, I Corinthians 13, has a line that seems made-to-measure here. "Love always protects." Of course, the whole chapter fits with this verse, but that line really focuses on what this proverb teaches. He who covers over an offense promotes love. This may be an offense against you personally, but in the context, it seems to be an offense against someone else.

To cover over does not mean to deny it, but rather to not capitalize on it. We talked earlier about the wise in heart knowing when to refrain from speaking. When an offense has been committed, what value will there be, and who will benefit by your talking about it? This would include gossip, but could also refer to just simply remembering the offense from now on. Our verse says: "cover over." The 1 Corinthian 13 teaching is that love "protects" the offender and keeps no record of wrongs. Whatever else, cover over is a deliberate action to help and restore the individual who may already be embarrassed by his actions and be ready to crawl under a log. God loves the offender as much after, as He did before the offense, and here our love for God can truly shine as we in love do for the offender whatever is appropriate to his/her well-being. Our text says this promotes love. How well we do that is an indication of our real character.

The easiest thing to do is also the wrong thing, and that would be to repeat the matter. Repeating the matter, which is gossip, may be perfectly correct in content and wording, but the absolute worst way to deal with an offense. Generally, this will "separate close friends." No matter what excuse we may claim for ourselves when we repeat something of a degrading or defaming nature can only aggravate an unfortunate situation. Love does not, cannot, and will not do that. Love "does not delight in evil but rejoices with the truth." "Beloved, let us love one another," 1 John 4:7.

Proverbs 17: 10

*"A rebuke impresses a man of discernment more than
a hundred lashes a fool."*

I do not know a lot of people who go around fishing for a rebuke. In
fact, I don't know any, myself included. None of us enjoys being rebuked.
We don't even like to admit it to ourselves when we make a mistake. I tend
to get mad at myself when I have to admit "I was wrong." Probably we
would admit that at times we need a rebuke, so long as we don't need to
be specific about it. That is like saying "nobody is perfect, but I don't make
mistakes, at least not of the severity that would make a rebuke appropriate."
That is "natural man" speech.

The truth is, to the degree that we have gained a measure of wisdom,
we will listen to, and consider a rebuke when it is given. Our text says "a
rebuke impresses a man of discernment." A man of discernment is a wise
man. When the rebuke comes directly from Scripture, we have a hard time
arguing; we may simply try to ignore, and maybe even declare ourselves
"not guilty." Sure, the rebuke is valid for those who need it, but it just does
not apply to me. Even with such mental gymnastics going on, we need to
be listening to the Holy Spirit to see if He wants to apply the rebuke to
us. However, when the rebuke comes personally directed at us by another
person, it may be even harder to accept. Our defense mechanism will
immediately kick in, and we may ask ourselves "who does he/she think
they are? What gives them the right to rebuke me? A wise man, a man of
discernment, will at least consider it. We may still think they are wrong,
but it is wise to hear them out, and then to honestly examine ourselves.
Even a rebuke given with evil intent may merit being heard.

The fool simply will not consider a rebuke, no matter the source. Even
a hundred lashes, which was more than twice the legal limit, won't "get
through" to one who is foolish. Among such fools in Scripture was king
Ahab of Israel.

With a rebuke heeded, the wise become wiser still; with a rebuke
rejected, the fool becomes more foolish still.

"As evil man is bent only on rebellion; a merciless official will be sent against him. Better to meet a bear robbed of her cubs than a fool in his folly."

We can readily assume that the evil man of verse 11 and the fool of verse 12 are one. Central to his whole being, an evil man is bent on rebellion against God. Such a man simply cannot expect to go unpunished. As far back as Numbers 32:23, we are warned "be sure your sin will find you out." For the believer, sin will find you out by the Holy Spirit bringing conviction of sin. We then need to confess and repent; the death of Jesus Christ was the payment for that sin.

Keep in mind that God loves the unconverted, rebellious sinner too, and if he continues in his rebellion, God will bring a "merciless official" against him if necessary. Other translations of this "merciless official" are "cruel messenger" or even "messenger of death." Whatever the translation, the point is clear, God will not allow such rebellion to continue forever. If there is no change of heart in this life, eternal punishment awaits the evil man.

Now the warning against meeting such an evil fool is really for everyone. Stay away from him at all costs! I have never met a bear out in the wild who had been robbed of her cubs, and I hope I never do. It was enough to meet a bear in mid to late summer when it was well fed. We left each other alone. But God says it would be better to meet a bear robbed of her cubs than to meet a fool in his folly. This warning is to freshman college students on a secular campus, since there are bound to be an abundance of fools around. And they probably will not *appear* foolish; in fact, they may appear very "nice." If they are fools of the variety of this proverb, they will seek to turn you away from God. The bear would be safer. The warning is also for all the rest of us.

Proverbs 17: 14

"Starting a quarrel is like breaching a dam; so, drop the matter before a dispute breaks out."

Some people find it a lot easier to give this advice than to take it. "But is it a good idea to drop the matter while the other person still thinks he's right? I'll drop it if he drops it first. I don't particularly want to quarrel, but I sure won't sit by idly while he is . . ."

Let's look at the text again. "Starting a quarrel is like breaching a dam." Once a dam is breached and the water starts to get through or over, it doesn't take long before the dam is totally gone and the water gushes freely. Quarrels do that. Calm, deliberate discussions can resolve issues; quarrels can't. Maybe the flood water is at the verge of overflowing, and just one more little jab will do it. Stop and think, what will I really gain if I proceed and give just one more verbal jab? And what will I gain if I don't?

Well, for starters, you may avoid an uncontrollable flood; a flood that will cost you your self-respect. Possibly that flood, if allowed to develop, will become a raging torrent that will produce an irreparable, un-resolvable dispute. This in turn may cost you a friendship, never again to be restored, as well as the trust and respect of the community. Not to mention what it will do to your personal "walk with the Lord."

OK, so maybe you not only think you are in the right on this issue, you actually are right. Is it wise to insist on your right, in view of the personal cost? I'm just asking. You need not say "OK, you are right," when in fact he is not right, just "drop the matter" before the dam gives way. You will have a rewarding "inner peace," and perhaps also have retained a valued relationship.

Solomon had watched the dam give way among his own siblings, with the horrific aftermath.

Proverbs 17: 17

"A friend loves at all times, and a brother is born for adversity."

How many **reliable** friends do you have? Furthermore, how reliable of a friend are you to others? How long-term are your friendships? If you had a friend whose friendship only lasted until the first personal difficulty came up, you really did not lose much.

The kind of friendships our text has in mind are dependable in all circumstances. Casual friendships are fine; in fact, probably all friendships begin on a casual basis when we first meet this new friend. Blessed is the person who has many friends at this level. Among these many friends, it is healthy to develop a few close friends with whom you can share at a deeper level. But then you also need one or two friends of the kind that our text refers to; a friend with whom you can share failures as well as successes, A friend who "loves at all times," will be true, even when you have truly "blown it." This will be "the brother born for adversity," whether he is a sibling or not. This is the friend with whom you can share even your shame, without fear of rejection.

There are far too many people, even among Christians, who really do not have any friends like that and never will if they continue on their present course. They want to have friends, but they are not willing to be a friend—or perhaps they just don't know how. Deep down, some people are extremely selfish and have an overall negative outlook on life. That does not attract friends, at least not real friends.

Proverbs 18:24 basically teaches that someone who wants to have friends must show himself friendly. That verse also says that a man of many companions may come to ruin. That might be because casual friends come and go. A true friend will stay with you, but to **have** a friend, one must **be** a friend.

"A man lacking in judgment strikes hands in pledge and puts up security for his neighbor. He who loves a quarrel loves sin; he who builds a high gate invites destruction."

To "strike hands in pledge" means to be a guarantor for a loan or a debt. When I planned to go to Bible College, I did not have the money, so I went to our local Credit Union. They of course required some security that the debt would be repaid. My friend's father was a member of the board of directors, and he spoke in my behalf and became my guarantor. Had I not re-paid the loan he would have had to.

This proverb does not say it is a sin to "put up security," it simply says it is inadvisable. If Psalm 24:1 is correct, and the earth and all that is in it really is the Lord's, (and it is) and if Jesus Christ is Lord, (and He is) then we are merely stewards or managers of all that He has entrusted to us. Therefore, we do not have the final word on whether or not to put up the Lord's assets as security for another. Generally, it is unwise to do so. Our text says such an act is due to a "lack in judgment."

The writer seems to imply that the neighbor in verse 18 defaulted on his debt, and so an argument ensued. Here verse 19 continues with "he who loves a quarrel," (which this guarantor evidently did because he willingly put up the security) loves sin." Evidently there was a considerable amount of *pride of possessions*, because he readily co-signed, maybe in hopes that a quarrel would develop. Because of his wealth, he was a powerful man, and possibly had a law-firm on retainer for such eventualities. The "high gate" suggests a walled estate with a security gate and all that goes with it. In other words, he had it made. His coming to ruin because of burglary is highly unlikely; even if that did happen, he would have been well-insured. A successful lawsuit would also be unlikely, because his lawyers could take care of that.

His ruin or "destruction" would be related to his life in the here and now. Isaiah 48:22 tells us "There is no peace, says the Lord, for the wicked." And what about "what shall it profit a man . . ."

Let us be wise!!

Proverbs 17: 22

"A cheerful heart is good medicine, but a crushed spirit dries up the bones."

The Psalmist wrote "we are fearfully and wonderfully made." Psalm 139:14. That thought should always inspire us to awe and wonder. We understand lust a little of what it means, and does not mean, to be made in the image of God, but we believe more than we understand. God said it, and that is enough for faith. We also understand a little of the connection between the body and physical health, and the spirit and attitude. Medical science understands that better than the rest of us. Science can study the connection, but they still can't see how God made it so that it works the way it does. However, the text is there. Take time to read it again.

So, a cheerful heart is, in itself, good medicine. I am on several "prescribed medicines," but whether I get one month or three month prescriptions, none of them do me any good unless I take them, and take them as prescribed. All right, then how do we take the medicine of a cheerful heart? Let's consider the cheerful heart and its opposite, a crushed spirit, together. Actually, a cheerful heart is quite independent of external circumstances, and so is the crushed spirit. I believe we always have either one or the other at any given time. We cannot have both simultaneously.

It is imperative that we accept the Sovereignty of God. He is Sovereign, whether we believe it or not. He's got the whole world in His hand, and He has all our circumstances under His control. Now the issue for you and me is, will we trust him. Will we be content. Often there is a disconnect between what we have or feel physically, and what we think we would like to have and feel. That results in discontent and a crushed spirit. We can blame lack of resources, or lack of physical well-being for our crushed spirit, but it really is a spiritual matter. Discontent or a crushed spirit produce stress, leading to heart trouble and many other diseases. A cheerful heart is one that trusts God, regardless, which often entirely avoids stress related matters, and may even result in reversing medical conditions. "Miraculous healing can come from learning a cheerful heart That really is good medicine.

Proverbs 17: 26

"It is not good to punish an innocent man, or to flog officials for their integrity."

On the surface, this proverb might seem unnecessary, almost absurd. Why would anyone want to punish an innocent person; what would you punish him for? Yet that is precisely what we have degenerated to as a nation. Isaiah 5:20 tells us: "Woe to those who call evil good and good evil." Once we started down that path, it wasn't too long before we began to prosecute police for enforcing the law. But who is doing this? Well, **they** are. And who are they? That would be the government: the Executive Branch, the Legislative Branch and the Judicial Branch for starters. We could also name different organizations. Notice that all of this points the finger at others, because ***we would never do anything like that.***

But how did all this get started, and who started it? That is a good question. Again, there is much room for finger pointing. But think about this; what would you and I gain if we could accurately pin-point where this problem began. I suppose we could then with a clear conscience say "Well, he started it," but beyond that, how would that change anything. Originally of course it began with Satan, and God is going to deal with that, but isn't there something we can do now about our problem in America? Thank you for asking.

What we can**not** do is to change the hearts of Presidents, senators, judges and legislators or anybody else. Nor will condemning them accomplish anything. All that is God's territory. So, what **can** we do? Long ago God said: (2 Chronicles 7:14) "if my people. Who are called by my Name will humble themselves and pray and seek my face (done that?) and turn from their wicked ways, (that too?) then will I hear from heaven . . ." Maybe you are thinking like one church leader who said he had nothing that requires "turning away from." Well, that is the precondition God laid out. When we, each of us individually, do that, then God can change my heart—and the hearts of kings and dictators and others. It is not a group thing; rather, it is individuals within the church or group. We must begin with each of us as an individual.

PROVERBS TO LIVE BY

Proverbs 17: 27-28

"A man of knowledge uses words with restraint, a
man of understanding is even-tempered. Even a fool
is thought wise if he keeps silent, and discerning if he
holds his tongue."

This is good advice for anyone of any age, at any time. The motor-mouth is generally not perceived as wise, and wisdom is our goal in the book of Proverbs. In Matthew 6:7 Jesus said "they think they will be heard because of their many words." To use many words for words' sake, Jesus called "babbling." In our text the words "knowledge" and "understanding" are used jointly and imply "wisdom." Therefore, the wise man, even though he may have a huge vocabulary, will not use words to impress. Using words "with restraint" indicates both the appropriate choice of words and the amount of words used.

The Apostle James gives some further insight. In the first chapter he tells us "everyone should be quick to listen, slow to speak, and slow to become angry." Then in chapter three he tells us that none of us do this to perfection. The perfect man, he says, is never at fault in what he says, "able to keep his whole body in check." Taking our text and the James teaching in tandem, therefore, indicates that to use words without restraint leads to an uncontrolled temper; to quick outbursts of anger. The less control you have over your speech, the less control you will have over your temper. How does that square with your experience or understanding?

Let us not be like those who listen with restraint, if at all, and then speak loquaciously.

Verse 28 is not suggesting that fools tend to keep silent and hold their tongue, and that therefore we need to be always talking. Rather, even a fool, if he keeps silent **appears** and will seem to be wise as compared to the "motor-mouth." My pastor is fond of saying "you pay me to talk," and he does that very well behind the pulpit, but I have learned that in private conversations and discussions, he is a very good listener. Everyone can learn more by listening than by talking.

"God is in heaven and you are on earth, so let your words be few." Ecclesiastes 5:2

PROVERBS TO LIVE BY

Proverbs 18:1-2

"An unfriendly man pursues selfish ends; he defies all sound judgment. A fool finds no pleasure in understanding but delights in airing his own opinions."

It is safe to say that generally an unfriendly man is one who has no friends. He is therefore a loner, and as such he pursues "selfish ends." We saw a few days ago that to have a friend, one must be a friend, so we need not pursue that today. This unfriendly man not only pursues selfish ends, he also defies all sound judgment. How sad! Why would anyone choose to live like that? Simple answer? He is a fool. The Moody Bible Commentary tells us: "A person needs others to be wise."

When a person cuts himself off from friends for whatever reason he is making a foolish choice. He may think he is reacting to a friend who proved to be untrustworthy. "You just can't trust anybody these days." How often have you heard that line? A person may be unfriendly because he thinks he is superior to others—or because he thinks he is inferior to others. The point is, when he isolates himself, he cannot see beyond "selfish ends." Well, he could, but by now he defies all sound judgment. I never met or even heard of the Harry Truman of Mt. St. Helens fame until after the eruption on May 18, 1980. He was warned about the coming eruption, but figured the mountain was his best friend and it would not hurt him. He defied **ALL** sound judgment.

Not only is a person who cuts himself off from friends unwise, he is a fool. We may all do a foolish thing every now and then, but to be a fool and to remain a fool is another matter. "A fool finds no pleasure in understanding, but delights in airing his own opinions." We all delight in pleasurable things, though not all pleasurable things are good, and a fool delights in airing his own opinions. Whoa! Does that mean if you delight in "airing your own opinions" you are a fool? Well, the text does not say it in that way, so you decide. Would you rather pontificate your own opinion, or discuss an opinion with an open mind and find the pleasure of understanding? If you reject the opinions of all others, then it seems there is a fool in the mix.

Proverbs 18:4

"The words of a man's mouth are deep waters, but the fountain of wisdom is a bubbling brook."

Other translations have a semi-colon where the NIV has the word "but." I believe that is preferable, so try reading it without the "but." That would now indicate that both the "deep waters" and the "bubbling brook" represent the man's wisdom.

When I was a kid, we had two water wells, the deeper one had better, cooler water and was less affected by periods of drought. There was a more plentiful supply. The deep waters in our text suggest a bountiful supply of wisdom. When this man of deep wisdom speaks, he is worth listening to. His advice reveals deep insights and is therefore worthy of consideration. He won't tell you everything he knows and/or understands—there is not time for all that. He will however, tell you enough to whet your appetite, and you can then pursue the matter further with pertinent questions. You can be sure that shallow questions will elicit shallow replies, and insightful questions will bring insightful answers.

The Apostle James wrote: "if any of you lacks wisdom," (and we all do,) let him ask God." Very often God answers that prayer for wisdom through one who, while not all-wise, has sufficient wisdom to be God's answer to your prayer. It is wise therefore, to make friends of wise people. Iron sharpens iron.

Our text goes on to inform that the "fountain of wisdom is a bubbling brook." As children in Sunday School, we learned the little chorus: "Running over, my cup is full and running over." There the theme was the joy and happiness "since the Lord saved me." The change in our text is that we are dealing with wisdom, and instead of just an overfull cup, we have a bubbling brook, whose source is the deep-water supply. It is not that the wise man is always talking and spouting wisdom, we have already seen that always talking is the purview of the fool, but the wise man has something wise to say whenever called upon to do so. The brook is there to tap into.

One does not need to have full technical knowledge in order to impart wisdom. Back to our James verse, God "gives generously to all, without finding fault."

PROVERBS TO LIVE BY

Proverbs 18:8

"The words of a gossip are like choice morsels; they go down to a man's inmost parts."

Let's think about this for a minute. We all know intuitively that gossip is bad, and we generally disapprove of anyone who is known for spreading gossip. Gossip can be the spreading of absolutely false information about someone. It can also be totally true. Probably most often it is at least partially true, and therefore more believable. Generally, the purpose of gossip is either to discredit another person, or to enhance the perception of the gossiper—perhaps for his acuity in getting the information ahead of others. When the word gossip is used to describe or define a person, (he is such a gossip) my dictionary says a gossip is: *a person who habitually reveals personal or sensational facts,* and I would add *or information,* because gossip is not always factual. In our text the gossip is a person, but the proverb relates to such a person's words.

First of all, "choice morsels" are sweet, delicious treats, like a favorite candy bar. In what way, and to whom are those words like "choice morsels"? Well, it seems they are choice morsels to the gossip himself. He enjoys sharing this information, because he sees himself as the first in the group to "know this. Information." Lest we get too comfortable thinking that it applies only to the gossip himself so we are off the hook, I doubt very much, that was the writer's intent here. If the gossip had no favorable, appreciative listeners, he would soon tire of speaking words that nobody wants to hear. The truth is that some people gossip because other people like to hear gossip. The gossip relishes speaking them; he revels in seeing the eagerness of his listeners to catch every word, true, but It is the listeners who encourage him by their eagerness to hear every word.

Personally, I don't need that piece of carrot cake; I just enjoy it on the way down. After that the calories work against me. The choice morsels of the gossip are "choice" only briefly, and once ingested they begin do their damnable work of destruction. So now let's read the proverb again, and whether you are a gossip, or think you are not, consider what gossip is and does.

Proverbs 18:10

"The name of the Lord is a strong tower; the righteous run into it and are safe."

This is a marvelous verse to know every day of our lives. When you stop to think of it, it is amazing how many times we need the Lord's strength and protection. Of course, there is never a time when we do not need it, but sadly, when the pressure is off, we seem to forget. Often times in our praying we may begin with "Dear Lord," and thus we are calling on His Name. But the "name" in this verse does not refer to His title but to His character. When you call my name, either on the telephone or in physical proximity, you can say "Harry" and I will think you wish to speak to me and not to my brother. When you call the Lord, you are not really calling Him as opposed to calling the angel Gabriel. You are literally calling on the entire Godhead with all that entails: His love, His power, His holiness, His grace and all that He is. So it is not so much that His "call letters" are a strong tower, He is.

The verse says He is a strong tower. That would speak of safety and protection. When Jesus taught on prayer in Matthew 6, He included "deliver us from the evil one." We constantly need protection from the evil one. At times his assaults are very obvious, and we may unwisely try to handle a situation by ourselves; at other times he comes in a very deceitful disguise and we don't even know we are in danger. So, we might not even think of calling on Him. Our proverb then says "the righteous run into it, and are safe." How do you run into a name? You don't, you run into Him, into His protection, into His power, into His holiness. We can never call on Him before we need Him because we always need Him, but we can and should call on Him before we **know** and **feel** we need Him.

I'm afraid many of us have the notion that to **call** on Him is just "HELP!" However, basking in the joy of the awareness of His presence is to "run into it" and be enveloped in his safe protection. Then if a moment later we encounter a special need, we are already there, and need only to thank Him. He is the strong tower, and when we are in Him, we are in the tower, and need only to be consciously aware to enjoy the benefits.

Proverbs 18:11

"The wealth of the rich is their fortified city, they imagine it an unscalable wall."

This proverb is really connected to the previous one. Really it is the Lord who is the strong tower as we saw yesterday, but this proverb is true only in the minds of those who trust in riches. That is why the text says "they <u>imagine</u> it an unscalable wall." Wealth, when submitted to the Lordship of Jesus Christ, is a marvelous provision and a great blessing—both to the holder of the wealth along with his family and friends, but can reach out and bless others to the ends of the earth. In the aftermath of hurricane Harvey, at least one wealthy person donated a million dollars to the relief effort. (He was too public of a figure to remain anonymous as he prefers to be.) Others, who have wealth, may not have been directed by the true Owner of their wealth to do likewise. The benefits of wealth can be enormous when managed by a wise steward.

However, in my experience in dealing with people, I have found many people of rather meager means who very much "imagine wealth, even if merely longed for, to be a fortified city with unscalable walls."

The "righteous," have the Lord as their strong tower as per verse 10. By contrast, there are those who see wealth as the strong tower as per verse 11. These are the unrighteous, the unwise, or the foolish. Wealth can have great advantage, but it provides nothing for eternity, and is not reliable even down here in certain difficult situations. For some people, a valuable exercise might be to draw up two lists regarding money: (1) what it cannot do, as well as (2) what it can do. This can help provide a realistic perspective. With such perspective, consider what the Lord has enabled you to do, and then consider the next of Solomon's books of wisdom, Ecclesiastes 9:10: "Whatever your hand finds to do, do it with all your might." If that includes accumulating wealth, go for it. Any wealth accumulated is not your strong tower, the Lord is. Colossians 3:17 teaches "Whatever you do, whether in word or deed, do it all in the name of the Lord Jesus, giving thanks to God the Father through him."

"He who answers before listening – that is his folly and his shame."

We've all heard some version of the old saying: "My mind is made up, don't confuse me with the facts." Maybe we did not know just how old that saying was. I am not suggesting that we must listen to everyone who thinks they have something to say that we need to hear. If we did that, all our time would be taken up listening to hucksters and would-be salespeople. So, what is this proverb telling us?

First of all, this is another Old Testament version of James 1:19 about being "quick to listen and slow to speak." It is pure foolishness to mentally prepare your reply while the person is speaking. If you want to reply, do not only wait your turn, but truly listen in-depth to what is being said. At one point in my ministry, I was enrolled in a formal classroom training in "how to listen." I am not claiming astounding success for myself, only to say that I did become a much better listener, and still am to this day I benefit from that training. But we don't need classroom training; just determine to listen for the purpose of understanding what is being said.

Some people, I have found, will interrupt a conversation or direct question to give their answer. They must be super impressed with their wisdom and insights; I thought it was only God who knows what we are thinking "even before a word is in our mouth." Others, perhaps most of us at times, seemingly "listen" just for the purpose of answering. Actually, they may be "hearing," but they are not listening. When we do that, we are not seeking to understand what is being said at all. That could fall into the category of "don't confuse me, my mind is made up."

Unless we listen to understand, we may be hearing, but we are just not listening. Our text says that this is our "folly and our shame." Now a probing question: Does this ever happen when God is speaking? Honesty says Yes! It happens in church, in Bible study, and even in personal Bible reading. James said "be quick to listen, and slow to speak."

Proverbs 18:20-21

"From the fruit of his mouth a man's stomach is filled; with the harvest from his lips he is satisfied. The tongue has the power of life and death, and those who love it will eat its fruit."

A person's words have consequences for both himself and for the listener, whether they are good and helpful words or selfish and destructive words. Usually when we hear about "eating your own words" it has negative connotations, but let's look at the positive approach first. Wise words are satisfying to both the speaker as well as to the hearer. Have you ever had someone thank you for a comment, and then come back sometime later and thank you again because it was so very helpful? You can never get enough of that kind of harvest. Both you and your listener will be more than satisfied with the harvest produced by those words.

Proverbs 25:11 fits here as well. "A word aptly spoken is like apples of gold in settings of silver." That is the proper sowing of word seeds, and will be followed by a glorious harvest. Solomon is talking in terms of this life. Like apples of gold in settings of silver is not referring to "smooth" talk, or a good vocabulary and grammar to match. It's more like gracious words, helpful and encouraging words. The rewards will be great. And we haven't even hinted at the eternal harvest yet. No, we won't harvest an entry into heaven by words "aptly spoken," but for those who are going there because of the marvelous grace of God, demonstrated in Christ Jesus, heaven will in some way be sweeter for you because of your helpful speech. The tongue has the power of life and death and those who love it will eat its fruit.

To think that the tongue has power of life and death is truly awesome and it is serious. James said "whoever turns a sinner from the error of his ways will save him from death, and cover a multitude of sins." Could death be the consequence of "careless" words? It could, if our careless words turn someone away from an interest in the things of the Lord. What about the one who says "If that is Christianity, leave me out.

Let us seek to find "aptly spoken" words, and honor the Lord.

Proverbs 18:23-24

"A poor man pleads for mercy, but a rich man answers harshly. A man of many companions may come to ruin, but there is a friend who sticks closer than a brother."

This world has many rich people and many more poor people, and perhaps no two of them are in identical situations. At least in America, people may be poor for many different reasons. The poor man in our text is generic, and not a specific person. Let's think of him as being poor because of a lack of diligence—we have countless people in that category; maybe he is lazy, maybe he keeps making unwise decisions, but his poverty is really self-imposed. Our "welfare system" keeps producing more and more people like that.

Now this man goes to a wealthy man and begs for financial help. The man is wealthy because he is wise and diligent. Will he, or should he even help the poor man? No, he need not be "harsh" but it would be unwise to re-enforce the poor man's life-style by giving him something for nothing. He is poor for a reason, and will still be poor after someone bails him out. A lady came to our church one day in an older model, beat-up car with several children, asking for money to buy gas. At the end of her story, I reminded her that she had been to a neighboring church with the same story two days earlier. As she left, she cheerfully said, "I guess you can't win them all."

Some people of course are poor for reasons beyond their control, and legitimately do need help. Both the wealthy and the not-so-wealthy should help such people.

Our text continues, "A man of many companions (a wealthy man, perhaps? (Proverbs 19:4) may come to ruin." After all, wealth is uncertain as taught in 1 Timothy 6:17. The poor man in this context has already come to ruin. Both however need to be reminded that "there is a friend who sticks closer than a brother." This friend is Jesus. It is fine for a poor man to have wealthy friends and visa-versa. But no friend on earth is totally reliable, because none is omniscient or omnipotent. Let's put our trust in the One who cannot fail, for He is God, and He has promised to meet all our needs "according to His glorious riches in Christ Jesus." Philippians 4:19

"Better a poor man whose walk is blameless than a fool whose lips are perverse."

There are numerous "better this than that" proverbs. These are never the only two alternatives. Intrinsically, poverty is never better than wealth, and the Bible never suggests that. As in all of Scripture, ethical character is always better than any other alternative. That is the point of this proverb. If you happen to be poor, and if you had the choice of becoming wealthy by simply altering the truth a little, you would be foolish to choose wealth on that basis.

When we think about "perverse lips," we may think of politicians. This is unfair, because not all politicians are liars. However, where else can one of very modest means take a modestly-paying job and a few years later come out a multi-millionaire! But before we cast any stones, let us examine our own personal integrity. Whether rich or poor, we need to consider the depth of our own honesty. Which do you think is worse in God's eyes, to be honest in our major financial affairs, but yet keep the extra change when it is mistakenly given, or to be an embezzler of thousands of dollars? I'm just asking, and if you don't know, don't ask me—ask God.

Now I know that Scripture says "we all stumble in many ways," including in what we say. That includes both you and me. See James 3:1-2. "If anyone is never at fault in what he says, he is a perfect man." I for one do not claim perfection. So, if at times we are all guilty in what we say, what does our text mean by perverse lips? A good question! Are we then all fools "whose lips are perverse? Or is there another alternative? Falling into sin differs from living in it.

We would probably all confess to being sinners, so why not be specific and say we are liars and ask God to help us live contrary to our natural inclinations and become people of true integrity. We are forgiven in Christ if the Holy Spirit resides within. Therefore when (not if) we do fail, we must confess and repent, and by the grace of God endeavor to be people of greater integrity. We must by an act of will, determine to trust God by being blameless in our walk with Him. We will become noticeably different from the one with perverse lips.

PROVERBS TO LIVE BY

Proverbs 19:2

"It is not good to have zeal without knowledge, nor to be hasty and miss the way."

Some people get most of their daily exercise by jumping to conclusions. They hear an idea, or they get one on their own, and immediately jump into action. I remember my first year of Bible College; near the end of the semester. we were challenged in a class to do personal evangelism. A challenge requiring thought, prayer and action. One classmate boldly announced that during the summer break he would lead a person to salvation every single day. Commendable—perhaps, but it is the Holy Spirit who brings people to salvation. We are privileged at times to be facilitators in that process. Coming to our second year in the fall, he was one quiet individual. One could not fault his zeal, but it was a zeal without knowledge.

I do not recall what ever happened to that classmate, but such a sudden dose of reality can sometimes completely derail an individual. According to our text, an ill-advised hasty decision can cause one to miss the way entirely. Because of the grace of God, such a move is not beyond redemption. It can however trap one in discouragement and despair, and one might then determine to "never try that again." Maybe not to the same degree as my school friend, but at least to some degree, many of us have attempted to move forward on something with a zeal devoid of knowledge. It could be job related, family related or almost anything else, but can you see yourself in a similar situation? Some have been cautioned not to proceed in a determined direction, and have listened and gained needed knowledge, others have ignored the caution to their own peril.

We know the saying, "haste makes waste." For me, one such act of haste cost me 23 stitches in my hand, with ongoing problems beyond. The spiritual costs can sometimes be much higher. Let's rejoice in zeal, especially God-given zeal, but then take time to gain knowledge commensurate to the need. Whatever else may be required, prayer is first on the list.

*"A man's own folly ruins his life, yet his heart rages
against the Lord."*

This proverb proceeds directly from the previous, and is so reflective of
everyday life. Everything in life may seem to be going so well, and moving
in the direction we want to go. The scholastic goal, the career goal, the
relational goal may not be what God wants for us, we just think it best for
us. We even want God's will—so long as it agrees with what we think.
That is because we cannot see what lies beyond. He loves us so much that
He always wants what is best for us. So, when He keeps us from making a
drastic mistake, we may think He is depriving us of the best. We think "I
know best, after all, it is my desire we are dealing with." So, we just proceed
with our own desires and suffer the consequences.

At other times, God has such a so much better goal in mind for us that
He allows us to suffer a personal loss now, to obtain a much better gain
later. When that happens, we will be eternally grateful. Our text deals with
pursuing our own desire and suffering the consequences.

In either scenario, however, the last part of the text applies to either
loss: that of suffering the consequences of the loss that came because
of God's protection now, or suffering the consequences of the loss of
God's best by proceeding with our own determination. There <u>will be
some reaction</u> to the consequence, and we decide how we will react. One
reaction would be to submit to God's dealing with us and prayerfully seek
to understand and follow what He is doing. He **IS** doing what is best for
us. By doing that, we will earn an "A+" in the course. Another reaction
can be to "get mad at God." We can respond with something like: "God
how can you do that to me! If that is how you are going to treat me, then
just leave me alone. (That was the advice Job got—from his wife.) That is
what many people, including Christians, choose today.

Maybe someone who is reading this has made such a choice at some
point in life. You are not beyond redemption; your life is not beyond
redemption. God can take you and make something good of your life,
even yet, and even in this life and on into eternity.

Proverbs 19:6-7

"Many curry favor with a ruler, and everyone is the friend of a man who gives gifts. A poor man is shunned by all his relatives—how much more do his friends avoid him."

Although "ruler" or "prince" is an acceptable translation of the original, I prefer the NASB which is also correct in saying "a generous man." The Matthew Henry commentary uses "prince," but then says this proverb is a commentary on verse 4. The whole context here deals with the friends of both the rich and the poor. The idea here then would be "many curry favor with a generous rich man." Thank God for generous rich people. Many ministries could not continue if it were not for those whom God has blessed with wealth and with a burden for ministry.

Charitable fund raisers sometimes speak of "friend-raising" as opposed to "fund-raising." This is fine and acceptable, depending on what is meant by the term. Both wealthy and relatively poor people need to become friends of a ministry before they can wholeheartedly support its mission. But that is not what this proverb is addressing. This is talking about the many who seek to be friends with a generous, wealthy person for personal gain. The Moody Bible Commentary calls such "friends" sycophants. Now to us average folk, if you have a friend who is wealthy, treasure the friendship, but avoid his "treasure." That is his—not yours.

The same people who seek the friendship of the wealthy for potential financial gain and personal status, will also **avoid** friendship with the poor—even their own kindred. They do not wish to condescend to associate with "those" people.

Wise people, whether rich or poor, will see through hidden motives and agendas. Let the sycophants find their own level of discontent, so that in their misery they might reach out to God and find that His grace is sufficient—even for them. Any true friend deserves to be treated as valuable and precious. I cannot help my wealthy friends financially, sometimes I can help others. But if I live my life as God has planned, I can be a blessing to anyone He places in my life. Let's choose our friends, and let them choose us—wisely.

Proverbs 19:8

"He who gets wisdom loves his own soul; he who cherishes understanding prospers."

Jesus never said "to all who gained enough wisdom, he gave the right to become children of God." He did say "to all who received him, to those who believed in his name . . ." But what is wisdom if not to heed the best advice ever given. Our text says it is wisdom to love your own soul. God loves your soul; He died to save it from eternal separation from Himself.

But our text is not what it takes to get to heaven, it is talking about how to live joyfully and happily in this life. Eternal life is not something that will be given us when we get to heaven; eternal life was given to us the moment we "became children of God." Eternal life is something that we are to live out as we continue to live this temporal life. So, if it is wisdom to believe and receive Him, and thereby receive eternal life, then wisdom is to live that life now. We already know that we do not have all wisdom, and that more wisdom is available to us by asking and receiving.

We can study any subject to obtain more knowledge, but what can we study to obtain more wisdom? Our text tells us that wisdom is understanding. Is there a textbook on understanding? Well, yes and no. The book provides the information, and as we apply the knowledge of that information to life situations, we gain wisdom. We can, and should also study life as it is lived, and not just books, and we'll gain even more wisdom and gain it more quickly. "If this, then that," and it applies both positively and negatively.

When we ask God for wisdom, He will give it, generously, says James 1;5. But He may just give us the raw material, and allow us to learn wisdom while processing it. That can be a slow, arduous experience. But, "he who cherishes understanding prospers." This is not a promise of material prosperity. Isaiah wrote (55:11) "it . . . will achieve the purpose for which I sent it." The King James says "it shall prosper in the thing whereto I sent it." In the immediate context, "it" refers to the word of God, but can equally be applied to anything that God sends. In our textual context "it" can be the raw materials of circumstances that God send to teach us wisdom.

Proverbs 19:11

"A man's wisdom gives him patience; it is to his glory to overlook an offense."

To many of us, patience belongs back in the dark ages. We have no time for it. Back then, there was no hurry; if you needed a doctor quickly, you abandoned your chores and hitched up your fastest horse and drove, however far, to town to get him. OK, so let's not make the first application of wisdom relate to gadgets. Apply them to life—your life. God's word is still true in every age, but we never lived in the dark ages, although in the truest sense of the word, today may be darker than it was ages ago; God looks on the heart. But where do you lack patience? Where do I?

Our text is seems to say, insofar as we lack patience, we lack wisdom. That is convicting! How does your patience hold up when there are unexpected delays due to traffic jams? How does it hold up when you are on time for the meeting, but the chairman is ten minutes late? Or the sermon is five minutes too long? Or the annual report was not at all prepared? How does it hold up when dinner is not ready as promised? Or the kids are late coming in? Or the plumber said he would be there by nine, and at 10:45 you are still waiting? Those, and other patience-trying situations happen to all of us from time to time. Is God there in any of this? Is He trying to get our attention? Well, He is, but we can be too focused on ourselves and our frustrations to notice.

All of the above can happen without any bad intent on the part of anyone who caused the situation. Each of those could have been entirely beyond anyone's control. But what about when someone offends you? That, of course could also be unintended, but you don't know that. Now where is your frustration level. I remember talking to one of our deacons one day, and another church member came and falsely accused him of something. I may never forget this. He graciously said "I'm sorry you feel that way." And the matter was closed. It is to a person's glory to overlook an offense. Wisdom gives patience, and I dare say many besides me have not yet arrived. My deacon has gone to glory, but the glory of his response lingers.

PROVERBS TO LIVE BY

Proverbs 19:13-14

"A foolish son is his father's ruin, and a quarrelsome wife is like a constant dripping. Houses and wealth are inherited from parents, but a prudent wife is from the Lord."

This duo tells us that our family and home life is critical. While both verses deal with family relationships, the second also includes some potential consequence in the future.

A dysfunctional home life can make all of life miserable. We must be careful here to not read absolute cause and effect into this, so let's consider carefully. The first misery refers to foolish and disobedient children. A loving, well-run home will tend to result in wise, obedient children. But there are no absolute guaranties. A foolish, disobedient son is that by his own choice, even in the wisest and most loving, even godly, of homes. It is the son's choice. If he persists in rebellion against God and parents, his efforts may well bring destruction to the home. In a godly home, such a foolish child has a better likelihood of seeing the error of his ways and return, like the prodigal in Luke 15. Such a son or daughter is not beyond the reach of God's grace, but to receive that grace, there must be a change in the pattern of choices. The text says this son **IS**, not might be, but **IS** his father's ruin. Our text implies a dysfunctional home, which is the "breeding ground" or environment, most likely to produce a foolish son or daughter.

A second misery that awaits a dysfunctional family is marital failure. A failed marriage need not end in divorce; it can continue in misery until "death do you part." By a quarrelsome wife is like a constant dripping" we understand this to be an ongoing condition. This may sometimes result from a husband's neglect, but the issue here is a "quarrelsome" or nagging, bossy wife. If there is to be any finger pointing, point to self and talk to the Lord about it. The verse ends with "a prudent wife is from the Lord," as is also a wise, godly husband. Neither one is perfect—but some day we will be. In the meantime, we can and should be growing in Christ-likeness.

Instead of excuses or blame, let's all move on to learn personal holiness.

PROVERBS TO LIVE BY

Proverbs 19:17

"He who is kind to the poor lends to the Lord, and he will repay him for what he has done."

When we think of "the poor" we probably tend to have our own stereotypes. We may think of those on welfare; we may think of indigent people, or street people, or beggars. Each of those categories no doubt includes poor people, but may also include some fairly wealthy ones. But let's back up a little. The reference in this text undoubtedly includes providing financial assistance. The wording however, is to be kind or gracious to the poor. This speaks to me of attitude. While finances and giving may be involved in this issue, they are not **the** issue. The real issue here is a matter of the heart—kindness. I do not believe God is overly concerned about the size of our bank account. He is still the one who looks at the heart while we look at the outward appearance. We know that appearances can be deceiving, so we need the Lords perspective; He sees the heart.

Sometimes a financial donation can also be a most unkind thing to do for a poor person. Such donations may be given as the quickest and most convenient way of getting rid of this person. A kindness might be to listen to him instead, to offer advice and encouragement, perhaps to offer an opportunity for usefulness.

I'm thinking of Glenn Payne's signature song: **Then My Living Will Not Be in Vain.** The basic message of the song is that if I can help somebody as I pass along, if I can do my duty as a good man ought, if I can bring some sunshine into the dark world of a needy person's life, then my living will not be in vain. Thank you, Glenn. Our text says that not only will my living not be in vain, but to be kind to the poor is literally a lending to the Lord. And guess what. He may not refund you the money or the effort spent, but He will reward you for what you have done. He said so.

I am now in my third official retirement, (and so far, it is holding,) but when I reach my final retirement from this life, what else is there but to have done my duty in integrity before God? Then comes the final pay-day.

PROVERBS TO LIVE BY

Proverbs 19:18-19

"Discipline your son, for in that there is hope; do not be a willing party to his death. A hot-tempered man must pay the penalty if you rescue him, you will have to do it again."

This harks back to verse 13. Have you ever been to a restaurant and had a young family seated at the next table (I'm sure you have) and within the first few minutes it became evident that age 5 and 6 children were in charge? That is so sad. Those young children are being ruined for life. They are in desperate need of some firm, loving discipline. In verse 13 it was the foolish son who was ruining his father, but here it is the parents ruining their children. We have a window of opportunity to "train up a child in the way he should go, and once that window closes, we are too late. In Bible College I knew a young man whose father bought him a new Thunderbird as a Christmas gift. He came back to school, and was very disappointed; he had wanted some family love and togetherness.

There is hope for a son who is consistently and properly disciplined. No question, we need to be compassionate and understanding, but compassion to the point of failing to correct can be disastrous. That is not real compassion. Too often I've been asked to counsel couples whose thirty something son is still financially dependent because he won't keep a job because this job is "beneath his dignity." The parents pay his rent, pay for his car, and pay for his children's needs as well. Perhaps his wife has already left him. Now the parents want help in teaching their son to take responsibility. That should have been done thirty years ago. That failure may now consist of being a party to his death.

A hot-tempered man, (that is also a selfish, irresponsible man) must pay the penalty. If you rescue him, you'll just have to do it again. Actions have consequences. Failure to take action also has consequences. In such cases it may be a kindness to let him get evicted and have his car re-possessed. However, some of these men end up at a ministry like Teen Challenge, and by the grace of God, their lives are changed. God's grace is always greater than our sin.

"Listen to advice and accept instruction, and in the end you will be wise."

I would like to ask God for wisdom today, and then be permanently wise tomorrow. Unfortunately, it does not work that way. Wisdom comes as a step by step process. And even then, it is not an uninterrupted, smooth road. There will be bumps and stumbles and failures along the way. Solomon was the wisest man in his day, and even he pulled some real boners along the way.

Our text tells us that first we must listen to advice. There are many sources where advice comes from. Since God's word tells us to ask God for wisdom, our primary source of advice must be God's word—however delivered. But that is really not what our text is referring to. Furthermore, on many issues in daily life the Bible has no direct advice to offer. If you need advice on specific matters, you need to find someone conversant with such matters. But our text implies that you must ask for, and listen to the advice of a person already wise.

Next, our text indicates we must "accept" the wise instruction. Have you ever listened to advice and then ignored it? I have too, just don't ask me how many times. Some of the advice we will hear, even from a wise person, may not be good advice because the person is not all-wise. The King James version translates Prov. 11:14 as "in the multitude of counselors there is safety (or wisdom)." In a democracy, the majority opinion rules, but not so in a theocracy. Because we are all sinners, no so-called theocracy can properly run a country. But we are citizens of heaven, so we must learn to sort out the various opinions and advice, and then get our final word from the King.

This sounds like a lot of hard work, and it is. That is why no one becomes wise in a day. Our text says "in the end," ultimately, near the end of life, after years of pursuit, "you will be wise." So, the young initiate, and the experienced old sage are still "becoming" wise. But the promise is that if you follow the rules (God's rules) you will eventually (in the end) get there.

PROVERBS TO LIVE BY

Proverbs 19:21

"Many are the plans in a man's heart, but it is the Lord's purpose that prevails."

No doubt we have all experienced failed plans. We eagerly looked forward to a thing or an event that never materialized, and in retrospect, we may have grieved the loss, or rejoiced in the prevention of a disaster. I've heard people say they will simply stop making plans and avoid the disappointment. That is not wise; in fact, it is very foolish. Without plans, even though some of them will inevitably change, we can never know the joy of fulfillment.

The Bible does not lecture much on the process of planning or goal setting, but a closer look shows over and over again, that His servants were inveterate planners and goal setters. We don't know how long Joseph planned the ultimate family reunion, but as we see it taking shape and eventually become a reality, we can see careful long-range planning in it all. Unless eternity will reveal it, we will never know how long and how often Joseph dreamed and planned for such a day. One of those dreams and plans was God's purpose, and that prevailed. In God's plan, that was essential to the fulfillment of His ultimate Redemption plan. In Isaiah 50:7, Jesus had already "set my face like flint." Talk about long-term planning. He knew the costs as well as the rewards, and His purpose prevailed.

Among the many "plans in a man's (in your) heart," some will come to fulfillment. And the more carefully and prayerfully the plans are developed, the more we will see which are in line with "the Lord's purpose" and will therefore prevail.

In all my "Goals Setting" sessions in seminars, one verse was always included, and that is James 4:15. Essentially it says "you should make plans, counting on God to direct you." It is all too common for Christians to ask God for direction, and then proceed to rely on our own limited insights and wisdom in the planning process. Then, when it fails, we wonder why, after all we prayed about it. We need God's direction in the planning process, if we want the purpose to prevail in the outcome. That is just common sense. That is wisdom.

Proverbs 19:26-27

"He who robs his father and drives out his mother is a son who brings shame and disgrace. Stop listening to instruction, my son, and you will stray away from the words of knowledge."

To rob one's father and drive out his mother is very extreme and rare—if taken only in a very literal sense. Even so, it does happen. By looking a little more closely, it may not be all that rare. He might "rob" his parents be simply ignoring their teaching, or by accepting their financial support in College, but then living contrary to their values and teachings. He could drive out his mother by the same means. He would be driving her away from any involvement with her, or with any form of family life. Such behavior indeed brings shame and disgrace to himself, but also to his parents. Any parent wants to be proud of their offspring, but a disobedient, rebellious son or daughter can rob them of that desire and opportunity. The parent can still love the foolish rebel, but that does not remove the shame and disgrace.

From such a scene, the biblical writer now moves on to show how or why such a sad situation can and does happen. When someone stops listening to correct instruction, he begins immediately to stray away from the words of knowledge. Such straying may be slow and gradual, but can also accelerate very quickly. With the moral decline in our culture, such a stoppage of listening to correct instruction can happen very easily. We used to decry the denial of truth in our secular universities; now that not only is the norm, it is prevalent right down to the lowest grades. Children in kindergarten and first grade are subjected to blatant denial of the truth of God. And that falsehood is very cleverly and attractively presented. Satan has never been known for his fair-play. He is a liar "from the beginning, and is the father of all lies." God, of course, is able to keep and protect our children and young people, but the warning of our text is to the children themselves; "My son," when you stop listening to accurate, godly instruction, the downward spiral has begun. You are now, already, straying away from words of knowledge. Without a change of heart, it just continues to get worse.

Proverbs 20:1

"Wine is a mocker and beer a brawler; whoever is led astray by them is not wise."

While the Bible does not condemn all drinking of alcoholic beverages, it absolutely condemns all drunkenness. This text does not specifically mention drunkenness, but rather talks about the foolishness of those who are led into the traps of drinking too much. No one has ever become an alcoholic without taking that first drink. Neither wine nor beer are intrinsically evil or righteous. The problem is, or can be, with those who partake. This text touches on the potential dangers. At the same time and also from the pen of Solomon, there is a call to "eat your food with gladness, and *drink your wine with a joyful heart.*" Other Scriptures, including the New Testament, also indicate drinking of wine for both medicinal purposes and as a beverage. But no Scripture endorses drunkenness.

As to being a mocker, too much drinking, and you come to think unrealistically about yourself and/or your surroundings. It seems drinking to excess is almost expected in our society. Our laws try to restrict the amount of alcohol consumption only in regards to driving a vehicle. If/when you get drunk, just get some relatively sober person to do the driving.

In the first church I pastored I had a deacon who in earlier years had been an alcoholic. To hear him tell it, alcohol had made him a "brawler," so when he was born again and remained sober, this verse became one of his favorites. The drink itself is to some people a mocker; it deceives them into thinking that just a few more drinks will make them "the life of the party," or make them happy, or feel good. Some think a few drinks will cause the problem to disappear, or else be solved all together. Those who "are led astray by them are not wise." Proverbs is a Book of Wisdom.

Some people who are wise will abstain completely; others who are wise will know their limits, or better yet, will know the limits of the drink itself. Those who are wise will know what drinking can do. But wise people will not drink to excess, because God said, "Don't!"

Proverbs 20:2-3

"A king's wrath is like the roar of a lion; he who angers him forfeits his life. It is to a man's honor to avoid strife, but every fool is quick to quarrel."

Throughout the ages, kings and dictators have had absolute power of life or death over their subjects. In recent decades, some dictators have excessively exercised such power. Since absolute power belongs only to the Lord, those who usurp such authority seem to use it only for evil. With that in mind, please read verse 2 again. Keep in mind that God does have absolute power, both to save and to destroy, James 4:12.

Such a king's wrath or displeasure, is like the roar of a lion. A lion's roar is a death-knell to any potential prey in the vicinity. The roar itself cannot kill, but the one roaring can—and is planning to. So, escape if you can, while you can. It is important to differentiate between the Lord's roar of warning, which is Scripture, calling us to repentance, and the devil's roar, seeking whom he may destroy. How do you know if/when you anger the Lord? When you deliberately disobey? Yes, God is love, but He is also just and will exercise His justice. His wrath is against sin, so in mercy He already exercised his justice by providing "payment in full." Now, the only ones needing to fear are those who have not accepted that payment in their behalf. For them, justice will be required at the Judgment.

Now look at the rest of the text. It seems like the wisest thing we can do, after we have received Christ, is to avoid strife. Avoiding strife also seems like the hardest thing to do. But "every fool is quick to quarrel." There is a vast difference between disagree and quarrel. The first of my daily Psalms this morning begins with "The fools says in his heart, there is no God." Many of us would never, ever say that with our mouth, but what does the heart say when you refuse to obey the Lord on some issue? And don't we all refuse to obey at times? And doesn't that apply to those who tend to quarrel? For those who not only believe in God, but also claim Him as their Father, for them such failure is followed by confession, repentance, and forgiveness. Grace is greater than our sin!

Proverbs 20:4

"A sluggard does not plow in season; so, at harvest time he looks but finds nothing."

A Merriam-Webster definition would tell us it means a person who is habitually lazy. Sometimes I feel lazy, and just want to take a nap, but I don't think that makes me a sluggard, especially in the biblical use of the word. Biblically the sluggard is more a fool than a lazy person, although one can readily be both. The sluggard in this verse plows, he just does not do it in season. He has no foresight. I remember a year when we had a late spring, and could not get out on the land in time. Wise farmers then made an adjustment and prepared for a crop requiring less time to mature. At harvest time they still found a harvest, but perhaps a different one from what they had originally planned. The sluggard prepares the land late, because of lack of foresight, and yet expects a regular harvest. I believe Dr. Swindoll would call this man a procrastinator. That sluggard is a fool.

How many people seem to live by the motto, "not today, maybe later." There is a story about a man who, when the 1938 model cars came out, took a special liking to the Buick. He couldn't afford it right away, so he began to save up, and sure enough, in 1988 he was able to buy that same car for cash. No matter if there is any truth to that story, at least he took immediate action. In the matter of salvation, many people keep putting it off to a "more convenient time." Not wise!

Many readers of this page have already received Christ, and are assured of their eternal destiny. But what about other matters in daily living? Maybe are you putting off action on career issues, on education, on personal preparation for some event, on talking to your children about values and life decisions etc. Failure to act now will result in a loss at "harvest" time. What you had hoped for just will not be there. What is it you know you should be doing, but you just keep putting it off? Solomon wrote in Ecclesiastes 9:10 "Whatever your hand finds to do, do it with all your might." Don't put it off. Do it with zest and enthusiasm. Don't be a procrastinator. Don't be lazy. Do not be a sluggard or you will miss the harvest.

"The purposes of a man's heart are deep waters, but a man of understanding draws them out."

Some translations translate this: *Counsel in the heart of man is like deep water."* In that sense, both the men in this proverb are wise: the one who has the counsel and the one who draws it out.

The one who has the counsel buried is wise, and has a deep reservoir of wisdom and counsel. Much of that is buried deeper than his own conscious awareness, and he cannot possibly bring all of it to mind at any given time. In a well or a pool or a pond or an ocean, there is water right on the surface, but there is much more water deeper down. The counsel or the purposes are not so much "deep water" as they are *like* deep water in the sense that there is much more beneath the surface than is readily apparent. Like any wise person, he is not always trying to flaunt wisdom to all within earshot, so much of his wisdom lies beneath the surface.

As we get older, we tend to forget some of what we once knew, even quite apart from any form of dementia. This is probably equally true of "wise people." But do not despair, much of the forgotten can be retrieved. I find myself sometimes giving deeper insights and wiser answers than I knew I had, especially when someone "probes" correctly. This brings us to the second man in the proverb.

A man of understanding is also a wise man, as we have seen in some earlier proverbs. Like the first wise man, he is not all-wise, so he is seeking insight from a second source to gain further understanding and information. He has observed wisdom in his friend, and understands that there is more beneath the surface. So, however he begins, he then has sufficient understanding to know that proper probing will bring up further wisdom. As a trickle of wisdom begins to come out, he listens and absorbs and pursue further with additional questions.

So, for those of us who lack wisdom, sure, ask God, but then learn to ask probing questions. Once the process is started, learn to hone you questions to greater effect. Most of the extant wisdom is well beneath the surface. Let's learn to dig for it.

Proverbs 20:6-7

"Many a man claims to have unfailing love, but a faithful man who can find? The righteous man leads a blameless life; blessed are his children after him."

In spite of cues from some Hollywood celebrities, we might say most people make that claim. Yet, some wedding vows have been changed from "as long as we both shall live" to "as long as we both shall love." That basically frees people from any real commitment. However, I believe the point of this teaching is broader than just the divorce rate, although that would be included. This really talks about all of life, and that then brings us to the issue of character.

In Luke 16:10 Jesus said "Whoever is dishonest with very little will also be dishonest with much." Our text points to love to make the point, but Jesus broadened it to include those who may be faithful in love, but are not faithful in other areas of life. Probably no one is unfaithful or dishonest in every area of life, at least not simultaneously. So, to all who have good, though imperfect, family and love relationships, it might be wise to take inventory of faithfulness in other areas of life. Our text asks "Who can even find a faithful man?" Always one hundred percent faithful? Nobody! Except Jesus, the God-man.

Next our text mentions a blameless life, which is not the same as a sinless life. This reminds me of Psalm 112 where we read "Blessed is the man who fears the Lord, who finds great delight in his commands. His children will be mighty in the land; the generation of the upright will be blessed." Sinless of course means absolutely perfect, which for us happens when we receive our glorified bodies. Blameless refers to this life, which is where Proverbs is focused. Psalm 112 equates it with the fear of the Lord, and delighting in obeying His commands. While such a person still stumbles, his walk is one of integrity. That is, he seeks at all times and in all ways to please the Lord. By the grace of God and the power of the Holy Spirit, we can live in such a way before men that they will recognize complete honesty and integrity. And where we at times fail, Jesus never fails. For each temptation "He will also provide a way out so we can stand up under it."

"Who can say I have kept my heart pure; I am clean and without sin."

This morning in my devotional time with the Lord I spent some time in Romans. The glorious truth that "Therefore there is now no condemnation for those who are in Christ Jesus" became precious to me all over again. Later, when I turned to our current text, I had to review it again.

Our text reminds us of our human depravity, which I readily recognize in my own life. Jeremiah 17:9 tells us "The heart is deceitful above all things and beyond cure" in the NIV, or "desperately wicked" in the King James. No matter the translation, the point is clear. We may not like the description of desperately wicked or beyond cure, but like it or not, that is your heart and mine. Now wait a minute: "Beyond cure?" Yes, beyond any human cure. Through Ezekiel God said (36:26) "I will give you a new heart, I will remove your heart of stone and give you a heart of flesh." Obviously, the discussion here is not the organ in your body that pumps blood. Rather, it is talking about our sin-nature, our "heart" of unbelief or of faith. "If anyone is in Christ, he is a new creation, the old has gone, the new has come," says 2 Corinthians 5:17. So even God does not repair it—He replaces it.

I trusted Christ for salvation at ten Years of age, and I have no idea of the depth of depravity I could have sunk to, but I know myself well enough to know it would have been deep. I used to disagree with the saying: "There, but for the grace of God go I." I used to think "I would never do **that,**" in reference to certain sins. Some of you have probably been there. Our text asks further "Who can say I am clean and without sin?" The implied answer is, no one! Many of us thank God for the truth of 1 John 1:9, but look back just one verse. "If we claim to be without sin, we deceive ourselves and the truth is not in us." So, let us thank God daily for what He has saved us from, but then ask Him to show us what He has saved us for. It is not a matter of what He saved us to **do**; He saved us to **be** or become "conformed to the image of Christ." How is that working for you?

251

Proverbs 20:10-11

"Differing weights and differing measures—the Lord detests them both. Even a child is known by his actions, by whether his conduct is pure and right."

Verse 10 takes us back to the theme of honesty in business transactions. Apparently, that is a big deal to God. That must mean then that dishonesty is a BIG trap for us—all of us. Receiving Christ has not made us immune. Our hearts too are "deceitful" above all things. The specifics in this text was something like this: The buyer might use a 17 ounce weight to purchase his pound of merchandise, and/or then use a 15 ounce weight when he sells to the consumer. We can do something similar when an hourly employee gives the employer 55 minutes of work per hour of employment. On many jobs, this can easily be done without fear of detection. You take it from there.

Even a child is known by his conduct. Where does the child learn his conduct? Yes, the child (even the cutest and most and precious child) too is born with the old sin nature, but he learns by observations. "Like father like son" is more than just a cliché. It contains a great deal of truth and probability. An honest father may end up with a dishonest son, but the probability of the child becoming an honest adult is greatest when that was his model while growing up. A Christian home and family may have a non-Christian, or even an anti-Christian member in the family. But an ungodly couple will most likely raise children who grow up to be ungodly adults. "Whether his conduct is pure and right" implies there is an alternative, so we can say "pure and right, or not."

So how long must we seek to provide a godly teaching model, till the child leaves home? By the time the child becomes an adult, our parental authority has changed, but our responsibility (not necessarily our liability) is for our full lifetime. Our children are still watching us, whether or not they follow our example. In the final analysis, Jesus did say "no one can come to me unless that Father who sent me draws him," John 6:44. Even though my earthly father was a minister, I had to trust Christ personally, and so did my children, and so do yours. Their actions will reveal their choices.

Proverbs 20:12

"Ears that hear and eyes that see—the Lord has made them both."

This one requires a little investigation; it reaches a little below the surface. Ears that hear and eyes that see represent perception. We have all experienced hearing without really "hearing," and we have at least looked, if not seen, without truly "seeing." What is the problem?

Generally speaking, God has given eyes and ears to each of us, even though some people may be physically deaf or blind. So why do we, who can hear and see, sometimes fail to perceive? In a word: wisdom! Understanding! I remember a particular "work of art" in a museum, thinking it absurd. I suspect a real art critic would have a different perception. Obviously, I lack an understanding of art, but this is too superficial an observation for this text.

In our "seeing and hearing," it takes wisdom and understanding to "get the message." When our text says that the Lord has made both the ear and the eye, it is not so much talking about His creative activity, but rather that true, insightful hearing and seeing come from God. So, we are back to square one, "if you lack wisdom, ask God." Since God has already made both physical hearing and seeing, as well as the true understanding and wise hearing and seeing, and He has already given us both, what are we to do! If we can hear physically without understanding, and we can see physically without perceiving, how much of the problem rests with us personally? All of it! Since we are to love the Lord with all our mind, let me suggest we must also trust Him with all our mind, our mental capacity. That will take work and effort. We must begin to deliberately look beneath the obvious; to look beneath the surface.

A favorite Psalm is #19. I suggest you read the whole Psalm, but look with me at the opening. "The heavens declare the glory of God, the skies proclaim . . . There is no speech or language where their voice is not heard." It is there, do you hear it? Do you see it? Look again! Do you lack wisdom? Ask, and then look again; try to understand, try to see. Ask, knowing that God gives generously to all, including you and me.

PROVERBS TO LIVE BY

Proverbs 20:13-14

"Do not love sleep or you will grow poor; stay awake and you will have food to spare. It's no good, it's no good! Says the buyer; then off he goes and boasts about his purchase."

In a way, this one is almost a continuation from the previous verse. However, it points back to integrity in personal and business affairs. The love of sleep to the point of neglecting to provide for his own and/or family welfare could simply be called laziness. However, it is probably coupled with personal foolishness, evidenced in the lack of insight in seeing the consequences of action or inaction. A wise person could not possibly neglect either planting or harvest, a certain road to poverty—and even hunger.

God has given eyes and ears and a mind to know what needs to be done. A man with a measure of common sense, one type of wisdom, would go to work to provide for his own and family needs, even when he does not feel like it. The one with eyes that actually see, will be diligent to stay awake and prepare the land and sow the crops when it is time to do so. People who are habitually late to everything may not be physically asleep, but are definitely asleep in regard to the import of their actions. Instead of thinking and planning ahead, they are more focused on their own, immediate desires and concerns.

When our oldest son entered the workplace after college, the company HR department had an informational meeting to acquaint new employees with investment and retirement opportunities. He was amazed to find that many of these new recruits were "planning," or rather wishing to win the lottery as their retirement plan. They were included in verse 13.

Then there is the outright dishonesty of verse 14 which again looks only at the immediate, ignoring the future consequences. Such a one looks only at his own selfish desires and ambitions. James 3:16 tells us "Where you have envy and selfish ambition, there you find disorder and every evil practice." Not wise.

When He was a boy, Jesus **grew** In wisdom. Are you growing? Am I? Even as we get a little older? We have not "arrived" yet.

Proverbs 20:15

"Gold there is, and rubies in abundance, but lips that speak knowledge are a rare jewel."

This proverb is easy to understand; Wisdom is better than wealth. For those of us who believe the Bible to be the word of God, it is easy to say we believe that. And in a sense, and to a degree, that is no doubt true. But my question to myself, and to anyone else who might be interested, is this: How strongly do we believe it?

James 2:18-24 explains that faith apart from action is useless. Using Abraham as his example, these verses conclude that Abraham's "faith and his actions were working together, and his faith was made complete by what he did." It was after that, that "his faith was credited to him as righteousness." In the context of our text, can the measure of our faith be determined by our actions? Are our faith and our actions working together on this?

The lips that speak knowledge belong to a wise person—not necessarily to a well-educated one. And that wisdom is more precious than unlimited quantities of gold and rare jewels. I'm reminded of the story of a very wealthy church member who invited his not-so-wealthy friend and fellow church member to his house. In the course of the visit, the rich man told his friend about his great wealth and showed him his financial statements and all that was in his safe, and then proudly exclaimed "what do you think of that?" The poor man said "well, I'm just as rich as you are. You have your wealth just to look at, and now I've seen it too." Of course, a wise man's wealth, surrendered to the Lordship of Jesus Christ can be enormously beneficial, but not wealth for its own sake or wealth limited to personal enjoyment and selfish pride.

Wisdom and lips that speak knowledge are more appealing than mere wealth. It is more beautiful, it is more attractive, it is more valuable. Wisdom is more rewarding and benefits both the possessor as well as the observers. Wealth of itself does not produce wealth, but wisdom can, and generally does, go on to create wealth. So, wisdom can benefit everyone; wealth in itself cannot.

Proverbs 20:17

"Food gained by fraud tastes sweet to a man, but he ends up with a mouth full of gravel."

Where I grew up on the farm, we had no refrigeration except what was provided by nature. In the winter, our basement temperature was below freezing, so storing up the freshly baked cookies for Christmas was no problem. Neither was finding a reason to go down into the basement if a watchful eye happened to notice. And yes, those cookies tasted sweet—perhaps even better than those that survived until Christmas Day. But this proverb is not just about cookies at Christmas. It is dealing with a serious principle.

Some translations say, "bread of deceit," or "bread of falsehood." The food is called "deceptive" because deception acquired it. That is clearly stated in the text: "food gained by fraud . . ." It could also be called deceptive because it deceives the one acquiring it by fraud, so, it is the deceiver who is being deceived. He thinks he is getting away with it, and there will be no consequences. But, "he ends up with a mouth full of gravel." So, in the end he did not get away scot-free.

It could also be called deceptive because it tends to deceive those who notice the fraud. If you observe someone acquiring what he wants by fraud, and he seems to get away with it, one could begin to think "that's not too bad." Such a person is being deceived. Human nature, with a little help from the enemy of our soul, can reason "I didn't actually steal it, nor did I tell a direct lie, so it should be OK." That is just another of Satan's wicked schemes; he gets us to believe a lie.

Now look at the mouth full of gravel. Of course, this is not literal, so what is it? First it is a guilty conscience. Living with the knowledge that the acquired "thing" was wrongfully obtained makes it **unpleasant, not sweet.** The misery will continue and grow until we finally make it right. Psalm 32:3 assures us when we keep silent, our "bones wasted away through my groaning all night long." The solution lies in confession, repentance, and forgiveness, resulting in the joy being restored. "Restore to me the joy of my salvation." Psalm 51:12

Proverbs 20:18

"Make plans by seeking advice; if you wage war, obtain guidance."

You may remember we were on this theme in Proverbs 19:21.

That must mean there is more to be said on the subject. The word used here is "seeking." First of all, that tells me we do not always and only go to the same source for advice. We are familiar with the phrase "jack of all trades." Certainly, some people seem to be capable and knowledgeable in multiple skills but not necessarily in the matter you are currently pursuing. Sometimes what we call seeking advice may in reality mean we are seeking approval or confirmation, rather than further insights. Our text says make your plans **by** seeking advice. I take that to mean before as well as during the actual planning process. That points out a common error people make, and that is to lack clarity of purpose. You must know your destination before you can profitably consult a road map.

Clarity of purpose and/or destination must come from God. That too may require advice from fellow pilgrims, but you need to know that this is what God wants. Once that is determined you can begin the planning process by seeking advice. Now this advice is not necessarily to come only from fellow Christians, but may also include other sources of wisdom. Nor should we blindly follow every piece of advice we get, even if it seems good.

I have much left to learn in this matter, but let me give you one personal example. Just weeks into my 3rd retirement I was asked to produce study material on a subject with which I was not at all familiar. That this was God's purpose for me quickly became evident, but talk about needing advice!!! And advice was forthcoming from both expected and unexpected sources. With the goal in place and the plan in process, specific guidance came directly from the Lord, with periodic input from one of His servants in particular.

Remember, you can't steer a parked car, and it seems God has chosen not to do it either, so let's get going. Once we begin to move in the direction of our assignment or goal, God can and will direct and/or re-direct to keep us on the right road. But we must take that first step of obedience.

PROVERBS TO LIVE BY

Proverbs 20:19-20

"A gossip betrays a confidence; so, avoid a man who talks too much. If a man curses his father or mother, his lamp will be snuffed out in pitch darkness."

One dictionary defines a gossip as "one who shares casual or unconstrained conversation or reports about other people." This would indicate that not all gossip is necessarily false. So, our text says a gossip betrays a confidence. When we were children, we sometimes accused our friends in school, or our younger siblings of being "a big mouth." A person who "talks too much" may inadvertently say something he had no intension of saying. Since the mouth was going already anyway, this little addition just "came out" along with the rest. No wonder James tells us to be quick to listen and slow to speak. Pre-school children sing "be careful little mouth what you say"; at least I learned it when I was that age. As we get older, too often we forget that good advice.

A well-practiced motor-mouth often does not have the time to verify the truthfulness of what he is reporting—or sharing "as a prayer request." Have you ever disseminated a morsel of gossip? If we are honest, we would probably all reply "have I ever? Yes." But hopefully we have advanced beyond "being a gossip." In our fast-paced, instant information culture, even the news media often forgets (?) to double check their facts. I for one, no longer accept news reports carte blanche. When we know a person is prone to such gossip, our text advises us to avoid them. We really don't need to hear what they have to say if we can't depend on its accuracy or truthfulness anyway.

Perhaps verse 20 is the logical, or inevitable direction for one who "talks too much." I know there is a day of judgment waiting for each of us, but the kind of behavior warned about in our text is inviting early judgment in this life, and then we still face God's judgment at its appointed time.

Failure to heed this speech warning is failure. Maybe today would be a good day for someone to take a personal inventory.

*"An inheritance quickly gained at the beginning will
not be blessed in the end,"*

A few of my ministry years were spent in Stewardship and Development, or Charitable Fund-Raising work. Much of this involved assisting people with their estate distribution planning. This proverb was one of my standbys. By good planning, and using a few good distribution methods, it is possible to leave a significant charitable distribution to your church and/or other ministries, and still leave the heirs—especially young heirs, the whole estate distributed over a period of time. At that time, and it may be worse now, a national statistic by the IRS claimed that "on average, an inheritance—regardless of size, is totally spent in 6 months."

Our proverb says nothing about the reasons the inheritance, when given too soon, will not be blessed. It is just given, by God, as a fact to be dealt with wisely. That is how it normally is. Solomon inherited the kingdom from his father David; we don't know what others in the family inherited, but Solomon probably did. Being the wisest man in his era, he had probably seen too many who received a sizeable inheritance early in life, and then never did learn to be productive contributors to society. That certainly is one of the potential pitfalls in our day. A possible contributor to such misuse of sudden wealth is that the children were not properly and adequately taught the value of work as well as of money. God has made us— He has designed us to work and to be productive. If we have not taught that to our heirs-to-be, we can compound the problem by giving them too much.

One example from Scripture is given by Jesus in Luke 15 in the parable of the "prodigal son." There is no mail-order house that dispenses wisdom; it must be learned, and it takes time. Learning wisdom can be facilitated by the help of wise people, usually of the older variety. When godly wisdom is imparted to young people by wise parents who model it every day it is a blessing beyond price. Those who are wise can continue to impart wisdom, even to older and mature children and grand-children. May God help us to be wise.

PROVERBS TO LIVE BY

Proverbs 20:22

"Do not say, 'I'll pay you back for this wrong!' Wait for the Lord, and he will deliver you."

This verse obviously speaks to the matter of personal revenge, which is never condoned in Scripture. It does not in any way restrict governments and instituted authorities from administering justice including punishment suitable to the crime. The Old Testament rule of an eye for an eye was a clear restriction on the amount or extent of punishment that was permitted in administering justice. In fact, injustices may well occur in any justice system, but this verse does not speak to that.

If and when we are personally wronged, there may well be occasions when turning the matter over to proper authorities is in order. Before that happens, however, there may be opportunity to negotiate with the offender and avoid involving the courts. If negotiation fails, it may be in order to go to authorities, or, better yet, it may be an opportunity for the sake of peace, to "suffer the loss." The context of 1Corinthians 6:7, "Why not rather be wronged," is appropriate here. So much for loopholes.

The plain teaching, re-enforced in Romans 12:17-20, is "do not take personal revenge." This would include harboring vengeful thought and wishes. Vengeful thoughts may be just as bad for your blood-pressure and on your relationship with the Lord as the action when carried out. The Romans passage includes not only do not take revenge, but also "Be careful to do what is right in the eyes of everybody." And "if it is possible, as far as it depends on you, live at peace with everyone." One can't be making efforts to live at peace while also planning revenge.

Our text admonishes us to wait for the Lord. He will deliver you—but on His terms and in His time, not ours. We tend to want God to be patient and merciful when we have failed, but want speedy justice without mercy on those who have wronged us. The reason that can't work is because God loves those other sinners as much as He loves this sinner. So, let's learn to wait. "They that wait upon the Lord will renew their strength." Isaiah 40:31

*"A man's steps are directed by the Lord. How then can
anyone understand his own way?"*

Scriptures frequently advise and encourage the wise to make plans. However, advance planning by even the wisest of all men, can never negate the absolute sovereignty of God. We can, and must, believe in both the sovereignty of God and in the free will of man, because Scripture teaches both. At the same time, we will never fully comprehend or reconcile both truths. So then, what do we do with this text?

First of all, we must ask God for wisdom and insight to learn whatever it is we need to learn from this verse. For any who just go "drifting along with the tumbling tumble weed," with an attitude of "whatever will be will be," they might just need to learn to take responsibility for both planning and action. God has designed us to work and to take responsibility, and when we do, He will direct our steps in the process. One of my oft repeated sayings is that you cannot steer a parked car, and God cannot direct the steps of one who is not taking any.

Beyond just the matter of working for a living, for most of us this will often mean we need to take the next step in our walk of obedience with the Lord. When we are stalled in our Christian growth because of an act of disobedience, we cannot continue to receive new instructions and guidance. When we fail (or refuse) to walk as He directs, how can we possibly hope to understand our own way. We can't! Thus, people come to the end of their career, and whether or not they accumulated a measure of wealth and comfort, they face some probing inner questions like: Is that all there is? Why was I even here? What's the point?

The good news is that it is never too late to begin again, and to find fresh purpose and meaning in life. A new or renewed commitment of obedience to the Lord is the first step in such a reentry into purposeful living. Once a walk with Him has been established, He can and will "direct your steps." And yet we will not fully understand how we got there because God says: "My ways are higher than your ways, and my thoughts than your thoughts." Isaiah 55:9.

"It is a trap for a man to dedicate something rashly and only later to consider his vows."

Quite possibly Solomon had just recently read Deuteronomy 23 or more likely Judges 11 before writing this proverb. The Deuteronomy section deals with making vows, which were voluntary, and the Judges section tells about a godly man who made a rash vow and then could not get out of it. When one makes a vow, he must keep it and fulfill it. Again, the Deuteronomy section says it is not wrong to refrain from making the vow in the first place, which tells me it is wise to give it some careful thought.

It seems to me we rarely, if ever, would consider what we do a "vow to God," but what about a hasty promise? You may not ever have done this personally, but have you ever heard of someone telling God something like this: "Lord, if you will get me out of this mess, then I will _____ "? And just how does that differ from a vow! The Deuteronomy passage teaches that to make such a promise, and not fulfill it, will be considered by God as sin.

It seems to me that the main point of our text is to not be too hasty to make any kind of promise. That is not to say one should not consider it, even discuss it with the Lord. Isaiah 1:18 invites us to go to the Lord and reason with Him about your sin problem. If He is willing for that, does it not stand to reason that He will gladly reason with you about anything else that is a concern to you?

Our text talks about dedicating something rashly, implying that this was dedicated to God. However, if that is unwise, then what about our dealings with others? That would also be wise counsel in regard to making rash or hasty promises concerning issues or interactions with our fellow earth travelers. It is easy to make a quick promise without considering the possible consequences. A hasty promise may well be made with good intentions, but still be unwise or even impossible to keep because not all factors are known or considered. Often it might be better to make a conditional promise like: if this happens, then I will see if I can do what you need. In other words, we need to carefully consider before we make a promise, a pledge, a commitment. That is wise.

"The lamp of the Lord searches the spirit of a man! It searches out his inmost being."

In a church-school cafeteria there was a sign by the supply of cookies that read "Take only one; Jesus is watching." At the apple section, a kid said "Take all you want; Jesus is watching the cookies." Too many Christians think God is like a school monitor, always watching to see if He can catch us doing something wrong. That is not God. And that is not what this verse is saying.

The main point of our text is that God knows us, inside and out. He knows my weaknesses, not so He can exploit them, but so He can help me through them victoriously. He knows my strengths, so He can encourage me and guide me to make the best of them. He knows the dangers I face so He can protect me in the tough times. He knows, but we really don't. Well, if He knows, why does He need the search light? Why does He examine us? See Psalm 26:2. True, we need to examine ourselves as well, but we tend to grade on the curve. Furthermore, we do not have 20/20 vision, especially when we look below the surface.

The lamp of the Lord is a powerful searchlight that shines into the deepest crevices of the heart and mind, and brings to light hidden and forgotten things for our benefit—not for His. If we look at this text with a negative or selfish mind-set, we will miss out. Yes, the light may reveal some things that need confessing and forsaking, and for that we should thank the Lord for His mercy and grace. But far beyond that, the light will reveal who and what we are in Christ. It will show us better ways of using our innate abilities, it will show us how and where we can best fit into all that God has planned for us to be and do.

The Psalmist wisely prayed in 139:23-24 *"Search me, O God, and know my heart, test me and know my anxious thoughts. See if there is any offensive way in me, and lead me in the way everlasting."* God's search-light is the way for us to know true peace and joy. He is in process of making us to be more like Jesus Christ.

PROVERBS TO LIVE BY

Proverbs 20:28

"Love and faithfulness keep a king safe; through love his throne is made secure."

This verse is not just a promise for kings, presidents, prime-ministers and other rulers. The focus is not on the elite; the focus is on operating in the wisdom of love and faithfulness. The safety and security promised is therefore for the citizenry as well as on the ruling class. Since love and faithfulness provide safety and security in the extreme cases and unique challenges of rulers, how much more will that apply to the rest of us! No one can claim this promise who operates out of selfishness, greed and deception.

The first application might well be that it is the love and faithfulness of God that is in view here. That is most certainly true. We only love because He first loved us, and any faithfulness we find among us mortals is only because of His faithfulness to us. It is God's love and faithfulness that keeps us in any and every situation and circumstance of life. God's love never overlooks evil. Rather, it has made atonement for evil. God's faithfulness is steadfast and unwavering toward us in all the vicissitudes of life. He never changes, whereas we repeatedly change. So, let's hear it for God's love and faithfulness.

There is another application for us as well, though. We are indeed kept safe and secure in His love and faithfulness, but we may place ourselves in a position of danger and conflict by our own unfaithfulness and lack of love. The great revival Psalm, number 85, first of all reviews God's love and faithfulness in the past, verses 1-3. That constituted revival. Then the Psalm pleads for a renewed revival in verses 4-7. The rest of the Psalm reveals God's answer, and that would take a whole sermon series to exegete. But notice what is required of us in verse 11. Our response to God must be faithfulness. "Faithfulness springs forth from the earth," (that would be our faithfulness) which is met by God's righteousness looking down from heaven. Our faithfulness must be to God, demonstrated by our faithfulness to other people.

Proverbs 20:21:1

"The king's heart is in the hand of the Lord; he directs
it like a water course wherever he pleases."

Today's proverb is again dealing with the Sovereignty of God. The first question that came to my mind was: How often do we need to be reminded that God IS Sovereign? and the answer came just as quickly—constantly! The problem is not so much that we constantly forget, but rather that we fail to focus. We tend to think more about our own sufficiency and our own resourcefulness. So, let's look again.

Our text says the Lord directs the king's heart wherever (and we could say whenever) He pleases. And of course, we believe that – sort of. But then why doesn't He do something sovereignly drastic to change the direction of our nation? Hmmm, now that's a tough one! Could it be that He is Sovereign and we are not? Sometimes we can see "the wind of the Spirit" blowing and moving, but like Jesus said, you cannot tell where it comes from or where it is going. And so, when things are not to our liking, we (or should I say I) tend to get impatient. The reference to king in our text causes me to think in terms of politics, so let me just say that corruption in our system is rampant. Of course, it is easy to see that we need a major "course correction," so "Lord, here is the problem, and this is the solution, so why don't you do something." Excuse me, just who is sovereign here?

Let's go back to basics: God iS God. So, He is Sovereign, He is All-Wise, He is Love, He is Righteous, He is Just, He knows the end from the beginning. So, let's let God be God, and when by our measurements He delays doing what we have asked, He is still God. However, we must not allow our knowledge of His sovereignty to keep us from praying within the context of our observation. We may not always be right in our praying, but we are never wrong to pray. In Isaiah we are told to give God no rest "till he establishes Jerusalem . . ." He may never change my circumstances to my liking, but He is always true to His Word—even in relation to national events, so we can pray confidently for the end result, and leave the rest up to Him.

Proverbs 21:2-3

"All a man's ways seem right to him, but the Lord weighs the heart. To do what is right and just is more acceptable to the Lord than sacrifice."

This text is not saying that man cannot discern between right and wrong: rather, it is more like we can justify almost anything. Surely, that is not talking to Christians—or is it? Can we ever be deceived into doing something wrong, thinking it is right? If that is possible, does it ever happen to you personally? Now I'll go to meddling. Do we ever knowingly do something wrong just because we really want to, and it really is not all that bad anyway, (we think) and besides, we can explain. If you can quickly say "not me" to that last thought, maybe it is time to ask the Lord to search your heart. Think of Jeremiah 17:9 "The heart is deceitful above all things, and desperately wicked." Is that literally true? Even after you have been born again? No matter what you may have heard someone say, or what you think about yourself, or what you believe, what does the Bible say?

Now back to our text. "The Lord weighs the heart." That truth impacts both positively and negatively. The Lord is not just searching for things to condemn and punish in the Christian; He is searching for things to commend and reward. He is Love. He is looking for reasons to say "atta boy" or," atta girl". And He is perfectly fair and just and right. Always! Now, with any possible mess cleaned up, let's look at the encouragement in vs. 3.

God is more interested in what we are in our hearts than what we are in our heads, than in what we do with our hands. In the Old Testament, approach to God required one to bring a sacrifice. In the New Testament, approach to God requires that we come in the Name of One who already brought The Sacrifice. Now, what is acceptable to God is that we do in our hearts what is right and just. Then we can follow that up with actual deeds. Early on in my ministry I learned that God is always more interested in the worker than in the work. He is more interested in what we are, than what we do.

"Haughty eyes and a proud heart, the lamp of the wicked, are sin."

I will let the scholars debate the best interpretation of a specific word used in this context, and focus on the message of the verse. The Good News Bible does that for us by giving us the "meat" of it like this: ***Wicked people are controlled by their conceit and arrogance, and this is sinful."***

My reading of this verse tells me that the wicked have no objective source of input into different life situations. Basically, they are left to figure things out for themselves because they have ruled God out of their lives. The only lamp, the only source of light to illuminate their calculations is their own "haughty eyes and proud heart." As the Good News Bible has it, they are controlled by their conceit and arrogance. That being said, not only will they come to the wrong and sinful conclusions, their process of getting there is itself sinful.

We could of course just leave it there and move on. By excluding God, they have "made their own bed, now they have to lie in it." Or, we can take a second look to see if there is something for believers to learn and benefit from. Let' take the second alternative.

Believers share in many of the same life situations, circumstances, and difficulties with the rest of the world. In dealing with these issues, however, believers have a choice. We have another resource. We not only believe in God, we have Him residing within our very lives in the Person of the Holy Spirit. So, when we face any life situation that has us stumped, and we don't know what to do or which was to turn, we have this assurance: when we lack wisdom and insight we need but ask of God who gives generously to all, "and it will be given to him."

The deliberation of the wicked who exclude God is sin. Similar deliberation by believers who include God and enquire of Him, will obtain wisdom and insights far beyond their own to navigate the rough roads we travel. So now the meddlesome question: How often do we as Christians include, or exclude God, in our planning and decision making? I'm just asking.

Proverbs 21:5

"The plans of the diligent lead to profit, as surely as haste leads to poverty."

In this text, diligence is contrasted with haste, not with laziness as one might expect. Laziness would seem to be a pretty sure way to achieve poverty; haste would seem to agree with our cultural wisdom of "the early bird gets the work," and thus be an ally to diligence. Our text, however, states that haste leads to poverty, so what is going on here? Perhaps our view of "haste" has been somewhat corrupted by investment marketing techniques.

Let's look at some implications of what it means to be diligent in the investment industry. I do not have a degree in finance or investing or even in marketing. My understanding of investing comes mostly from the study of Scripture. Doing "diligence," as used in the text, refers to obtaining all the facts and implications possible before "jumping in." The first thing to consider is your own motives for wanting to "make a profit" which is, by the way, commended in our text. Ecclesiastes 5:10 can be a help here: "whoever loves money, never has enough money, whoever loves wealth (or wants to get rich) is never satisfied. . ." It may be helpful to study this verse along with 1Timothy 6:6-10.

To study investment techniques, turn to Ecclesiastes 11:1-6. All we can do here is look at a few concepts and define them in terms of contemporary nomenclature. The first verse deals with investing for the long term, as opposed to "get-rich-quick gimmicks. Verse 2 speaks of diversification, and verse 3 adds that not every option will perform equally well. In verses 4-5 we are cautioned against what is now known as "market timing." It is always profitable to buy low and sell high, but only God really knows where those "high/low" points are. Another critical consideration in diligence is what is commonly called "dollar-cost-averaging.

A would-be investor needs not only to understand terms like these, but more importantly, understand their impact on investing. So, take time to do due diligence, and don't worry about possibly missing a "golden opportunity," you may have missed a "too good to be true" prospect, ending up in a disaster.

Proverbs 21:6-7

"A fortune made by a lying tongue is a fleeting vapor and a deadly snare. The violence of the wicked will drag them away, for they refuse to do what is right."

Wealth, and the desire for wealth is a very subtle thing. Everyone can see the benefits of it, and most of us would want more of it than we presently have. Just start thinking of what I could do with an extra $ XXX right now, and you can fill in the amount. Once your thoughts have gone that far, it is easy to just let the imagination run wild until you become absolutely obsessed with what you don't have. Desire can be either a bane or a blessing. When desire equals motivation, it can be very good. Too often, as in our text, the desire is not a motivation to improve, but rather to obtain.

Let's look back at 1 Timothy 6 and read verse 6; "godliness with contentment is great gain." It seems to me that as Americans, we have lost the whole concept of contentment. All we want is more! And we are willing to go to almost any lengths to get it. The trouble with getting more is that the **desire** for more is not abated. That, it seems is the point of this text. We could re-phrase the concept as: "a fortune honestly made is a blessing, but a fortune made by a lying tongue . . ." Any fortune dishonestly made involves lying in some way, even when no specific lie is spoken. Sometimes, as in the case of the recent "biggest ponzi scheme ever," the perpetrator may watch his wealth disappear from his jail cell; at other times he may remain respectable in the eyes of outsiders, but in the longer scheme of things his wealth is still "a fleeting vapor."

Can contentment with, and improvement of, our financial station in life co-exist? Absolutely! It just requires a proper prioritizing of values. What values are most important to you, what relationships, what assets, what accomplishments? Do you value people above things? Jesus advised that we "seek first His kingdom and His righteousness, and all these (other) things will be given you as well. There is an old song that says "I am satisfied with Jesus, Is He satisfied with me." Until we have learned to be content, nothing else will satisfy.

"The way of the guilty is devious, but the conduct of the innocent is upright."

Remember what God said to the prophet Samuel when he went to find a successor king to replace Saul? "Man looks at the outward appearance, but the Lord looks at the heart." 1Samuel 16:9. We know that to be true, and yet, there is a sense in which one can tell a lot about the **heart** simply by observing the outward appearance. A little child has not yet perfected the art of deception, so the mother can tell what has been going on in secret. I remember one time at about age 3 or 4, finding it advisable to try deceiving my mom, and she asked me "what if I were to check?" Since I did not know whether or not she actually would check, I replied "in that case I don't know." I must confess that by now I would be much more adept at deception.

According to our text, there are tell-tale outward signs of internal goings on. The way of the guilty is devious; it just is. Such "deviousness" may not be evident to all, and it may not be *clearly* evident even to the most astute observer, but it is clearly evident to the Lord. Once in graduate school our class was assigned to interview an under-grad, and to take careful notes, including some exact quotations. In the next class session, one of us was to write a quotation on the board; after the professor left the room. I wrote mine. After he re-entered, he read the first three words and then began to "analyze" the individual, and he quickly came to the same conclusion I had reached after an hour of interview. Can God do as well? He does not determine by what He hears, or by observing shifty eyes etc. He just looks at the heart. He knows whether or not we are trying to deceive.

The guilty person is not just trying to deceive someone about one thing or another, he is not just trying to "pull one over" on us, he **IS** devious in his person. He is just behaving like his lord, the devil, who is a liar from the beginning. The conduct of the innocent is upright. He is seeking to be like his Lord, the God of truth and righteousness. Since he still has a sin nature, he too often still "blows it," but the bent of his life, his desire, his goal is to be upright.

Proverbs 21:10-11

"The wicked man craves evil; his neighbor gets no mercy from him. When a mocker is punished, the simple gain wisdom; when a wise man is instructed, he gets knowledge."

Have you ever had a neighbor like the wicked man in our text? That's OK, as long as you are not yourself that kind of neighbor. We have probably all had a neighbor we would have rather done without. If only they would wear a sign to tell us that God is using them to "hone" us, but they never do. By the time we figure it out, we may have already said or done something that should have been left **un**said and **un**done.

The wicked neighbor in this text would be a terrible neighbor; he literally has a craving for evil. If only he would ignore us completely, we could return the favor, but too often people like that are so self-absorbed that meanness almost oozes out of their pores. There is no way you could ever expect a favor from him, unless it first of all benefits him. Now I am wondering, is that the neighbor God had in mind when He said "Love your neighbor as yourself. Could be, you now.

Of course, God is not going to let him get away with this. Actions have consequences—usually in this life first, and also in the next, unless they repent and accept Christ's payment on their behalf. So, let's assume he gets fairly quick justice in this life, some do. Our text tells us that the simple will see this and gain wisdom. It does not say *simpletons*, it says the simple. That would mean ordinary folks like you and me. Have you ever seen a "jerk," which means this neighbor, get what he deserves for his meanness? Good! What did you gain: wisdom? or gleeful personal satisfaction.

If you are one who is already on the way to obtaining wisdom, our text suggests you take what the wicked neighbor is experiencing as instruction for yourself, and you will get further knowledge. Knowledge, when processed, leads to increased wisdom.

Perhaps our text is not so much about the wicked neighbor, as it is about how the "normal" neighbors respond. Has God placed that jerk on our street so that he might see Jesus in action? It's a point worth considering.

PROVERBS TO LIVE BY

Proverbs 21:12-13

*"The Righteous One takes note of the house of the
wicked and brings the wicked to ruin. If a man shuts
his ears to the cry of the poor, he too will cry out and
not be answered."*

The Book of Proverbs sometimes uses the terms "wise man" and "righteous man" somewhat interchangeably. In this text, the Righteous One clearly refers to the only Wise God who is perfectly Righteous. If you grew up going to church and Sunday School, you may remember being taught that God sees everything and knows everything. Thank God, that is true. Here, for the more sophisticated adults, we are told that The Righteous One takes special note of "the house of the wicked." Terrorists are taught how to blend into a neighborhood and community without attracting undue attention. That works with people. Not with God. God takes note, He sees and He knows, and He will take action according to His own timetable. He has never adjusted His plans to suit our calendars or our preferences. He says He will bring the wicked to ruin. At just the right time!

What is it that He is looking for in the context of this proverb? This text says "if a man shuts his ears to the cries of the poor." He takes special note of things like that. To shut one's ears, as used here, simply means he does not respond. He becomes aware of a need, and has the wherewithal to help, but fails. He decides, not to do so. We are familiar with the saying "what goes around comes around." It seems to me God is saying that will be true for those who refuse to help when they can. Some people have sufficient material wealth, they will never be financially in need. True, but a time will come when they are in need—whatever that need may be. It may be a need only God can meet, but as I read this, for those who refused to help others, a time will come when even God will not help them.

Yes, I know about the grace of God; grace that is greater than all our sins. I also know that our God of love and mercy is at the same time a God of justice and righteousness. So, when God gives a warning, all I can do is heed it, and pass it on. So, give it some thought.

Proverbs 21:14-15

"A gift given in secret soothes anger, and a bribe concealed in the cloak pacifies wrath. When justice is done, it brings joy to the righteous but terror to evildoers."

This verse, taken by itself, might appear to approve of bribery. After all, we know it works. "Every man has his price" is a universal truism. Because of our innate greed, people are willing to excuse or condone almost anything—if the price is right. For Sergeant Schultz of Hogan's Heroes fame, the price was often two chocolate bars. But at whatever level, be it national security information, private business, local politics or personal relationships, wherever bribery works, justice has been discarded. But, because God is God, justice will prevail. At all levels! Bribery only works temporarily, and only with people who are willing to give up honesty and integrity. Both the one giving the bribe and the one accepting it must be willing to forsake truth and justice.

Our text refers back to the wicked man in verse13 who refused to provide, in his case perhaps justice, for the one in need. Now, to cover up the whole matter, he comes to the offended person and offers a monetary gift to keep the matter hidden. In our case, whether we are offered a bribe, or are tempted to offer one to someone else, or else accept a bribe to "forget what we saw," the issue is the same. It is basic honesty. Oh, we might rationalize and agree that this is not right, but then, it is probably better than the alternative.

For the here and now, when justice is done, it brings joy. One reason to hate bribes is because we should love justice, and we cannot love both. God is justice, and He loves to see us doing and being just and righteous. One of the joys of heaven will be the fullness of justice. One of the joys in this life is to see specific justice done as we interface with it. Romans 12:18 tells us "as far as it depends on you, live at peace. . ." Let's adapt that to today's concept, as far as it depends on you, have nothing to do with bribes, be honest in your dealings with others, even if and when they are not. We cannot control what others do.

OCTOBER 1

PROVERBS TO LIVE BY

Proverbs 21:16

"A man who strays from the path of understanding comes to rest in the company of the dead."

Proverbs keeps referring to the path of understanding versus the path of foolishness, the path of righteousness versus the path of wickedness. Here we have the path of understanding versus the un-named one which is the default away from the path of wisdom or understanding. They all refer to the same two paths. Those really are the only two available in this life. There are rich and poor, sick and healthy, religious and irreligious on each of the two.

Proverbs is dealing with matters of how to live life on earth, and it is always evident that the path of wisdom, whatever it is called in each context, is the only one to choose if you want to get the most out of life on this earth. Although Proverbs has eternity in view from time to time, the focus remains primarily on life here on earth. The idea of "laying up for yourselves treasures in heaven did not come into clear view until Jesus taught it.

In this text we have a man straying away from the right path, and it must be understood in its proper context. This is not talking about a Christian wandering off the path of righteousness, and thereby losing his salvation. Neither was this man necessarily ever actually on the path. Very possibly he was confronted by a choice between the two paths, and he turned down the right one. He wandered away by following what appeared to be easier at the time. Many Christians wander or stray away from the right path; in fact, we all do it too often even when we are on it. I like the phrase "live with eternity's values in view," but that just is not the language of Proverbs. Proverbs wants us to live life to its best advantage in the here and now. That means life in the way that would be best for any of us personally here on earth. Of course, we look forward to heaven, but that is not in view here in this text.

To stray away from the path of understanding is to land in the graveyard; not a good choice. I would not recommend it. Even if such a one lives to a ripe old age, his quality of life ends up being meaningless, unfulfilling, purposeless, and that is death.

Proverbs 21:17

"He who loves pleasure will become poor; whoever loves wine and oil will never be rich."

Let's take a surface look at this proverb, and then see if there is something a little deeper down. "He who loves pleasure will become poor." In the context of this verse, the word poor means lacking in material possessions, just like the word rich means an abundance thereof. So, the question arises, what is wrong with pleasure? I mean really, who does not love, or at least enjoy pleasure. In fact, 1 Timothy 6:17 tells us that God Himself has provided "everything for our enjoyment." Indeed, Scripture is full of admonitions to joy, enjoy, rejoice and take pleasure in a variety of things and situations and people. In fact, just two verse back we were told that justice brings joy to the righteous, and the word joy in verse 15 is the same basic word as pleasure in verse 17.

So maybe the difference is the degree of pleasure. It is good to have pleasure, but not to excess, or perhaps it is good to take pleasure in some things but not in others. We should take pleasure in good things but not in bad. That sounds sort of reasonable, but that can hardly be the issue here. In this text he who loves pleasure—without qualification, will become poor. And yet in I Timothy God gives "for our enjoyment, or pleasure. Hmmm!

So maybe the key is in the word "loves." The same text goes on to say that whoever loves wine and oil will never be rich. Wine and oil here refere to luxurious living, which means they are probably already rich. If so, they are rich only in money, and that will diminish if the living is beyond their actual means. Whoever loves the luxurious lifestyle, will never be rich—or won't remain there. So, what about the word love. It is not an issue of agape love versus phjle'o. What this love denotes is an all-consuming self-love. It is a matter of loving pleasure and/or the luxurious lifestyle to the degree that it is their primary purpose for living. Those who love "stuff" in that way will be poor in meaningful family and social relationships. They will never be rich in kindness and good deeds or in any of the fruit of the Spirit.

*"The wicked become a ransom for the righteous, and
the unfaithful for the upright."*

We understand "ransom" as it relates to the payment demanded for
the promised release of a kidnapped person. Such a ransom is demanded
by wicked people for the release of someone more righteous than they. The
wicked person has captured or kidnapped someone more righteous than
themselves, and this ransom is to be paid by someone else who is also more
righteous than they.

We also understand, to a degree at least, the ransom that was paid for
our salvation. In Matthew 20:28 Jesus said that he came to "give his life as
a ransom for many." We cannot fully understand the measure of the cost,
nor can we fully understand the willingness to pay such a price, but we
can sort of understand how it worked. The payment price for sin was the
sacrifice of the sinless One. Now add to that Psalm 49:7, which tells us that
"no man can redeem the life of another or give to God a ransom for him."
Animal sacrifices were insufficient payment for the offense of sin, and so
would have been any (sinful) human sacrifices, had they been offered.

Now to the problem raised by our text. Here the wicked become a
ransom for the righteous, and the unfaithful for the upright. But how
can the wicked become a ransom for the righteous? This may possibly be
referring to the wicked bearing the brunt of a national judgment meted
out by God. If that is the thrust, it must surely be referring to end-time
judgment because we certainly don't see that happening in today's world.
I keep coming back to Deuteronomy 28:7-14 where God promised His
people "The Lord will make you the head and not the tail." This has to do
with the righteous people providing the leadership, even when they are not
necessarily elected to leadership. Jesus said "You are the salt of the earth,"
which simply means we are the preservative in a rotting society. Right
now, in our nation it seems like wickedness may have the upper hand. But
their time is coming. Recently a few senators declared that born-again
Christians are not fit or qualified for public service. But they do not have
the final word on anything, God does.

Proverbs 21:20-21

"In the house of the wise are stores of choice food and oil, but a foolish man devours all he has. He who pursues righteousness and love finds life, prosperity and honor."

The story is told of a lady visiting her doctor. The doctor advised her to eat more fruit and vegetables, so she said "I ate 7 apples yesterday." Why 7,? asked the doctor, to which she replied well, "the recipe called for 7 apples in the pie." Personally, I might have left some of it for the next day. That may make an OK joke, but is really not a wise thing to do in life.

We should never live IN tomorrow, bringing all its worries and concerns into today, but we should plan for tomorrow. James 4 tells us go ahead and plan for a new business venture in another town; just make sure you subject your plans to the Lord's will and direction. (That is a loose paraphrase of verses 13-15.) In other words, go ahead and start a college fund for your child right after birth, but not at the expense of tomorrow's groceries. Good planning and hard work will normally result in sufficient food on the table at all times, and some to spare. That is the path of wisdom. The foolish person spends it all as it comes in. He fully indulges himself as far as each paycheck will allow. This man has strayed away from the path of wisdom, which is not to say he was ever on it. Possibly he just did not get on the path of wisdom when he had the chance.

The one who pursues righteousness and love recognizes where the real values of life are to be found. Life, prosperity and honor do not find him so much as he finds them, or receives them, in the process of wisely following the guidance of wisdom, righteousness and love. Wisdom makes you get a job instead of depending on welfare, whether provided by the government or a wealthy relative or family member. No honor has ever come to the man who refuses to work. In a diversified culture like ours, both wisdom and foolishness have a multitude of avenues of expression. However, wisdom always wins out in the end. And if that is true in relation to this life, think of how much more so it will apply to the next. And remember, we never get a second run at life on earth.

PROVERBS TO LIVE BY

Proverbs 21:22

"A wise man attacks the city of the mighty and pulls down the stronghold in which they trusted."

Power can be found in many areas of life. Some have said that knowledge is power, and there is truth to that. Others have said money is power, and they try to live by their own golden rule: "he who has the gold makes the rules", and there is truth to that. I believe that the power of wisdom trumps them all and today's text would support that view. Proverbs is a Book of Wisdom. As early as in 2:6 we learn that "The Lord gives wisdom," as well as knowledge and understanding. So, we come to the text of the day which gives a vivid picture of the power of wisdom.

The city of the mighty is obviously a major, important city, and it is very well fortified. It is called a stronghold. There must be restricted access to it with security screening. The mighty ones in the city probably command quite an army. What can one man do against such odds! Such a "stronghold" surely houses much corruption and evil of many kinds. All well entrenched and facilitated by "the mighty" within its walls. Are you seeing any similarities with current events and conditions in our own country? Are you seeing any strongholds in your own life, or in our country? And are you finding that naming specifics in relation to our country is much easier than naming the spiritual ones in your own life? If so, we are on the same page. So, I ask again, what can one person do?

The wise man in our text attacks the city and pulls down the stronghold, but it never tells us just how he did it. I'd like to see a plan of action, but none is given. Why is that? What did Luther and Zwingli and Calvin do five hundred years ago? Well, they took a stand, but how does that relate to today. OK, wisdom comes from God, and they individually went to the source. We can get some knowledge by studying what they did, but not wisdom. Wisdom comes from God. As we pray for our national and personal concerns, could it be that besides asking God to do something, we should also ask Him for wisdom to know what we personally must do? We all know what is wrong; only God knows how and where to move on from here. Dare we ask Him for wisdom? Why not!

Proverbs 21:23

"He who guards his mouth and his tongue keeps himself from calamity."

In Matthew 12:37 Jesus said "By your words you will be acquitted and by your words you will be condemned." Words are very important, once spoken, they can never be unspoken. They can be excused or explained or regretted or denied or remembered or forgotten, but what you have said can never be unsaid. That thought alone should be sufficient to make us cautious of what we say. For many people it is; for others not so much. God's Word also says that "we all stumble in many ways. If anyone is never at fault in what he ways, he is a perfect man, able to keep his whole body in check." James 3:2. So even for those who are very cautious, we are not always careful enough.

According to our text, the better we guard what we say, the better we will keep ourselves from calamity. But that is not to say we ought not to speak. True, many times it is better to listen than to speak, but we must be careful of what, when and how or why we say what we do say. Mark Lowry jokingly says that he has to hear himself, before he knows what is talking about. That of course is not true, but then again, sometimes that may be true for all of us.

Speaking unguardedly would include repeating something you've heard without knowing its accuracy, or repeating something that should not be repeated—perhaps never, perhaps not here and now, or to this particular person. It could include speaking accurately about something you know, but doing it too authoritatively. You might be perceived as a "know-it-all." For some of us who are aggravated by the incessant solicitor's calls, it may well mean speaking angrily and unkindly to the point of speaking hatefully. I am trying to learn to speak kindly, if at all, or to simply hang up the phone. But that is not who I am naturally. My human nature is constantly trying to assert itself. I think of the Apostle Paul who said "I do what I hate to do." (Romans 7:14-20)

Our text tells us to guard our speech, but it does not give us the power to do it. For that we have to go to God. He provides that power through the indwelling Holy Spirit.

Proverbs 21:24

"The proud and arrogant man—Mocker is his name;
he behaves with overweening pride,"

Proverbs has frequently referred to the proud and arrogant as well as to scoffers and all those who oppose wise and righteous people. Here they are kind of lumped together, and given a name. The idea of a "Mocker" in the context of Proverbs is not the unpleasant kid on the children's playground that we knew in elementary school. This title of "Mocker" is in fact a very serious charge. By any human standards, there would surely be degrees of seriousness in behavior warranting such a charge. If we had a group discussion on this matter, there would be many different opinions as to which types of behaviors are the most egregious. So, let's not go there.

It seems to me our text implies that many evils are born out of pride and arrogance. Whether they are greater or lesser evils is not my concern at this time. My call to self-examination is not so much to see whether or not we would classify ourselves a "Mocker," but rather to see if we have a measure of "pride and arrogance" hidden in the inner recesses of our hearts. For the "Mocker" that seems to be a lifestyle, day in and day out. That is who he is. That is what he is. So "he behaves with overweening pride. Overweening pride, as I understand it, is excessive, or exaggerated arrogance. That would be someone who at a practical level really believes that certain laws, restrictions, or guidelines do not apply to him. Somehow, he is above that sort of thing. I remember someone saying in a discussion: "those of us in the inner circle . . ." Interpretation: ordinary people would not be able to understand, or ordinary people need that kind of control imposed on their behavior.

Any of us who operate from that kind of a mindset, even if briefly, are submitting to pride and arrogance. When we notice or recognize that in ourselves, we need to make a U-turn, in other words, repent and confess. If any selfish pride and arrogance is permitted to remain unchallenged, we are exposing ourselves to unintended consequences. Arrogance and intimate fellowship with Jesus Christ cannot co-exist in any individual.

"The sluggard's craving will be the death of him, because he refuses to work. All day long he craves for more, but the righteous give without sparing."

The dictionary says a sluggard is one who is "habitually lazy." That does not mean he does nothing, but rather that he does nothing productive; he shirks his responsibility, he does not do what he is supposed to do. On the other hand, what he does is to daydream, he desires to have and to be what he does not have, with no action to obtain it. He probably sees others achieving and obtaining what he desires for himself, and his desires merely increase and intensify to the point where they become all consuming. He thinks he knows what he wants, but is unwilling to pay the price—or even to consider what would be required to achieve his desires. This is what our text calls "craving."

The cravings of a sluggard are normally associated with material things and possessions. I believe they can just as well apply to spiritual matters. Let's look at some issues like "being a better Christian" that are almost ubiquitous among Christians. Many are not even willing to define for themselves what they mean by that phrase, let alone get down to any specifics of personal life changes. Consider the matter of prayer. I don't know that I have ever met anyone who considers his prayer life adequate. The number of Christians actually doing something about it is another story. Their desire for a consistent prayer life may even be considered a craving.

When I first became serious about prayer in my own life, I bought *and read* a number of books on the subject, which provided excellent information of the subject. A good start? Perhaps! But before there could be any real change in my prayer life here had to be a beginning; I had to DO something. I had to begin putting into practice what I was learning. (That is the difference between knowledge and wisdom.) I had to begin to pray. The issue is not how far I've progressed since then, but am I progressing now. So, I ask: Do you desire progress in your Christian walk? Are you making any effort toward progress? The cost may be high, but the rewards are and will be GREAT.

Proverbs 21:27

"The sacrifice of the wicked is detestable—how much
more so when brought with evil intent!"

Of course, we don't bring sacrifices as in the Old Testament, so we have to look to see how this applies to us today. Since "all Scripture is given by inspiration of God and is profitable for teaching, rebuking, correcting and training in righteousness," there is something for us in this text for today. The Old Testament sacrifices had to follow a very strict, meticulous set of rituals. But even with all the rules and regulations and outward performances, God was always after the heart of man. The whole system was designed to show mankind their need in light of their sin, and to find the answer to that need in God alone, not in the rituals. That has never changed.

But why would the "wicked" even bother to bring sacrifices? Thanks for asking. Among those whom we might classify as wicked, some never would. So, what is the text saying here? And why would these sacrifices be detestable if they followed correct procedures? Because, God was never interested in performances, except as they were brought as a heart response to God. Therefore, anyone bringing a sacrifice merely for its own sake would be included with those whom this text calls "wicked." They are wicked because they are leaving God, and a desire for a relationship with Him, out of the equation.

If this is so, then what is intended by bringing sacrifices with "evil intent"? Perhaps this would refer to their motives for bringing the sacrifice, which could be to impress others with their own piety, or to curry favor with whomever.

Move ahead to today and consider our "performances" of worship with a few rhetorical questions. Why do I join in congregational singing? Where is my mind during the pastoral prayer? If this is a contemporary style of service, what did I notice about the band? What did I think of the person who sang off-key? What or why did I contribute in the offering? How was my relationship with God enhanced during the worship experience today? Was God pleased with my worship today, or was it "detestable" to Him.

PROVERBS TO LIVE BY

Proverbs 21:28-29

"A false witness will perish, and whoever listens to him
will be destroyed forever. A wicked man puts up a bold
front, but an upright man gives thought to his ways."

In our culture, the first phrase would automatically draw our attention to a court case. Such a witness might slant his testimony to favor one side or the other of the case at hand. He might even claim to have seen and heard what in fact he neither saw nor heard. All of that would rightly indict him as a liar. Since there are more liars outside the courtroom than inside, means we need to focus where we are.

Our text says liars will perish, which draws us to Revelation 21:8 which says in part "all liars . . . will be in the fiery lake of burning sulfur." This is very unambiguous, and the only exception is the redeeming grace of God. The difficulty comes in the next phrase. Is this saying that anyone who listens to a liar will suffer the same consequences? That would be true if it means following the liar's lead. Sometimes the word "listens" carries with it the idea of absorbing and obeying. At other times, as may be the case here, it has the idea of listening to discern and evaluate. Here the newer NIV translates the last part as "but a careful listener will testify successfully." Taken in the second sense, no matter how translated, he listens to discern and will speak truthfully and victoriously.

The wicked man in verse 29 is still the same liar as in verse 28. Here he now puts up a bold front. He steels or hardens his face to avoid any detection of his lies. He tries to sound confident and objective so as to be believed. His lies are carefully planned and polished for the best possible benefit to himself at this moment. Never mind the potential adverse consequences down the road. "But an upright man gives thought to his ways." His speech is thoroughly considered, thought through, and evaluated for truth and accuracy before his mouth utters a sound. He knows how this will be perceived before the throne of God. If his current hearers listen and respond as he did, they too will be guided toward the same consequences of the truth speakers that he faces.

Does your speaking and listening need re-evaluating?

PROVERBS TO LIVE BY

Proverbs 21:30-31

There is no wisdom, no insight, no plan that can succeed against the Lord. The horse is made ready for the day of battle, but victory rests with the Lord."

We in the West are generally so determined to be self-sufficient that we find it difficult to accept the opening words of this text. Just look at what we've accomplished all on our own: I started this business with nothing but determination, skill and hard work, or I put myself through school and maintained a 4.0 GPA, or a little more inclusively, we made this country into the greatest nation on earth, you should see my IQ score, and such bragging could go on almost indefinitely. We always want to take credit for something. We are so wise, so perceptive and so ingenious that nothing we set our mind to can fail. We are quite willing, even anxious to agree with Frank Sinatra: "I Did It My Way." Look at all my accomplishments! Nobody helped me, and I didn't ask anyone for advice, I am the king of my castle. A former President once said "You did not build that!" and in a way, he was right—just not the way it was intended. Neither the government nor socialism in general facilitated that achievement, but God did. Even if you did not acknowledge Him then, or ever, He did it. Without Him are and can do nothing.

No wisdom, no insight, no plan can succeed against the Lord. If God says NO! then the answer is no. He is Sovereign, He is in control, and even though at times He has us on a very long leash, He retains control.

The next verse is an illustration to show us what He means. We can plan and prepare and threaten and declare our military might to scare would-be nuclear nations, but we cannot win any war without the Lord's permission and aid. We never have; we never will. So nationally or personally, go ahead and form your alliances and sign your treaties, but know this: "Nothing will succeed against the Lord." Of course, no nation, no church denomination, no family can trust the Lord as a unity; only its individual members can do that.

I've got an idea, why not you and I, beginning today, start trusting the Lord more fully. Are you willing to try it? He is.

Proverbs 22:1-2

"A good name is more desirable than great riches; to be esteemed is better than silver or gold. Rich and poor have this in common: The Lord is the Maker of both."

Throughout the Book of Proverbs, material wealth is made to appear desirable and Solomon should know. There is no way of comparing his wealth with modern day billionaires, but he was wealthy. However, wealth is never made to appear as the highest value—except in greedy people's minds. Wealth may indeed be preferable than poverty, but in today's text we get a challenge to proper valuation.

A good name, or we could say a good reputation, is more desirable than great riches. There is nothing to keep a person from having both, but the priority should be set. The good reputation or name in this text do not so much refer to what people think of you, as to what you are. Through careful manipulation, people can temporarily achieve a good reputation and be held in high esteem by their fellow people, but such manipulated achievements are very tenuous. With God it does not work at all. Wisdom, the theme of the book, can enable a person to earn a good name, as well as wealth to go with it. Wealth, on the other hand, cannot buy a good name, and any reputation of being a truly good person that is purchased with wealth, will not endure.

"Rich and poor have this in common: The Lord is the Maker of both." Therefore, the poor should never envy the rich, and the rich should never disdain the poor. Both should pursue wisdom, and through wisdom obtain a good name, or a good reputation, which is of greater value than any amount of wealth. Of a wise person, it can always be said "he's as good as his word; she's as good as her word." They are dependable; they are reliable. They will definitely do what they have promised. Titus 2:14 tells us Jesus Christ "gave himself for us to redeem us from all wickedness and to purify for himself a people that are his very own, eager to do what is good."

Now that is a good reputation.

"A prudent man sees danger and takes refuge, but the simple keep going and suffer for it."

The word "danger" is intentionally broad. It can include moral danger or evil, it can include physical danger, and it can also include material danger such as a potentially bad investment. When we are looking at wisdom for daily living on this planet, danger of every kind is to be avoided. Proverbs 27:1 simply says "you do not know what a day may bring forth." Only God knows the future.

Consider with me first the spiritual dangers. This proverb again contrasts the wise with the foolish, here called the "prudent" and the "simple." A wise person does not always need a specific Bible verse to tell him a thing is wrong, or even potentially wrong. He is wise enough to see danger and potential danger. The foolish person says "hey, that looks like fun" and off he goes. Just because a thing is not an outright sin does not mean it is a wise thing to do. I remember a young man refusing to learn a particular activity because he figured it could become too time-consuming. For him that was a wise decision, even though it was not a bad thing. We all know that we should always avoid what is sinful, but the prudent person can see potential future implications, and "plays it safe."

There is no guide-book, including the Bible that can warn us of all potential physical dangers in life. Therefore, no other person can do it for us either. Some things we know intuitively, some things are rightly proscribed by law, most things require us to make our own choices, and for that we need to consult Wisdom, and often that requires seeking counsel from others with experience.

We have touched on financial matters above, but beyond Scripture, it is usually wise to consult trained investment advisors, keeping in mind they need to sell in order to make a living. Not all of them give good advice, so again you need wisdom.

The more intimate we are with the Lord, the better we will discern his still, small voice in all matters of life. He always wants what is best for us, and will never "steer us wrong."

Proverbs 22:4-5

"Humility and the fear of the Lord bring wealth and honor and life. In the paths of the wicked lie thorns and snares, but he who guards his soul is safe."

In the previous verse, the difference between wisdom (prudence) and foolishness (the simple) was given in a single verse. In today's text, the results or rewards are given in a verse for each.

Here wisdom is described as "humility and the fear of the Lord." In its essence, wisdom **is** humility and the fear of the Lord. Wisdom is never proud; it cannot be. The two are antithetical. Therefore, when a relatively wise person behaves pride-fully foolish, he has at that moment abandoned wisdom. That is really not too hard to understand and accept—so long as we keep it in the 3rd person. However, when we make it personal it takes on a more significant dimension. Why would anyone ever behave pride-fully? To convince oneself of personal worth or value, or to impress others, are the only two reasons I can come up with. Yet the results are the exact opposite. And why would anyone neglect or abandon the fear of the Lord? Only to achieve one's own selfish desires and goals, and again it is counterproductive. The rewards of wisdom include riches and honor and life. Life is worth the living, just because He lives." In wisdom, all of life is enhanced.

Those called "simple" or "wicked" in verse 5, are those who lack wisdom. They think that by going their own way, they can have freedom to do anything, to achieve anything, and to have the best of everything. But they have never thought through all the way to consequences. And everything we ever do has consequences, even for eternity. The path of the wicked is littered with thorns and snares and all kinds of difficulties and heartaches, and it just keep getting worse. And there is no one or nothing on that path to which they can call for help. O yes, they can call on the Lord, but He is not on that path. In order to call on Him they have to leave that path.

The person of wisdom, who guards his soul, is safe. Not only he will be safe, he *IS* safe. God keeps him safe. Among the biggest potential derailments for believers in Christ, is pride and the neglect of fear of the Lord.

PROVERBS TO LIVE BY

Proverbs 22:6

"Train a child in the way he should go, and when he is old, he will not turn from it."

Even though this is perhaps one of the best-known of all the proverbs, it may not be the best understood. First of all, since it is a proverb, it is a statement of wisdom, related to a general truth or experience in life, and not an absolute promise of outcome. God has given to humans the capacity and freedom to choose, which we all exercise throughout life. This proverb is written to provide parents with wisdom in relation to training up their children. What parents and children do about that training instruction is their choice. So, what is this training in "the way he should go"? Should all children go in the same way? Does this mean taking your children to Sunday-School and church? If so, which church? When does this training begin? Or does it mean we are to train them in the direction of their latent skills and interests?

Many people believe this is a guarantee that if children are "brought up in church," and then in their youth turn away, "they will return when they are old." But this verse does not talk about any return. The Church was born about 1,000 years after Proverbs was written. Nor can it refer to training them in the direction of their talents. Many people "discover" their own talents and choose careers in mid-life. So, where do we turn for an understanding of this proverb? How about to the Book of Proverbs!

By its own declaration, the book was written "*for attaining wisdom and discipline; for understanding words and insights; for acquiring a disciplined and prudent life, doing what is right and just and fair; . . .*" 1:2-7 This purpose statement concludes by saying that it all begins with "the fear of the Lord." So, our text is saying that when you train up a child in the way of wisdom, to be a person of honesty and integrity, and all facets of wisdom, he will *most generally* live that way all his life into old age. So, the call is for us all, parents, children and grandparents, to live in wisdom, beginning with a true "fear of the Lord." There is no need to return if we have never departed. But by the grace of God, we can return at any age if and when we have strayed.

Proverbs 22:7

"The rich rule over the poor, and the borrower is servant to the lender."

The matter of personal debt is not a major Bible theme, though it is referenced in both Old and New Testaments. It can be, however, and for many people it is a very major issue in life. Our text merely gives a very strong caution, citing only the realities of life.

That the rich rule over the poor is evident throughout our society, and probably every society on earth. This is not intrinsically evil, neither is it necessarily meritorious. It is just fact. It is the *other* golden rule: "the one with the gold makes the rules." That is (generally) true at all levels of society, including church and community matters, and is also generally accepted; that's just the way it is. The Bible however, does give some specific rules. A section in Leviticus 25 forbids charging any interest in certain circumstance, and Nehemiah 5:10 forbids excessive interest. Jesus told us to not refuse those "who want to borrow from you," Matthew 5:42. These, and many others, are guidelines for the lender. Our text is given to teach wisdom to the borrower.

"The borrower is servant (slave) to the lender." Borrowing is spiritually, socially and nationally legal, but is potentially dangerous, and can become catastrophic. For most people, a house mortgage is their single biggest debt item, but credit cards are for many absolutely destructive. Statistics say that buying on credit cards results in greater spending by as much as 35%. And if you need to prove the validity of debt enslaving the borrower, just try missing 6 months of car payments. So, we also have a balancing Scripture; Romans 13:8 tells us "Let no debt remain outstanding." In other words, don't borrow more than you can afford to repay. A rule of thumb would be "don't buy on credit what you don't have equity to pay for at the time of purchase."

The verse in Romans continues: ". . . except the continuing debt to love one another." Our focus must always be more on giving than on getting. Let us strive to become rich in love, and in serving one another. I have it on good authority that "the coming of the Lord is near."

PROVERBS TO LIVE BY

Proverbs 22:8-9

"He who sows wickedness reaps trouble, and the rod of
his fury will be destroyed. A generous man will himself
be blessed, for he shares his food with the poor."

What does it mean to sow wickedness? We could hypothesize in several directions here, but let's look at the most obvious. When we see the word "wickedness," we think in categories that would include terrorism, murder, rape etc. Some translations use the word "iniquity," to which we might tend to ascribe a lower call of bad things, things that are more socially acceptable, like a little cheating, or shading the truth etc. The word translated "wickedness" or "iniquity" here in this context have more the idea of injustice. That however is not just aimed at the justice system of our land. This is talking specifically about our own justice or injustice in our daily interpersonal activities and relationships. Anyone of us who deals unfairly or unjustly with our family, friends, acquaintances and others with whom we have interactions "will reap trouble."

The result of this trouble is further expanded in the next phrase, the "rod of fury" used to deliver the injustice will be destroyed. That is to say, it will fail. You can't get away with a thing! Any success and appearance of not getting "found out" is at best temporary. Numbers 32:23 puts it this way: "your sin will find you out." That is because no one can "pull the wool over God's eyes," not even with a little thing for a little while.

"A generous man will himself be blessed." This is not talking about a generous act or deed, but a generous person. A generous person will be generous with his finances, and that is the point here, but also generous in life overall, including thoughts and deeds as well as words. This is a person who is self-giving. What he gives will be a blessing to the recipients, but the promise here is that he/she will be blessed personally. "Jesus himself said it is more blessed to give than to receive," Acts 20:35. And that is good for all time. A generous person does not need recognition from others to be fulfilled. Just doing, and knowing that he is doing the right thing is reward. Jesus will see to that Himself.

Proverbs 22:10-11

"Drive out the mocker, and out goes strife; quarrels and insults are ended. He who loves a pure heart and whose speech is gracious will have the king for a friend."

Some translations use scoffer where NIV says mocker. When you look at this kind of a person, you see that basically he is a troublemaker. He doesn't necessarily mock or scoff at God and the Bible, though that often happens as well with such people. Among other things, they are extremely selfish: in their own opinion, they are never wrong, try to always be in charge, and to have the last word on any issue. They are utterly judgmental and critical of anything and anyone except themselves. It is no wonder that strife goes out and ends when such people leave. The issue, or the problem have not been the problem. The problem has been these people.

Unfortunately, these people are found in any community, system or organization, including the church. When such people leave the church, it is often called "a blessed subtraction." The Martins sing *In The Presence of Jehovah.* The lyrics include: "Troubles vanish, hearts are mended in the presence of the King." Self-appointed kings cause the problems; their departure ends quarrels and insults.

Let us not be like the prideful Pharisee who prayed "I thank you Lord that I am better than the sinner," but rather strive to be like the one in verse 11 our text. "He who loves a pure heart and whose speech is gracious . . ." This is not an act, not a pretense; it is to be a demonstration of the reality of our own heart. A love of a pure heart, beginning with one's own, will result in gracious speech. When the speech is harsh, critical, demeaning and cruel, it doesn't matter that it may still be true, it is nevertheless of the "troublemaker" variety. The speech then, is not the problem—it is the expression of the problem, which is the impure heart of the troublemaker.

Proverbs 22:12

"The eyes of the Lord keep watch over knowledge, but he frustrates the words of the unfaithful."

This verse not only follows the previous, but I believe is closely connected to the gracious speech aspect of verse eleven. Whenever we read about the Lord's keeping watch over, it has a much deeper meaning than to merely observe. We already know that the Lord sees everything we do, but this means not only that He sees, but that He also protects. I can't tell you how many times His watching over me has protected me from going, saying or doing something wrong. (We are not going to talk about how many times I have failed in spite of His watch-care.) He is still leaving us with a freedom to choose.

But what does it mean when it says He is keeping watch over "knowledge"? It cannot mean that He does not allow us to forget. Most seniors could only wish that were it. How about this! How many times have you wanted to say something, perhaps in anger but also in simple conversation, and something just kept you from saying it? Then, sooner or later, you realized it would have been the wrong thing to say. Was that the Lord watching over your knowledge? You knew, though not right at the time perhaps, that what you wanted to say might have been true and even OK, yet in retrospect you see it would have been unwise at the time. Not everything you know needs to be told, and some things need to be held in abeyance until it is the right time. I sometimes jokingly say "now I've told you everything I know." But that is never true. A closer walk with the Lord will help us to better know when to speak and when to refrain.

The words of the unfaithful, are spoken purely on the basis of personal decisions and choices, without the protection of the Holy Spirit. The "unfaithful" in Proverbs usually means the unwise. And remember, the Lord is the source of all wisdom. People who have a reputation of always running off at the mouth, are probably speaking without the protection of the Lord's watch-keeping. For the believer, that protection is always ready and available to us. Let's pray and learn to remember to plug in.

"Pay attention and listen to the sayings of the wise; apply your heart to what I teach for it is pleasing when you keep them in your heart and have all of them ready on your lips."

This next section contains "sayings of the wise," but are nevertheless included Holy in Scripture. Solomon evidently, under the direction and inspiration of the Holy Spirit, gathered some of these sayings for inclusion. We must remember that all truth is God's truth.

Our text for today, which begins this section, is an exhortation to pay attention to these sayings, or proverbs. Such exhortation is applicable to each of us every time we open the Word of God and/or hear it proclaimed. Far too often we read or listen to Scripture, without paying attention to what it says. Worse yet, we can pay attention to the point where we also understand it, and yet do not allow it to impact our lives. Some people attend worship services and Bible studies only to learn something new. It is always good to learn something new in Scripture—providing we then also apply it to our lives. When our text exhorts us to "pay attention," it includes life application. Otherwise we fit into the category of those who, according to 2 Timothy 3:7, are "always learning but never able to acknowledge the truth." They have intellectual knowledge of truth, but they do not acknowledge it; they do not incorporate it into daily living.

The "I" in apply your heart to what I teach, obviously refers to the one speaking the "wise saying" and to Solomon who incorporated these sayings in his collection. However, since God, the Holy Spirit directed their inclusion, we can rightly take this to mean "pay attention to what I, God, teach." Without that, the Bible becomes nothing more than just a good book for us. All Scripture is God-breathed, and given for the equipping of the people of God.

The Proverbs are given to improve our live on earth, with implications for eternity, so our text continues. It is pleasing when you keep these wise sayings in your heart. To whom is it pleasing? It is pleasing to you, to those around you, and above all, to the God who uses these sayings in our lives to teach us wisdom. Let's wise up!

Proverbs 22:19

"So that your trust may be in the Lord, I teach you today, even you."

I have no idea what heaven is going to be like; anything I try to imagine is totally inadequate. Imagine the best you can, just know that it will be infinitely better than that. I can perhaps come a little closer to imagining what life on earth could be like, if I were not so prone to sin and failure. I do know that our quality of life on earth, as well as our life in heaven, is directly related to our trust in Him. Of course, it begins with our trust in Him for salvation, but from that point onward, our trust needs to grow and increase; it needs to be honed and fine-tuned. All of the Christian's life should be that of growing in faith, trust and in the knowledge of God, 2 Peter 3:18.

This text tells us plainly that teaching is for the purpose of growing trust in the Lord. And note that is very personal; I teach you, even you. You need to—I need to put my name into that one. We may at times think that we are too insignificant, and unworthy to merit such personal attention by God. But our "merit" never enters into our relationship with God. In any dealings with the Almighty, it is always His grace, and never our merit. The most profound truth in the Bible is: **JESUS LOVES ME.** O YES, "God so loved the world that He gave," but that is just me multiplied by enough billions. He loves each "me" individually and uniquely. A Gospel song says "he has no favorites . . ." and that may be true in one sense, but in another sense each one is His favorite. I like a phrase used by author Paul Young, when in speaking for God he says "I am especially fond of **you**." And you can put your name in that one too. However, you may choose to say it, that is God's truth. And because of that truth, our text says "I teach you today, even you."

He teaches each of us individually and He teaches us uniquely. Since He created each of us individually and uniquely, it stands to reason that He would teach us individually and differently from each other. It is relatively unimportant how much data we can intellectualize, it is vitally and utterly important that we learn to trust Him more. After all, He is God. If He wants to teach me trust, I want to learn trust. And you?

Proverbs 22:20-21

"Have I not written thirty sayings for you, sayings of counsel and knowledge, teaching you true and reliable words, so that you can give sound answers to him who sent you?

Commentators often lump verses 17-21 into one grouping. This would probably be best for a more in-depth study, be it the whole book or just this chapter. However, we are looking for specific "miniature lessons" for daily living in each day's text. Nevertheless, we cannot completely untie these two verses from the preceding. The whole section through chapter 24 begins with "Pay attention and listen." That is the beginning point for all life situations, whether dealing with people or with God and His Word, or even physical projects and endeavors.

Solomon is here writing thirty sayings that he did not compose, but rather adapted. These were known and accepted sayings and would be recognized by the readers in his day, even if they were somewhat edited to fit the purposes of the communicator. Truth remains truth, even when couched in different words to suit the present situation.

In this section, Solomon has written 30 sayings of counsel and knowledge for us, not so we can repeat them, although that could happen for those who then know what these sayings are. The next phrase tells us he wrote them—not to inform, but to teach. If we learn the truth of these sayings, and understand them, we will have the wisdom to apply them in any life situations. The last part of the text says "so that." That gives us the purpose. One of our current "wise sayings" is honesty is the best policy. Pretty much everyone in our culture knows that saying and can repeat it; far fewer practice it. In order for us to teach that as a true and reliable concept to others, we need to know that truth both intellectually and experientially. And that is the principle that works in all of life. We do not need a Bible verse for every life situation, we need Bible wisdom. With well-founded and well- rounded wisdom, we can help people with Scriptural principles as well as other life circumstances where we have some expertise. So, let's learn to "pay attention and listen."

Proverbs 22:22-23

"Do not exploit the poor because they are poor and do not crush the needy in court, for the Lord will take up their case and will plunder those who plunder them."

This saying, possibly based on a real-life experience, basically forbids ill-gotten gains. A wealthy, powerful person is taking advantage of a poor person by some nefarious action. He may possibly have taken care, with the help of his lawyers, to keep it pretty close to the limits of actual crime, but it was exploitation nevertheless. The poor man cannot afford the lawyers required to prosecute, and so he suffers the loss. One can easily fill in the details, whether real or imagined, to make this a complete story.

Most people of course would never be involved in such a scenario, but I believe every country and culture has myriads of similar instances of such goings on all the time. Yet if this is perhaps relatively rare, especially among those who seek to live by the teachings of the Bible, why take time and effort to deal with a problem you may never face. Because we can take both warning and comfort that "the Lord will take up their case." Actions have consequences. They may not be immediate, but they are certain. Both the exploiters and the exploited will receive the due rewards for their deeds. But let's get more personal.

The warning is for both exploiters and exploited, but also all who hear. So, you have, or have never exploited anyone. Probably not in financial or legal matters, but the Lord looks on the heart. What is your REAL attitude towards the poor, especially if they are also dirty and unkempt? And how well can you hide that attitude—from God? What sin are you, in your superior status, incapable of committing? The warning is re-phrased for us in 1 Corinthians 10:12 "So if you think you are standing firm, be careful that you don't fall." No sin is too great for God to forgive, nor for us to commit. We are kept only by the grace and power of God. And we can be confident we will continue to be kept, because Greater is He who is in you, than he who is in the world. We may be living for the next world, while in this, but we must be careful how we live in this world, because there still are eternal consequences.

Proverbs 22:24-25

"Do not make friends with a hot-tempered man, do not associate with one easily angered, or you may learn his ways and get yourself ensnared."

This saying is quite self-explanatory and straight forward, and it makes good sense when taken as written and intended. However, it is all too easy to read into it what it does not say. To not make friends with him or even associate with him is not a license to be rude, unkind, or standoffish. Many of us have probably indulged in such attitudes, if not behavior. We still have to balance it all with love. In another context, Paul instructs the church at Corinth about a sinful person in the church to "hand this man over to Satan. . ." 1 Corinthians 5:5. Then a few verses later he instructs them to not associate or even eat with such a person. In his next letter, referring to the same man, he says "the punishment . . . is sufficient for him. Now instead, you ought to forgive and comfort him. . ." 2:6-7.

Perhaps the most difficult age to sort out these relationships would be in the teen years. Here young people tend to form their own value systems and establish long term friendships. However, the warning or caution of our text is for all ages. We all tend to become like the people we hang out with. We learn their ways and they learn ours. Being that we are all sinners to begin with, we find the wrong things attractive and easier to learn. In that we also get a lot of encouragement and help from the enemy of our souls. In fact, he can be very pushy, in case you had not noticed. Therefore, the best advice seems to be to avoid falling into such relationships in the first place.

One may very well ask how we can hope to influence them for good, if we do not befriend and associate with such people. That indeed is a good question. Let me repeat that Proverbs is not a book to teach techniques for leading people to Christ, but on how to live this present life to the best advantage. So, this brings us to the main point of our text which is wisdom. To be a friend to a hot-tempered man or one easily angered, make sure you know who will be influencing whom. A wise person will point others in the right direction, which is where he himself is heading.

PROVERBS TO LIVE BY

Proverbs 22:26-27

"Do not be a man who strikes hands in pledge or puts up security for debts; if you lack the means to pay, your very bed will be snatched from under you."

It has been said that the Bible speaks more about money than about heaven and faith combined. I cannot verify that, but believe it is correct. However, even a cursory reading will show clearly that it is not because money is most important. Rather, it is because people are so important, and people deal with money, people need money to survive, and, unfortunately, people tend to over-rate money. People abuse, and misuse money. Money provides more opportunity for dishonesty of all types than almost anything else. Yet, money is needed and the Bible teaches proper valuation and handling of money.

Our text warns against securing someone else's obligations, especially when they are risky or the person's integrity is questionable or even unknown. I recently gave a small interest-free loan to a person in need in our church. My inner commitment was that if the person were unable to repay, it would become a gift. This text is not talking about those kinds of arrangements. This is talking about entering a legally binding obligation that could jeopardize you and your family beyond reason. After all, since God owns all the wealth and money in the world, it is His money we are placing at risk. However, this is not the Lord's eleventh commandment. This is a caution not to be unwise. Life on this planet is most blessed and enjoyable when we avoid doing foolish things with money. One financial planner used to say: "Money changes people, whether it is in lack, or in abundance. Money changes people."

I would read into our text that we ought not to take unwise risks (and I think that would include gambling) with God's money, even though He wants us to use it to gain more. That is why Ecclesiastes 11 teaches diversification, dollar cost averaging and investing for long term gains. If step #1 in obtaining wisdom is to ask God, then step #2 is obeying God. In today's text that is talking about wisdom in money matters.

Proverbs 22:28

"Do not move an ancient boundary stone set up by your forefathers."

This is a very simple, easy to understand prohibition. Exodus 20:15 puts it very succinctly in #8 of the Ten Commandments: "You shall not steal." The issue in our text is real estate or farm land. Property lines were not as carefully measured and surveyed as at present, nor were they recorded and the record kept in a land office or county seat. When first established they were simply marked by a marker stone at each end of the field. Honesty required that they not be moved.

Solomon was probably not concerned that someone would come at night with a front-end loader and move the stones twenty feet over onto the neighbor's property, thus significantly enlarging his own. More likely it would be to move it just a little, maybe a few inches a year; an inconsequential move, really. However, done repeatedly over years, it would achieve the same end result. Still, a move of a few inches would be morally and ethically the same as a few feet—or yards; it would still be theft.

In our culture farming, like any other industry, is so technologically advanced, it is not subject to the same hazards as in more primitive days. Besides, the vast majority of us do not live on farms but in. cities and towns. So, where does that leave us? It leaves us with the same restrictions and temptations as Israel back when this was first written, and differs only in the details of application.

Consider what has happened to moral and ethical standards in the Church in specific and in Western culture generally during the last 6 decades. We may have a difficult time differentiating between cultural mores and biblical standards, but just note that the degeneration happened over time. We did not move from "Leave it to Beaver" to "Sex in the City" overnight. Nor did we move from the biblical standards for the family overnight. We ceded a few inches at a time to the one who comes only to kill, steal and destroy. Never mind your neighbor, what do you & I condone in our lives that is contrary to God's standards in our attitudes or in our actions?

Just asking.

Proverbs 22:29

*"Do you see a man skilled in his work? He will serve
before kings; he will not serve before obscure men."*

By inspiration of the Holy Spirit, Solomon chose the word here translated "skilled." The King James version translates this word as "diligent." Far be it from me to replace any divinely chosen word, but certain words can be correctly translated in different terms. So, let us consider what is involved in becoming skilled.

We can talk about being born with certain skills, aptitudes, and mental capacities, and maybe even find certain biological proofs to support that. Even so, what we are is still by God's design. So, let's say God designed for you to be born with certain skills and aptitudes. Twenty years later, does that make you a skilled worker—or another ten years later? Thousands of years ago, when the first "Tabernacle" was built, God gave both Bezalel and Oholiab skill, ability and knowledge "in all kinds of crafts." Exodus 35:30ff. Perhaps neither one could bake a pecan pie. Read the Exodus passage, there is nothing there about baking a pie. So, did they start wood working while in their cribs? or what about right after high school? No matter when they began, they did not become "skilled" until after they got started doing the thing they were born to do.

Here is where I like the King James translation "diligent." We are familiar with the expression "practice makes perfect." That, of course, is not necessarily true. Maybe correct practice makes for perfection; practice doing a thing incorrectly until it almost becomes second nature, and it is still incorrect. But work at a skill diligently to continually improve, and you become truly "skilled." Now, instead of just working at a craft, let's apply this to life in general. But while we are in process, how do we know when we get it right? That is where the instruction manual, known as *Basic Instructions Before Leaving Earth*, or **BIBLE** for short, comes in. It is the guide to wisdom, and wisdom is the pre-requisite for success.

Colossians 3:23 tells us "Whatever your hand finds to do, work at it with all your heart, as working for the Lord, not for men."

PROVERBS TO LIVE BY

Proverbs 23:4-5

"Do not wear yourself out to get rich; have the wisdom to show restraint. Cast but a glance at riches, and they are gone, for they will surely sprout wings and fly off to the sky like an eagle."

Beginning with verse one, the point in this section is to exercise restraint, with the context relating first to a formal banquet with influential people, such as a king. It is highly unlikely that any of us will ever be invited to such a banquet—in this life. A tourist visiting London is not allowed inside Buckingham Palace gates, much less being invited to dine with the Queen. But is there an application of this passage for us ordinary people? Yes, I believe there is. Remembering that the Proverbs are written to give us guidance in living this life on earth, there has to be such an application.

Just as boorish behavior would be out of place at a formal banquet in the presence of a monarch, it is inappropriate anywhere and at any time for the People of God. So, verses 1-3 would also apply to us at a church pot-luck. But on to our text for today!

God has especially gifted some people in acquiring wealth, but most of the rest of us in America have more than we really need to live on anyway. What many of us need to learn is to show restraint, or rather, to **have** restraint. If God has gifted and called you to wealth, great! But there is more to life than just that. If God has gifted and called you to some service that does not lead to wealth, great! But there is more to life than just that. What we need to strive for, no matter what our occupation might be, is a well-balanced life. Here it is very difficult to be specific, because no two well-balanced" lives will be the same. However, for each of us, our personal relationship with the Lord must always take first place. Beyond that, each one has to apportion time and energy to a plethora of activities and responsibilities. And here is where "restraint" enters in. Some things will be more enjoyable than others, some we will deem more urgent, some more and some less tiring, and some necessary but downright unpleasant. Through it all, we need divine wisdom to keep everything in balance. May God give us wisdom to have and to exercise restraint.

PROVERBS TO LIVE BY

Proverbs 23:6-8

*"Do not eat the food of a stingy man, do not crave
his delicacies, for he is the kind of man who is always
thinking about the cost. Eat and drink, he says to you,
but his heart is not with you. You will vomit up the little
you have eaten and will have wasted your compliments."*

This passage deals with very earthy matters that very practically relate
to everyday living; hardly what you might expect in Scripture. But that is
Proverbs for you; it is very practical and non-religious. That is because, as
the old saying goes, "Nothing is secular when Jesus Christ is Lord." But
does that include going out to dinner? Yes! No one ever really eats alone
because the Lord is always with you, especially as a believer. Since He is
there anyway, you are best off to recognize and acknowledge Him. So, the
message of this text can be helpful to you, whether you are a host or a guest.

First the host: we don't know why a person like that would ever invite
anyone over for dinner, unless it was perceived as a kind of "social obligation."
Since they invited us over last month, we really have to invite them back.
Jesus mentioned that concept in Luke 14 and gave instructions about hosting
a meal. It should never be to "show off," or to obligate anyone; rather it should
always be to the glory of God, whether it is family, friends or strangers.

Guests do not need to accept an invitation if there appear to be ulterior
motives. If someone does accept an invitation, not knowing they really
won't be welcome, it will probably be very awkward. The best one can do
is to remain pleasant, but not to give insincere compliments. Be honest,
even if the host is not, and seek to honor the Lord, no matter how things
go. I've had VERY little experience in this regard, but I know you need to
pray a lot during the awkward silent times.

The one thing we can take away from this is to be very transparent,
whether issuing or accepting an invitation and watch your motives. Try
not to issue or accept an invitation merely out of obligation. And when
inviting strangers, which can be a great ministry, keep in mind that you
may be entertaining angels—or you might be their angel. Whatever you
do, do it all for the glory of God.

PROVERBS TO LIVE BY

Proverbs 23:9

"Do not speak to a fool, for he will scorn the wisdom of your words."

This does not mean you have to give him the "silent treatment." Rather, this is telling us there is no point in trying to reason with him. All he will do is ridicule and scorn the wisdom of your words. By implication, this would also indicate that is not the kind of person you want to hang out with. Psalm 1 speaks to this idea in verse 1. My paraphrase of that verse would be: *you are blessed if you do not hang out with the wicked and mockers or the scornful.* Proverbs 26:4 says if you answer a fool according to his folly, you will be like him yourself. Both experience and practical wisdom tell us we become like those we mostly associate with.

Our text is not necessarily suggesting that the reader is prone to associate with fools who think themselves wise. It is really saying don't even speak to him. If the person is a stranger to you, you have no idea about whether or not he is a mocker, so you would greet him/her cordially and see whether that leads to an opportunity for some meaningful interchange. But our text seems to indicate how we should relate to known "fools." Perhaps you had a previous experience of trying to talk to him, and the response told you what to expect any time you try it again. If, however, we then ignore the person, or treat him like an enemy, you have lost any chance of influencing him to think sensibly. The Holy Spirit has reached and redeemed many a person whom his acquaintances and other contemporaries considered to be irredeemable.

I believe our text is basically telling us not to engage in any sort of argumentative reasoning. We can use Scripture to prove ourselves right and the other person wrong, and that is the approach that will call forth scorn, mockery and rejection from the fool. Whether he verbalizes it or not, he will probably classify you as one who thinks himself high and mighty, a goody two shoes. He may feel you are trying to condemn him, and that is a good way to make enemies and influence them away from the Lord. More than hearing what we say, they need to see Christ in our attitude. I am preaching to a standard higher than I have attained, but let's aim.

Proverbs 23:10-11

"Do not move an ancient boundary stone or encroach on the fields of the fatherless, for their Defender is strong; he will take up their case against you."

This text is an expansion on 22:28, so let us focus on the expansion. Israel in the time of Solomon was an agrarian society, and property lines were the sight-line from one boundary stone to another. If Isaac wanted to extend his holdings, and neighbor Ezra was unwilling to sell, Isaac might go during the night and move the boundary stones a few feet at each end of the field and "Wa-La" he had enlarged his farm—at no extra cost. That would be bad enough, but if he did it to Ezra's family after death, that was much worse. It is hard to imagine (?) anyone would do such a thing, but it evidently happened often enough for this prohibition to make its way into the Word of God. More than once. Do you remember the song that asks "Does Jesus care . . ." and then answers "Oh yes, He cares."

Almost everything about our culture has changed in the intervening 3,000 years, **in**cluding our laws, but **ex**cluding our greedy hearts. Sin is still sin. Enter verse 11 of our text. The Defender of the oppressed is strong, and He will take up their case—your case. He is both the Prosecutor of the offender and the Judge: He is simultaneously the Defender of the oppressed and their Judge. He who has the Almighty as his Prosecutor can't get away with a thing. He will make all things right. If Isaac, in our illustration above, confesses, repents and come to Christ for salvation, his crime is charged against Jesus Christ, and He has already paid the penalty. So, where does that leave the oppressed? They may not see the satisfaction of their hoped-for revenge, but then revenge is never ours to begin with. They will however see their Defender meet all their needs all along the way, and get reimbursement for their losses, and rewards for their faithfulness and trust.

PROVERBS TO LIVE BY

Proverbs 23:12

"Apply your heart to instruction and your ears to words of knowledge."

A lot of young people can hardly wait to finish high school so they can stop learning, others barely make it through college for the same reason. When does this all finally end? For some people sooner than others, but for all people, it should never end. It is just the formal classroom learning that ends, but that is when life learning begins—or should do so. I am reminded of the story about a certain employee who was repeatedly passed over for promotion. After a certain number of years, (let's say 10,) he was again passed over in favor of a relatively newly hired individual, so he went to see the boss for clarification. He said to his boss "I have 10 years of experience, and this one has been here barely a year, what gives? The boss replied, well actually you have just one-year experience, repeated 10 times. For anyone to gain and grow in wisdom, one cannot afford to ever quit learning. No one ever said this life was going to be easy, or all aspects of it enjoyable. For some people, book learning is a lot harder than for some others, but what is probably the hardest of all is to "Apply your heart to instruction."

Wisdom is hardly impacted at all, until the heart application happens. How often have you read a verse or a passage in your morning devotions that really hit you where you needed it—be it an encouragement, a blessing, or perhaps a correction. You hover over it for a few moments thinking wow, this is really good, but by noon you have forgotten what it was. O you remember there was something good there, but you can't remember what it was, or even where. If I had no problem in this regard, I wouldn't even think to bring up the subject. Some have progressed farther than others, but none of us yet arrived.

The last part of the verse says we must apply our ears to words of knowledge. That means we should always be looking for and listening for information to enter our minds, so we can process it into our hearts for the purpose of a change of life for the better. Our minds must then process the information to sort the "wheat from the chaff." Wisdom takes time and effort, but worth every bit of it.

Proverbs 23:13-14

"Do not withhold discipline from a child; if you punish him with the rod, he will not die. Punish him with the rod and save his soul from death."

There may possibly never have been a time in human history when this teaching was more needed than today. It seems the whole "western world" is hell-bent on teaching—even forcing, permissiveness as the only acceptable life style. To achieve such a goal, they know that young children need indoctrination. Some are now telling young children not to let their grandparents hug them, the reasoning being that this might lead to sexual harassment and abuse. God, who created little children and their grandparents, saw this coming. The section in 2 Timothy 3, foretelling the godlessness in the last days is very evident right now, and it is already getting worse. It begins with "people will be lovers of themselves," and includes children being disobedient to their parents. Because we are all sinners, that has of course always been true, but probably not to this degree. And now disobedience and disrespect is actually being taught in some schools.

The reference to the rod in this text is not talking about child abuse, nor beating with what we today would consider to be a rod; it is talking about discipline, including spankings when necessary. The biblical "rod of correction" would include all forms of discipline and training in righteousness. Anything and everything that would help the child to learn right from wrong. Indeed, parents of young children have the most difficult job in the world—and the most significant and important. Discipline will never kill the child; "he will not die." Rather, the discipline, when properly applied and heeded, will save him from eternal death, in some cases also from premature physical death, and in every case, make life on earth more enjoyable for both parents and children.

When the disciples of Jesus were threatened with death for obeying God, (Acts 5) they replied "We must obey God rather than men." That is still true for all of us today, especially for parents of young children. Obey God! Do it, even when the cost gets greater. Your commensurate rewards will be greater still.

PROVERBS TO LIVE BY

Proverbs 23:15-16

"My son, if your heart is wise, then my heart will be glad; my inmost being will rejoice when your lips speak what is right."

This proverb is among the thirty that Solomon collected and adapted to be included in God's book of wisdom. It occurs to me that it may well have a dual meaning. Surely, he is saying that his own heart will be glad if/when his son's heart is wise, and in that sense any parent can say that to a child. The son or daughter who receives this word, would normally take it in the same way, and for love of the parents, might well pursue wisdom in order to please his parents. However, since by the inspiration of the Holy Spirit this proverb is now the Word of God, it is also saying that when one of His children pursues a wise heart, God's heart will be glad.

With that perspective, this proverb speaks to each one of us, regardless of age. Now let's look at it again. My son or daughter, whether pre-teen or post eighty, "if your heart is wise, then My heart will be glad," says God. Quantum Physics may be related to a brilliant mind, but is unrelated to a wise heart. A wise heart is one that seeks to become more like Jesus Christ, seeks to fit into the plan God has for his career, for his personal relationships, his whole life and lifestyle. A wise heart seeks to know God better and more intimately. A wise heart desires to obey God, rather than follow personal desires. Many personal desires are not intrinsically sinful, but they may really not the best that God has for us at that moment.

"My inmost being will rejoice when your lips speak what is right." This is the expression of any wise parents regarding their own children, and it is the expression of God in regard to His children as well. Speaking what is right is the overflow of a wise person's heart. Have you ever thought of asking God out for a date? Just to be together, and to get to know Him better.

Proverbs 23:17-18

"Do not let your heart envy sinners, but always be zealous for the fear of the Lord. There is surely a future hope for you, and your hope will not be cut off."

Do not let or allow your heart to envy, because it is not wise to do so. In fact, it is rather stupid. Envy can never achieve or acquire what you want, it merely immobilizes you, and makes you internally miserable. A desire may motivate you to do something to reach its goal, whereas envy won't even allow you to enjoy what you already have. It just wants what someone else has. You may have a nice new car, that is totally adequate in every way, but if you envy your neighbor who has a new luxury car, you can't enjoy either one. Envy is one of Satan's most effective tools among Christians. The person with a wise heart, seeking to know God, will learn to be content. In Hebrews 13:5 we read: "Keep your lives free from the love of money (not the use of money) and be content with what you have." God wants us to be content, and it is wise to want what God wants. So, to this 1 Timothy 6:6 adds "godliness with contentment is great gain." Contentment IS gain. We gain when we are content.

Contentment and envy cannot co-exist. So, if we opt for contentment, so that we are "always zealous for the fear of the Lord," then there is a future hope for us. A hope that will not be cut off; a hope that is certain and guaranteed! God will deliver on every promise He has ever made. God will give us what we deeply desire, and more. Even in this life He will give us the peace that comes from trusting Him to care for us and meet all of our needs according to His glorious riches in Christ Jesus. He may not give us exactly what we had hoped for or imagined in every detail, but better than that, He will give us peace, joy and contentment. He will give us a joy and happiness that is more satisfying and fulfilling than any object of envy could ever hope to achieve.

A pastor friend bought a new car that was exactly what he wanted. He enjoyed it for a brief time before it was totaled in an accident. The car was gone; his peace and joy and trust and hope remained. And the best is yet to come.

PROVERBS TO LIVE BY

Proverbs 23:19-21

"Listen, my son, and be wise, and keep your heart on the right path. Do not join those who drink too much wine or gorge themselves with too much meat, for drunkards and gluttons become poor, and drowsiness clothes them in rags."

It sometimes amazes me how often the Scriptures exhort us to listen. This is true throughout both Old and New Testaments. This chapter uses the word "listen" only twice, but the concept runs throughout. "Listening" is a learned activity, and many highly educated people have never learned the art; they may politely keep quiet while someone is speaking, and hear the sound of speech, but they have not listened.

While it is true that some people listen better than others, the reality is that probably none of us have fully mastered the art of listening. According to this text, listening, really listening is a key—if not *the* key, to wisdom. The first basic of listening is to hear. After that, listening involves understanding what is communicated, then also why it is so communicated, and then there is the appropriation or application to life. One may at times listen to what is being said, and then coming to understand it, find that the best application of this communication is to avoid it. Other times one may find that the communication is indeed good, right and worthwhile, but still not appropriate it. Full listening is when, after we understand the "rightness" of a communication we then put it into practice, obeying its teaching. Here is where the listening keeps us on the right path.

Again, Solomon's applications relate primarily to this life, which has its applications to eternity and the next life. So here drunkenness and gluttony are seen to be unwise or foolish in this life, in part because they lead to material poverty. But there is more to it. Both lead to serious health risks, which WILL crimp lifestyles in one way or another. Neither hospitalization nor incarceration due to self-destructive lifestyles, are enjoyable; nor do they point anyone else to Jesus.

Listen, and keep to the right path, for your own and for Jesus' sake. That is the wisest course.

Proverbs 23:22-23

"Listen to your father, who gave you life, and do not despise your mother when she is old. Buy the truth and do not sell it, get wisdom, discipline and understanding.

The first of these verses makes it sound like the child is still very young when he first begins to listen to his father, and that he is a mature person by the end of the verse. If that is correct, then the admonition is that it is wisdom for a person to listen his parents throughout life. Even after the parents are deceased, the wisdom of their life and words remains. In my own situation, my parents have been deceased for over half my life, and I still find wisdom as I think about certain specifics. Like all parents, mine were imperfect. Yet, when I look back, there was a "pursuit of God" that became evident even when dealing with the aftermath of an error. Like Abel, being dead they still speak. Now I have to ask myself, what wisdom am I leaving for my children to draw on after I'm gone. And you?

To children of all ages the challenge is to listen. There is wisdom in just listening. Listen and learn when your parents are right; listen and learn when they are not right. Learn what to pursue, and what not to pursue. By learning from our parents' mistakes, we will be better equipped to learn from our own.

By careful listening we are learning to sort out truth from error. Now the advice is to buy the truth. Of course, it is not literally for sale at $5.00 for a single true statement and $25.00 for a whole true concept. Rather, in our vernacular we might say "buy into truth." It is not so much buying into a particular truth, but rather buying into truth as a way of living. To accomplish that we will need to deal with truth and with error in a multitude of different settings and life situations. Jesus Christ is THE truth—we are not, but for any of us to succeed in life, we must get onto that path. The Apostle Paul wrote "Follow my example as I follow Christ's example," 1 Corinthians 11:1. Many of us feel ourselves too inadequate to make such a statement, but unless we are at least on that path, we are failing our children.

Young people, get wisdom, discipline and understanding at all costs. It is the wise thing to do.

"The father of a righteous man has great joy; he who has a wise son delights in him. May your father and mother be glad; may she who gave you birth rejoice."

In yesterday's proverb we had a young child beginning to learn to listen to his father. Apparently, he learned well, because in the very next verse he has grown to become a righteous man, the joy of his father's heart. He is now a righteous man because he has become a wise man. This speaks to me of consistency. My Webster dictionary says of consistency that it is a "firmness of constitution or character." In the context of learning and pursuing wisdom and righteousness, this would mean doing a thing because it is right, not because it is convenient.

To the parent trying to instill principles of right and wrong, this takes a great deal of patience and seeking the Lord for personal wisdom and insight. Then when the child seems to begin to put into practice what he has learned, it will take truckloads of praise and encouragement to keep him "on the right path." Every child wants to please his parents, so each indication of accomplishment will serve as motivation to keep on the path. As the old hymn puts it: "each victory will help you some other to win." The pleasure the child finds in pleasing his parents is only equaled by the joy in the heart of the parent who sees the child become a righteous young adult. This whole process is a team effort, with the parent bearing the leadership responsibility. When eventually the grandfather sits in his rocking chair and observes the grandchildren teaching their offspring, his heart will almost explode with joy.

In verse 4 of his 3rd letter, the Apostle John said "I have no greater joy than to hear that my children are walking in truth." My experience after pastoring several churches fully agrees with that, and that joy is doubled when those spiritual children are also your biological children. Not everyone can pastor a church, but every parent can pastor his own family, his own children. The reward is great with joy inexpressible and full of glory.

PROVERBS TO LIVE BY

Proverbs 23:26-28

"My son, give me your heart and let your eyes keep to my ways, for a prostitute is a deep pit and a wayward wife is a narrow well. Like a bandit she lies in wait, and multiplies the unfaithful among men."

Initially this is the request of an earthly father to his natural born son. At a deeper level of course, it is the request of the heavenly Father to his earth-bound children. Both are valid. Let's look first at the natural parental level.

The father does not literally ask the young child to "give me your heart;" instead he might say let me show you how to do that, let me help you make that choice, let me explain why that would be dangerous etc. He is teaching the young child wisdom; he is showing how to keep on the right ways. As the father teaches basic concepts, and the child learns to trust the father's love and care, the foundation is being laid for that trust to be transferred to the heavenly Father.

The warning here, as earlier in Proverbs, is aimed directly at young men and refers specifically to "a prostitute," but includes all forms of sexual impurity and includes men and women of all ages. The consequences of such behavior are terribly destructive, and the writer says in effect "give me your heart" and let me guide you through this temptation. If indulged, this not only tears apart marriages and families, but is personally destructive to everyone who yields to it. This sin, more than many others, very quickly binds the offender with chains so powerful that he cannot extricate himself. Such a person has no inner peace, see Isaiah 48:22. There is forgiveness and deliverance ONLY by the grace of God given through Jesus Christ, but the consequences may remain for a lifetime.

The warning therefore is, avoid it—don't ever "try it just once." And the way to avoid prostitutes and all sexual immorality is with a large measure of self-control. "Self-control" is the concluding facet of the nine-part fruit of the Holy Spirit as found in Galatians 5:22-23, which begins with love. Such fruit is never the result of pure determination, but is produced in the believer by the Holy Spirit.

PROVERBS TO LIVE BY
Proverbs 23:29-30

"Who has woe? Who has sorrow? Who has strife? Who has complaints? Who has needless bruises? Who has bloodshot eyes? Those who linger over wine, who go to sample bowls of mixed wine."

This proverb begins with six rhetorical questions. The Moody Bible Commentary calls them "interrogatory riddles." However, these riddles are easily answered by people who have been there. An acquaintance of mine worked in a jail system in Canada, and his assignment was watching over about 30 prisoners who were alcoholics, some with called "Delirium Tremens." This may not have been an accurate diagnosis, but neither was it a medical treatment center. My friend told me one day that he understood what these men were going through because he "had been there." Alcoholism can take one there. (You should really read verses 29-35.)

Our text is a warning regarding the potential results of misguided behavior and unwise decisions. The six "who" questions have a single answer: "Those who linger over wine, who go to sample bowls of mixed wine". This text does not forbid any and all drinking of wine but it does give a strong warning against drunkenness, which can lead to alcoholism. No one can take a second drink until he has had a first. So, the problem is not simply taking a drink of wine but rather an over-indulgence in it. Our text mentions "lingering over wine," and sampling all sorts of wine and mixed drinks. It seems to basically boil down to the matters of motivation and self-control. For some of us, this may mean total abstinence.

The Apostle Paul's spiritual understanding came from his study and knowledge of Old Testament Scriptures. On top of that foundation, the Lord Himself taught him. To a carnal church Paul wrote "Everything is permissible for me—but not everything is beneficial." Before illustrating that point, he concludes the thought with "I will not be mastered by anything." 1 Corinthians 6:12. He knew what was right and wise and good, and he refused to deviate from that. The self-control required to keep us from getting into trouble on this, and other issues, is a work of the Holy Spirit. The fruit of the Holy Spirit is, in part, self-control. Where do you need self-control?

Proverbs 24:3-4

"By wisdom a house is built, and through understanding it is established; through knowledge its rooms are filled with rare and beautiful treasures."

The first 2 verses of this chapter are a warning against envy, especially when the person is deceitful and wishes to take advantage of his new would-be friends. What one might have gained from such a relationship is really better obtained through wisdom as is found in our text, verses 3-4.

The picture is that of a literal house being built and furnished through wisdom. That of course is literally true; it takes wisdom to produce the wealth required to build and furnish a nice place. The deeper implication of this picture, however, is the building up of a life. One may have envied the apparent success of another, not realizing that what he had was at best a façade. In the case of a literal house, it may be mortgaged way above actual value, or worse, obtained through dishonest means. That might not make the house or its treasures any less elegant, but it would nullify the enjoyment of what has been built or established.

Fanny Crosby wrote a song whose refrain echoes: *"We are building day by day, As the moments glide away, Our temple which the world may not see; Every moment won by grace, Will be sure to find a place, In our building for eternity."* Our text is focused on this life. We are doing the daily building right now, as the moments glide away; building at our work and at our play; and yes, building for eternity. It is only through wisdom and knowledge that our building is progressing toward being a truly beautiful life—filled with rare and beautiful treasures. Let's not be too concerned about how wisely and well anyone else is building, much less envy them. Rather, let's each one pay attention to our own building. A life well-built is a rare and beautiful thing to enjoy down here first of all, and then on into eternity.

Some of the rare and beautiful treasures to fill such a house are: love, joy peace patience, kindness, goodness, faithfulness, gentleness, and self-control, Galatians 5:22-23. That is what others long to see, and it is what the Lord desires to produce in each one of us.

Proverbs 24:5-6

"A wise man has great power, and a man of knowledge increases strength; for waging war you need guidance, and for victory many advisers."

We are familiar with the saying wisdom comes with age. That dates back to at least as far as Job; in chapter 12 and verse 12 the question comes "is not wisdom found among the aged?' That is not to say that every old person is wise; simply that it takes a lifetime to gain wisdom. Our text tells us a wise man has great power and knowledge increases strength. But isn't this something of a contradiction? And if not, what is it really saying?

When I was very young, I knew that my father was the wisest man in the world, even though I did not know what wisdom was. (He was also the strongest.) As I got a little older, I was not so sure, and before too long, I knew that I was wiser than my father. It really did not take too much longer before I realized this was not so at all. In a small measure I began to realize that wisdom does indeed come with age; I had simply been too unwise and immature to understand that. OK, so wisdom comes with age. Now we are confronted with the idea that with wisdom comes great power and increased strength. How can that be?

As we age, some people try with increasing effort but with decreasing success and zeal, to maintain the image of being youthful and virile. It doesn't take too long however, before the phrase "I'm not as young as I used to be" creeps into their vocabulary. That simply means they are no longer capable to do what they once did; they just don't have the strength. So, in practice, indeed wisdom ***comes*** with age, but physical strength and power ***leaves*** with age. There must be more than one kind of power and strength. The text continues that for waging war and obtaining victory one needs guidance and advice.

We are constantly at war over the control of our heart and mind. It takes the wisdom provided by God, appropriated by faith and obedience, for victory to be achieved. It takes the power of wisdom and the strength of knowledge to tap into the correct power source.

Proverbs 24:7

"Wisdom is too high for a fool; in the assembly at the gate he has nothing to say."

In communication we must seek to "put the cookies, or the gems and nuggets, on the lower shelf" so that everyone will be able to reach them. But that is too lofty an idea for the fool. He can't reach that level, so he tries to sound and seem wise by trying to impress. The fool is often the one who has something to say about everything, whether it is sports, business, politics, church or anything else. Our text says the fool will have nothing to say in the assembly at the gate, but that need not keep him from talking.

Let's look first at the phrase "at the gate." In ancient times that referred to the place where policies and practices were formulated, where judicial and governmental decisions were reached. Think of Boaz in the book of Ruth. That is where contractual and testamentary agreements were negotiated. At the gate involved the city officials, both as judges and as qualified witnesses as the needs arose. The fool has nothing to say in such circles although again, he may not always see it that way. We can talk about a Jack-of-all-trades, but no one is sufficiently knowledgeable and therefore wise enough in all area of life so as to speak authoritatively about each.

The Apostle James, in 1:19, tells us by inspiration of the Holy Spirit everyone should be quick to listen and slow to speak. The wise tend to follow that advice; the foolish tend not to. As a new member I recall my first meeting with the board of governors of a Christian University. I may have asked a few questions, but mostly I remember just listening. I also remember not all newcomers to the board taking that approach, and so those people did not remain on the board for long.

While listening is essential when entering a new or unknown environment, the advice of James is applicable in every relational contact. For some this may be a more difficult lesson to learn than it is for others, probably none of us ever learn and practice it to perfection. Please join me in the quest for increasing wisdom, simply by becoming better listeners.

PROVERBS TO LIVE BY

Proverbs 24:8-9

"He who plots evil will be known as a schemer. The schemes of folly are sin, and men detest a mocker."

The statement is pretty clear: he who plots evil . . . But who would want to plot evil? Maybe no one in individual comes to your mind, so think about *what kind* of a person would plot evil. Did you think criminals in general, or, to be more specific, perhaps bank- robbers. Perhaps you thought about politicians in general, or some other segment of society in whom you have little, if any, trust. Some may have thought about an individual who at some point wronged you or your reputation. Hmmm. Maybe evil scheming is more common than we would have guessed. So back to the opening question; who would want to?

May I suggest the answer is people, people who are born with a sin-nature and even as redeemed children of God are still prone to sin. That of course makes it all inclusive. Not that everyone necessarily plots evil, but the ones who do are people like you and me. So, before any of us cast a judgmental stone, let's take a closer look. Plotting to defraud or defame someone to their hurt or for personal gain is evil, but how does that differ from planning to shade the truth a little for our personal advantage? Are we not all guilty of a certain amount of scheming now and then?

Our text says the schemes of folly are sin. That does not mean the scheming is foolish, as in scheming that is ridiculous and could never succeed. The scheme itself may be brilliant. If it is foolish it is because it is morally or ethically not good; it is in some way not Christ-honoring. Such scheming deviates from absolute integrity. Now, it that includes you, then Solomon, or the Holy Spirit through Solomon, is speaking to you. Then this text is for you. And me!

In 1 Peter 2:12 we are admonished to "live such good lives among the pagans that, though they accuse you of doing wrong, they may see your good deeds and glorify God." We live in a society that is seemingly becoming more and more pagan all the time. The Bible tells us this will be so as we get closer to the Lord's return, but to what extent are our private lives pointing in one direction or the other? Probably much more than we think!

Proverbs 24:10

"If you falter in times of trouble, how small is your strength."

There may be different ways of saying the same thing. This text is pretty blunt. It does not allow for any extenuating circumstance or excuses. If you tell a 9 or 10 year-old boy that that his strength is pretty small, that is one of the greatest insults. Of course, he is strong; just ask him. Just because he can't beat up a 12 year-old bully, doesn't prove anything; the kid is older and bigger. To a kid strength is purely a physical thing, and unless he is the bully, he tends to compare himself with his peers. But of course, our text is not talking about a purely physical matter. Being that we are in Proverbs, the reference is to strength of character.

In the course of life, there are times when probably all of us feel like just giving up. Some are more prone to this than others. Since I am one who frequently faces this along the way, I ask myself why. If you ever falter, or stumble; if you ever feel like quitting or giving up, ask yourself why that is. Better yet, ask the Lord. If the answer were simple and easy, we wouldn't have that problem. Well, the answer is simply, it just is not easy.

First of all consider the biggest bully. He is bigger and stronger than anyone of us, and he wants to make any of us and all of us fall. Ephesians tells us we do not wrestle against flesh and blood, but against principalities and powers of this dark world. The troubles and trials we encounter, if not caused by our spiritual enemy, they are nevertheless used very effectively by him to derail us. Of course, we know that "greater is He that is in you than he that is in the world." The part we are most prone to forget is that He is **IN** us. We seem to think that "this is a problem I have to resolve." Not so! It is a problem that the Holy Spirit and I **together** have to resolve. And when we take that approach and do it His way, then the words of James 1:2-4: "The testing of your faith develops perseverance. Perseverance must finish its work (don't give up) so that you may be mature and complete, not lacking anything" (including strength) will become true in our lives and our strength increases with each trouble we encounter. God allows trials and troubles of many kinds to come into our lives so we can learn to depend on His strength.

PROVERBS TO LIVE BY

Proverbs 24:11-12

"Rescue those being led away to death; hold back those staggering toward slaughter. If you say, 'But we knew nothing about this,' does not he who weighs the heart perceive it?"

The thought of this text proceeds from the previous, concerning the lack of strength. Perhaps bodily strength could at times be included, but more significantly this refers to a lack of strength of character. A fairly precise picture of this can be seen in the case of the Holocaust during the previous century. In both the previous and current centuries, the slaughter of pre-born children is a very poignant application of the principle expounded here. Many of us are convinced that *some*body ought to do *some*thing, but we are very uncertain what, if anything, we can do about it ourselves. It is quite easy to find things we cannot do either legally and morally. Positive solutions are harder to come by, and besides, no single plan of action will apply equally and universally to everyone. So, besides prayer, which we all can and should do, what else can we do?

OK, let's answer the question with a question. What needs are there in your community, not only regarding abortion mills, but other kinds of wrongs being done to people? I can almost hear someone say "I don't know." Then let me ask, why not? Perhaps some of us are too cloistered in our own comfort zones. We need to become aware, and that means a lot of listening, along with a few probing questions. Perhaps "not knowing" may ease our guilt feelings a little, but consider our text: when we know "nothing about this, does not He who weighs the heart perceive it?"

Truth be told, each of us could fairly quickly make a lengthy list of things that ought to be changed, stopped or re-directed right in our own area or community. The real problem may just be that we lack the "strength of character" to get involved. However, if we simply fail to investigate or pursue the matter, then we rightly can "know nothing about it." The wise persons will at least deliberately become cognizant of needs, and perhaps of some efforts to do something. That in turn could lead to some involvement. Just because no one can do everything, maybe a few more of us could do something.

Proverbs 24:13-14

"Eat honey, my son, for it is good; honey from the comb is sweet to your taste. Know also that wisdom is sweet to your soul; If you find it, there is a future hope for you, and your hope will not be cut off."

I don't know of anyone who does not like the taste of honey. If there are people like that, they are probably a small minority, and always have been. In addition to the taste however, honey was considered to have medicinal value. So, the writer, without fear of contradiction, says it is good. Honey is also the only food that does not spoil with age, even without refrigeration. However, no matter the intrinsic value of honey, be it nourishment or medicine, in order to benefit from it, it must be ingested. To live without honey is to live without its benefits. Our text compares honey with wisdom.

According to our text, wisdom is sweet to the soul. Just like honey, however, its primary or initial benefit goes to the one who ingests it. Others will reap secondary benefits, no doubt but the person who is wise is enabled to live life with greater peace and joy; he is enabled to avoid pitfalls and foolish mistakes. That agrees with the whole theme of wisdom in Proverbs. The teaching on wisdom is to enable us to navigate our course of life—in this life on earth. Our army slogan is: "be all that you can be in the army." We can restate that as our slogan for Proverbs and say "be all that you can be in wisdom."

Our text continues: "if you find it, there is a future hope for you, and your hope (or that hope) will not be cut off." When you eat honey for nourishment, the taste is almost just an added benefit; sooner or later you will be hungry again. Not so with wisdom. Wisdom, once obtained and ingested, will be there for you tomorrow, and future tomorrows. By regular usage it will just continue to increase to your own success in life. That is why as early as 4:7 in Proverbs, we read "Wisdom is supreme, therefore get wisdom. Though it cost all you have, get understanding." "Your hope will not be cut off." Solomon wrote it, but God said it. Not only the ultimate acquisition of wisdom, but also the processes and the pursuit of wisdom is better than the taste of honey. Let's continue the pursuit, for in due season we will reap the harvest.

PROVERBS TO LIVE BY

Proverbs 24:15-16

"Do not lie in wait like an outlaw against a righteous man's house, do not raid his dwelling place; for though a righteous man falls seven times, he rises again, but the wicked are brought down by calamity.

The action indicated in this text is not restricted to armed robbery, though that would be included. Nor is the text suggesting that the reader of these words is an outlaw, for whom this might be standard procedure. Look at it again. It is saying don't act like an outlaw, thinking you can get away with it. You can't. Of course, don't be one rather. All right, then how could someone act like an outlaw if there is no thievery intended? Glad you asked. Although thievery may be indicated here, the broader implication could be that of taking unfair advantage. Period!

I'm quite sure that relatively few among those classed as "righteous" would go out and deliberately steal from another, although that is certainly possible. However, taking unfair advantage is quite another matter. I remember as a fourth grader trying to take unfair advantage of a class-mate who had not been listening to instructions. It backfired. But what about more recently? And for what purpose? It could be for personal gain in some way, and it could be simply to teach the other person a lesson.

Notice also that in the same sentence there is clear indication that the "righteous" do fall or fail. We are not immune to any particular kind of failure. Nor is anyone necessarily guilty of every kind of failure. That gives no one the right to "cast stones." But there is a difference. The righteous man may fall seven times. (Have you counted? It could also be more than seven times.) You may think he did that to me without any provocation. True! And what did you do to yourself or to someone else without any provocation?

Even though a "righteous" person falls many times in his primary area of weakness, yet, by the grace of God, he rises again. Our focus needs to be constantly re-directed back to God's redemptive grace and the indwelling Holy Spirit. He will pick us up again. Jesus said even seventy-seven times a day. Unlike the wicked, we are not ultimately "brought down." Failure is not final.

PROVERBS TO LIVE BY

Proverbs 24:17-18

Do not gloat when your enemy falls; when he stumbles,
do not let your heart rejoice, for the Lord will see and
disapprove and turn his wrath away from him."

These verses proceed from the previous, and merely broaden the insights and application. Unlike the teachings of some religions, we will never become gods; neither in this life nor in eternity. We cannot fully comprehend how God can love a specific sinner like He does, and simultaneously punish or "bring him down." This text tells me that God does not "gloat" when someone gets caught up in the aftermath of his own wrongdoing. All actions have consequences, both for the wicked and the righteous. Therefore, the attitude of glee when someone gets "a taste of his own medicine" is very dangerous territory, even though such an attitude is very prevalent.

We are all familiar with the concept of loving the sinner and hating the sin. We merely find we cannot consistently implement it. We may, and in some circumstances should, rejoice when justice is meted out, but our text clearly states "do not gloat when your enemy falls." A jail sentence may be imposed for a crime, and the guilty person be sentenced to serve in a "correctional institution." In theory, the purpose is to correct wrong behavior or lifestyle. With God, correction is always the goal. He is not willing that any should perish. So, any self-righteous attitude of "serves him right" on our part is dangerous. It may even interfere with, or oppose God's correctional purpose. Yet that is precisely the human tendency. Consciously or otherwise, it gives us a sense of superiority.

See the text, "The Lord will see and disapprove and turn his wrath away from them." Whoa!! Turn His wrath away from the person under discipline to whom, to the gloater? Read is again. That may be precisely what it means. We need to make very sure we do not rejoice in another's calamity in a self-righteous manner. Rejoice in that he is in God's hands? fine. Rejoice that another is finally getting what he deserves? Never! Such an attitude is beyond our pay-grade. God always looks and sees deeper than any outward appearances or verbiage; He looks at the attitudes and intents of the heart.

PROVERBS TO LIVE BY

Proverbs 24:19-20

"Do not fret because of evil men or be envious of the wicked, for the evil man has no future hope, and the lamp of the wicked will be snuffed out."

In the previous section we looked at our attitudes when God delivers justice and correction. Generally, we want God to administer justice to others, especially if they have wronged us personally in some way, but we want mercy for ourselves when we have done wrong. Hopefully we are at least learning to trust Him to help us have a right attitude toward offenders. Today we look at the opposite side of the coin. Someone has done something evil and wicked, and he seems to be getting away with it; God is not doing anything. That is so frustrating. We have waited and waited, perhaps for a whole week, and there is still no sign of justice on the horizon.

Here is where our text comes into play. Of course, we know that God is Sovereign, and He will do what is right and good. We know that, but we just don't quite believe it. It is really amazing how many things we know in our heads, but don't truly believe in our hearts. When God tells us to "relax, I've got it all under control," we would not think of saying "no You don't, this person is absolutely getting away with it." We wouldn't say it, but if our actions and attitudes of fretting and fuming mean anything, we often do not believe it what we think we know. But God is still so good. He knows what we feel, and He patiently says it again, "relax, I've got it all under control."

Today's text is for just such occasions. I know we can't see things from God's perspective, but let's try to see the bigger picture. All the wicked man has is the here and now, without any hope of a better tomorrow. He has no future hope. We do. In fact, many of us have had experiences that cause us to say something like "I don't know how I could have possibly made it without the Lord." That is true, but it relates only to the immediate. Most of us have heard Joni Erickson Tada speak to the matter. We can't see how she made it either, but her main hope is not to get out of that wheel-chair, but see her Lord. He is our hope, and all else is of lesser importance. "The lamp of the wicked will be snuffed out," so there really is nothing to envy or to make us fret.

PROVERBS TO LIVE BY

Proverbs 24:21-22

"Fear the Lord and the king, my son, and do not join with the rebellious, for those two will send sudden destruction upon them, and who knows what calamities they can bring."

When fearing the Lord and fearing the king are bundled together like this, we have the opportunity to take a fresh look Fear itself is either good or bad depending on the object of that fear. Scriptures give both warnings against fear of man, and instruction to fear as in our text.

To fear the Lord is to honor, obey, be in awe of, and worship Him. He is the Sovereign God of creation. To fear the king, or in our culture a Constitutional Republic or some other form of government, is very much the same thing—to a point. Certainly, the worship aspect must be missing in fearing the king; we worship only God. To honor, obey, and to be in awe however, is a fairly close parallel between the fear of God and the fear of the earthly authority.

The thrust of our text is to guide us into living law-abiding, exemplary lives. We could say the instruction is to "fear God" so you don't have to be afraid of Him; "fear the king" so you don't have to be afraid of him either. Also, fear the law so you don't have to be afraid of the enforcers of the law, both divine and human.

The warning of the text is against rebellion and its consequences. It is dangerous to rebel against authority—again either divine or human. Even if you are not the one who pulls the trigger or the one who drives the get-away car, it is dangerous to "hang out" with that kind of company. Both God and the law of the land can bring sudden destruction. In reality, we may often bring sudden destruction upon ourselves, or at least subject ourselves to it. This is perhaps most clearly seen in cases of extreme criminality, but is not morally different from deliberate minor infractions of the law. I have often wondered, what *really* is a little white lie? It is easy to find an acceptable definition, and besides, who cares anyway! Is this or that OK as long as no one gets hurt? "Who knows what calamities they can bring." This text does not provide a list of dos and don'ts, it merely issues a warning. The wise will take heed and figure it out.

PROVERBS TO LIVE BY

Proverbs 24:23-25

"These are also sayings of the wise: To show partiality in judging is not good: Whoever says to the guilty, 'You are innocent!' –people will curse him and nations will denounce him."

The remainder of this chapter has further proverbs that Solomon did not compose, but rather adopted and/or adapted. Since he was guided (inspired) by the Holy Spirit to include these, they are equally the inspired Word of God to us.

The initial application of this proverb is to the highest levels of government. The divine principle however is clearly for each one of us. Yet this negative perspective is exactly what we see happening across the whole spectrum of our society. Rules are being selectively interpreted for the benefit of some and to the detriment of others. This is happening in all sectors of society from education and family life to governmental and leadership bureaucracy. In fact, every type of social interaction is susceptible to the same temptation. An old, wise saying (our text) is: "that is not good," it is not wise, it is not smart, you won't get away with that.

But what does it mean to "show partiality in judging?" It simply means basic and complete honesty. That is by no means restricted to the court system. Of course, when the courts declare the guilty to be innocent, people will curse the judge and/or the lawyers and probably pretty soon the whole legal system. When it happens in the highest levels of government, nations will denounce them. Pretty soon nobody will trust anybody. Have we come to that point in our country? Some would say yes. Cursing and denouncing may indeed happen and is happening, but that won't solve the problem. What are we to do?

Whatever else we can do and maybe should do we have to begin with some introspection. And since we tend to be rather myopic in self-examination, we need to pray with the Psalmist in 139:23-24: "Search me, O God, and know my heart; test me and know my anxious thoughts. See if there is any offensive way in me and lead me in the way everlasting." Wise people do that, because they know they are imperfect, and as such are susceptible to dishonesty. When have you last had a complete spiritual check-up?

PROVERBS TO LIVE BY

Proverbs 24:25-26

"But it will go well with those who convict the guilty,
and rich blessing will come upon them. An honest
answer is like a kiss on the lips."

Obviously, verses 23-26 belong together, but we are considering them in two segments, first the negative (yesterday) and then this, the positive. While the negative lowers standards, changes standards and that ultimately eliminates standards, thereby bringing chaos and tyranny, today's text says "it will go well with those who convict the guilty," those who maintain that right is right and wrong is wrong.

Since there are no perfect people there can obviously be no perfect nations. Even our claim that "America is still the best country in the world" is open to question at the present time. What is not in question is that "it will go well with those who convict the guilty and rich blessings will come upon them." God said so! That being said, it is therefore incumbent on those of us who name the name of Christ to repent of our personal and national sins, and then return to and maintain biblical standards of right and wrong. The only way we can return the nation back is to turn back ourselves. In fact, that is the meaning of the word repent. It is like my GPS says when I have missed following its direction: "make a U-Turn."

Each one of us who individually makes the necessary U-Turn will experience the Lord's "rich blessings." It will go well with him. It will go well with each such family, each such church. That is the way God operates. A church I once pastored had made a bad mistake and brought shame to their Christian profession. In calling the church to repent, the elders came to kneel at the altar on Sunday morning as we prayed for forgiveness and committed ourselves to repentance. Those elders who brazenly claimed they had no need to repent soon left the church by their own choice.

If we want our nation to return to godly and biblical standards it is up to us to lead the way. "If my people, who are called by my name, will humble themselves and pray and seek my face and turn from their wicked ways . . ." says 2 Chronicles 7:14. Such turning must be done individually before it can be done corporately.

PROVERBS TO LIVE BY

Proverbs 24:28-29

"Do not testify against your neighbor without cause,
or use your lips to deceive. Do not say, 'I'll do to his as
he has done to me; I'll pay him back for what he did."

Probably every one of us experiences wrongs done to us by others. Sometimes these wrongs are real, at other times they are simply perceived. How often do we find ourselves truly seeking to understand the whole thing from the perspective of the other person before coming to a conclusion? Let's face it, too often we get our exercise just from jumping to conclusions. When that happens, we have most likely come to the wrong conclusion— in whole or in part. When that happens, we are subjecting ourselves to a situation such as presented in today's text.

It is probably best to take verse 29 as flowing from or out of verse 28, rather than as being two separate or independent issues. We begin with a caution, "do not testify against your neighbor without cause." This could certainly happen in a legal court case, but would much more often indicate internal accusations. Long before you might enter a court of law to give testimony this has already been done internally, and probably been discussed with a sympathetic ear of someone else. A person or an organization may have done what you perceive as a wrong, unless you are very careful you will probably build a case –a vengeful case, against him/ it. This can quickly grow into something rather major. Our text says do not use your lips to deceive. If you build a mental case against someone, and then discuss it with others to build a base of support, it is a natural step of progression to plan payback. Many a "church fight" has begun just like that.

Justification comes easily and logically. We have several different sayings to make this appear like acceptable behavior, such as: I'm just giving him a taste of his own medicine, what comes around goes around, I don't get mad, I just get even, he asked for it, and the list could go on. And it all begins in the mind. A prominent minister of a few decades ago was slandered for owning two Cadillac's, when actually he had two cataracts. He did not own a car at all. Let's make sure we know what we are talking about.

PROVERBS TO LIVE BY

Proverbs 24:30-32

"I went past the field of the sluggard, past the vineyard of the man who lacks judgment; thorns had come up everywhere, the ground was covered with weeds, and the stone wall was in ruins. I applied my heart to what I observed and learned a lesson from what I saw."
Please read the next 2 verses as well.

Some of us grew up on a farm, though we probably did not have a vineyard, but either way, our agricultural setting differed significantly from that of Israel 3,000 years ago. So, what lessons are we to learn? Certainly not agriculture! Diligence and the value of hard work, yes, but not primarily. We already learned some of that in chapter six. This text also shows us that we need to be observant and learn from other people's actions and mistakes as well as our own. There is always more to learn in that department. But let's look in a slightly different direction.

Instead of focusing on the obvious and the plainly visible aspects of the text, let us look for life-lessons in the spiritual realm. Let us look for these not only in today's text, but also in our own observations of people and life around us. For example, is there someone in your family or circle of friends and acquaintances who is a bit different? Perhaps he is overly aggressive, or maybe kind of lazy or lethargic. Consider! How does that seem to be working out for them? Does that seem to enhance or diminish their spiritual walk? Ask yourself if perhaps others see you that way. Solomon said he learned a personal lesson from what he saw. In the context of Proverbs that means he learned wisdom for personal living. Observing other people and conditions may cause you to consider changing your standards to line up with theirs. That could be either wise, or foolish and downright dangerous. Each one must make his own decisions and choices.

In all such observation, let us never fall into the trap of carelessness. "Whatever" is a good word, but not in this context. We must not interfere with other people's affairs good or bad, but if we are wise, we will learn from what we observe. Observation is the key to learning miniature life lessons.

PROVERBS TO LIVE BY

Proverbs 25:2-3

"It is the glory of God to conceal a matter; to search out a matter is the glory of kings. As the heavens are high and the earth is deep, so the hearts of kings are unsearchable."

In the same sentence, this text asserts that both God and earthly kings have glory. Not to the same degree by any means, but glory nonetheless. In the case of God, the heavens, and all creation, declare His glory. Most of creation is concealed to human minds and understanding, but we are slowly learning—a little. The glory of kings is to "search out a matter," not their political power. In fact, political power is often very inglorious. In the West we have very few "kingdoms" or "monarchies," and even England's is a constitutional monarchy. In the West we mostly have elected governments with Presidents or Prime Ministers as heads of government. So, where do we look for the glory our text ascribes to kings? In principle that remains unchanged, it is the glory of the rulers or heads of state, not to impose, but to search out. So again, it is not their political power, it is "searching out a matter." To re-phrase that, it is in providing honest and honorable leadership in searching out a matter. We could call that finding solutions to problems.

New Testament believers are told to submit to every authority instituted among men and to fear God and honor the king or the instituted authorities, 1 Peter 2:13-17. When we have good leaders, it is easier to be good followers. When leaders are not good, we can campaign for and promote change, but within the confines of what is legal, moral, and Christian. We can criticize bad policies and decisions, but we must be very careful to distinguish between the person and the policies. None of us needs to look very long and hard to find where we too made bad decisions. In many a Christian gathering where politics is discussed there are some very unchristian things said about certain leaders. Not only have I seen and heard it, too often I have also participated.

When we properly honor God and those in authority over us, we glorify Him and them. He has ultimate authority; they have delegated authority. Their authority can be challenged, His we must simply obey.

Proverbs 25:4-5

"Remove the dross from the silver, and out comes material for the silver smith; remove the wicked from the king's presence, and his throne will be established through righteousness."

This is an easy to understand proverb, but let's not pass over it too quickly. For some of us, the first thought is that we would like to remove a whole bunch of wicked from positions of authority and reclaim our country. Just wishing and talking alone won't do it, and neither will legislating protective laws or even engaging in physical battle. Armchair quarterbacks can usually out-perform the playing quarterback, as well as the coach. But armchair athletes never win any games; neither do they lose any because they don't literally get involved. This proverb does indeed speak God's truth, and provides a workable solution. It does not, however, provide us a battle plan for national or even state-wide implementation.

The enemy of our souls also understands this principle, and he is at work to remove the righteous from the mix and thus establish his own diabolical end-goal. According to some statistics, globally a Christian is martyred just for being a Christian every 5 to 6 minutes. The United States and Canada are not at that stage, but we are on a fast track to catch up. So how do WE overcome THEM? We don't! God has, however, given us a foolproof battle plan. In fact, He gave that plan to King Solomon in 2Chronicles 7:14: *If my people,* (that is you and I) who are called by my name, *will humble themselves and pray and seek my face and turn from their wicked ways* (removing the dross from our own lives) *THEN will I hear from heaven and will forgive their sin and will heal their land.* Before we say that is too simplistic or too slow a process, perhaps we should try it. The part about turning from our own wickedness? that would be removing the dross.

PROVERBS TO LIVE BY

Proverbs 25:6-7

"Do not exalt yourself in the king's presence, and do not claim a place among great men; It is better for him to say to you 'Come up here,' than for him to humiliate you before a nobleman."

Most of us have probably been in a setting where this principle of pride was on display. Jesus talked about such a scenario in Luke 14:1-14. He had been invited to a meal "in the house of a prominent Pharisee." He noticed how the guests picked places of honor for themselves and then gave a teaching on humility. He might well have had our text in mind. Surely, we all know that whoever exalts himself will be humbled (or even humiliated) and he who humbles himself will be exalted. Yet we often try to hurry the exaltation process to our own detriment or embarrassment. In Bible College there was a saying "the way up is down." That could apply in several ways. Those who want to be recognized as good or competent preachers and Bible study leaders need to spend more time praying than they do primping.

Have you ever noticed how some rather ordinary people like us, tend to inform others of all the famous, important people they have met? Some have made it an art form to get to meet the guest speaker.

I have noticed that meeting a rich person does not make one rich, meeting a political leader neither makes one a politician nor a leader, meeting a famous scientist neither makes one a scientist nor famous. In Jeremiah 9:24 we read "let him who boasts boast about this: that he understands and knows me, that I am the Lord, who exercises kindness." Perhaps, if you watch for it, you may find an opportunity today to boast about the Lord a little. You will find that exalting Him is much more satisfying and gratifying than exalting yourself. And if He wants to exalt you, He can do that far better than you could ever hope to do it for yourself.

John the Baptist had it right when he said of the Lord Jesus "He must increase, I must decrease." John never said he was insignificant or worthless. He simply had our modern-day army slogan right: Be all that you can be— for Jesus. He is all in all. Then let Him exalt you as highly as He chooses.

Proverbs 25:11-12

"A word aptly spoken is like apples of gold in settings of silver, like an earring of gold or an ornament of fine gold is a wise man's rebuke to a listening ear."

Two questions come to mind immediately, what is a word aptly spoken and what is a wise man's rebuke. The way they are paired together here would tell us they are basically the same thing. The words of a wise person seem always to perfectly fit the need. That is what is meant by their comparison to apples of gold, and the settings of silver would indicate they are spoken in just the right circumstances. A good or right word spoken at the wrong time may indeed be right, but it loses its value when it is drowned out by other noises and considerations.

Have you ever been in a group where a discussion is going on, when at some point you have just the right words to add, but too quickly the discussion takes a turn and your words are no longer needed? When that happens, don't force it. Your words may still be like apples of gold, if people would just give you a chance to speak them, but the setting of silver is gone. If you've ever observed someone coming in and belatedly adding his 2 cents worth, you know that the add-on fell flat, it did not really add anything. The wise person will soon learn that his "wisdom" is not essential in every situation. At times a word aptly left unspoken become like a rare diamond.

The wise man's rebuke is just another facet of his wise speech. In the course of life, rebukes are absolutely essential at times. We all need them. Often, we may think of rebukes as being negative, and they can be, but when given and heeded by wise people they are more likely to be very positive indeed. The Bible does not merely have a few choice selections of rebukes. All Scripture is given by inspiration of God and is profitable for . . . rebuke. At times a rebuke may be just a warning, possibly with some consequences enumerated. A wise person's rebuke is intended to correct or avoid wrong behavior and actions. Heeding a wise person's rebuke tends to make us wiser in turn.

Proverbs 25:13-14

"Like the coolness of snow at harvest time is a trustworthy messenger to those who send him; he refreshes the spirit of his masters. Like clouds and wind without rain is a man who boasts of gifts he does not give."

No farmer wants snow during wheat harvest, and that is not what this verse is saying. This is talking about something refreshing arriving in a time of heat and exhaustion. Farmers in Solomon's time did not have air-conditioned tractor and combine cabs. Picture a hot, cloudless day without a breath of air blowing, temperatures in the nineties even before lunch, all the dust seemingly settling right on the field worker and you still have most of the day ahead of you. That is pretty much a perfect prescription for absolute misery. He is enduring all that only because of the future value of the harvest.

Into that scene arrives a messenger with some great news. Remember, there are no radios or newspapers in existence, so all news has to be personally delivered. This particular piece of news may have been that the price of wheat has just gone up 10 cents a bushel. Wow!! That's as good as a cool breeze into the midst of the heat and dust. "For that I'll gladly continue harvesting right up until dark." Now, at this point you need to know that this "news" is not some kind of a sick joke; it had better be reliable. Next verse.

Different scene, same subject! We are still talking about trustworthy and reliable communication. The clouds and wind without rain keep us in the agrarian culture, but now transfer the issue to a church business meeting. A serious financial need has come up and there's not enough in the building fund to cover it. After an appropriate time of discussion, it is decided to ask the membership for a one-time pledge offering. After the pledges have all been counted, they are still $5,000 short. One member gets up and promises to add that amount to his pledge. That promise is no good unless there is follow through. Promises alone do not pay bills.

Now switch to any subject, anywhere, and you are the one to bring the news. If there is a drought you need rain, not just clouds and wind. What actually is your contribution bringing to the table? How reliable is your promise of action? Only you and God know.

PROVERBS TO LIVE BY

Proverbs 25:18-19

"Like a club or a sword or a sharp arrow is the man who gives false testimony against his neighbor. Like a bad tooth or a lame foot is reliance on the unfaithful in times of trouble."

The theme of reliable communication continues, which just underscores the importance of our speech. An authority no less than the Lord Jesus Christ Himself said: "By your words you will be acquitted, and by your words you will be condemned," Matthew 12:37. If that statement of Jesus does not wake us up to the seriousness of the matter, probably nothing else will. Some people might take a surface look at their own speech and conclude that since they have never lied under oath, none of this really applies to them. Oh Really! Are you absolutely sure you fit into the category of Jesus' words that "by your words you will be acquitted?" If so, that certainty is based on what, your self-evaluation?

Anyway, what did Jesus mean by being acquitted and/or condemned? He was not relating that to your eternal destiny. Your eternal destiny is never determined by your words, whether good or bad. That determination is made exclusively by what we choose to do with God's plan of salvation "by grace alone, through faith alone, in Christ alone." We are condemned or acquitted by our words in relation to the subject we speak to. Whether or not we can convince people, including lawyers, judges and juries, that we are giving truthful testimony is irrelevant. God is the final judge in such matters.

The reason I am taking time with this subject is because "it's in the Book." And that Book tells us in James 3:2 "We all stumble in many ways. *If anyone is never at fault in what he says, he is a perfect man, able to keep his whole body in check."* While I am writing these miniature life lessons, I keep thinking about my family and some of my very best friends, some of whom I consider to be spiritual giants, and like me, none of them are perfect. One fault is common to all, without exception, that: we all stumble in what we say at times. Proverbs 25 is in the Book for me, and let me suggest, it is in there for you as well. Check it out.

PROVERBS TO LIVE BY

Proverbs 25:20

"Like one who takes away a garment on a cold day, or like vinegar poured on soda, is one who sings to a heavy heart."

These are two quite different metaphors, but their relationship becomes evident with a closer look. They both suggest stupid or inappropriate actions taken in the face of unique circumstances, both of which would serve to exacerbate, rather than alleviate the problem.

For the first one I'm reminded of a story about a mother walking down the street with her adult son on a cold day. At least, the mother thought it was cold, and she told her son (as if he were still her little boy) "Close your jacket, I'm cold." Of course, <u>him</u> closing <u>his</u> jacket would not warm <u>her</u> up, but she was being a caring mother to her little boy again. Our text does not tell us who took a "garment" away from whom, nor does it say this ever actually happened. It is simply telling us that such would be a very inappropriate thing to do. Of course, you and I have never done anything that absurd, have we? But how often have we done something with perhaps only the best of intentions that in retrospect was absolutely the wrong thing to do. It may have been a relatively inconsequential matter, but we've all probably done it.

So now let's go on to the next metaphor. Why would one pour vinegar on soda? What would it accomplish, what would be the reaction to such a mixture? At best, probably the vinegar (or acid) would nullify or neutralize the soda. I can't imagine mixing vinegar with a can of Orange Crush soda. OK, so we simply would not do that. But how often have you met a friend or acquaintance who seemed to be "out-of-sorts" or perhaps depressed, and you had no idea about what was going on. Now what are you to do? First of all, you can't solve their problem, so don't even try. They may not even want to hear you, not even with a well-chosen Scripture verse; they may just need <u>you to hear them</u>—so listen, even to their silence. A hasty answer may be as inappropriate as vinegar on soda. We must prayerfully seek to become more sensitive to the needs and feelings of others, trusting the Lord for a heart of wisdom. Wisdom always listens before it speaks.

"If your enemy is hungry, give him food to eat; if he is thirsty, give him water to drink. In doing this you will heap burning coals on his head and the Lord will reward you."

I remember this text entering my 4th grade awareness when a 7th grade boy in our one room school house was assigned this text to quote in a play. In retrospect, I paid no attention to the method this text gives for heaping these coals, but figured I'd have to use some kind of a shovel so as not to burn my hands. I do remember having no enemies of the caliber to merit such treatment, but still thought it might be kind of fun. My 7th grade friend could have probably helped my understanding in large measure, but I never asked. And that brings up a very important question: why do so many still fail to ask for clarification and actively pursue and answer when we don't understand a Scripture? Why indeed!

As a percentage of the total population we probably have only a few who literally have no basic provisions. That is all the more reason we should meet these needs. We are well able. In other parts of the world the story is quite difference. But the hunger and thirst need not be confined to the physical only. People are hungry for love, for recognition, for some basic appreciation, for spiritual truth and reality. Stories are trickling out of some Muslim countries of people coming to Christ because of kindnesses shown them by Christians. The burning coals of conviction became irresistible, and they began to ask. Of course, we are not in a Muslim country, great; that makes it much easier to peddle kindness and love.

Of course, if our goal is to heap burning coals for purposes of destruction, this formula won't work. My 4th grade theology was all wrong here. God says to do deeds of love and kindness, expecting nothing in return, and let God take care of the rest. But we dare not simply *pretend* to love people, we must really love them; don't do deeds of kindness so you will be *appear* to be kind, just BE kind. When we are, or become, the real article, God has something to work with. When we learn to keep God as our Audience, and people as the objects of our deeds of kindness, everybody wins.

"It is not good to eat too much honey, nor is it honorable to seek one's own honor. Like a city whose walls are broken down, is a man who lacks self-control."

There are several different lessons to be drawn from these verses, and we can't pursue them all. Let's take them as a continuation of the previous verses with verse 28 as sort of a conclusion.

First of all, it is not good to eat too much honey, nor too much of anything else. It is simply not good to eat too much. Most of us would agree with that, intellectually at least, even though we might continue to indulge. Why? Because it is more than just a weight problem! To honor God with our bodies (1Corinthians 6:20) we must get down to something a little more basic than simply calories and weight. We have to get down to basic "purpose of life" issues. We must come to know and understand before God "why I am here." We are not here to build honor and acclaim for ourselves, we are here to honor God *with our bodies.* Our text is very specific: it is not honorable to seek one's own honor. Yet those who seek to honor God will be honored by God. God wants us to be honored, and to be honorable, so He established the rules. Pursuing God's objectives for ourselves by our own efforts is guaranteed failure.

Our text continues: without self-control, our lives are like a city whose walls are broken down, we are defenseless. Self-control will enable us to not eat too much, and will also enable us not to selfishly seek our own honor. People who tend to talk too much may well be attempting (subconsciously perhaps) to score some personal points in their own favor.

How then do we gain self-control? In a word, surrender! Surrender the control of your life to the Lordship of Jesus Christ. We do not "make Him Lord," He is Lord. We either surrender to His Lordship, or we seek to take control ourselves. And in that process, we are very definitely and vigorously involved. We are indwelt by the Holy Spirit, but yielding to His control is anything but passive. He works with us and in us and through us, but we decide to trust and obey moment by moment *ad on infinitum.* It is called the fruit of the Holy Spirit.

Proverbs 26:1

"Like snow in summer or rain in harvest, honor is not fitting for a fool."

The first part of this chapter deals primarily with descriptions or characteristics of a fool. As an introduction to these verses, verse 1 voices the conclusion first. Because of these characteristics and activities of a fool, honor ascribed to a fool is utterly out of place. So, let's examine the text.

"Like snow in summer or rain in harvest." According to the Moody Bible Commentary, grain harvest in Israel came during the hottest and driest part of summer. Both snow and rain are a vital, necessary, and desirable part of weather cycles. In order to grow crops, there must be rain, but to harvest the crops, the rain must hold off and allow for a normally dry harvest. Rain during harvest is inappropriate; snow when the temperature is 105 in the shade is unthinkable. It just does not fit. So, our text gives us two mutually exclusive alternatives; you can have snow, and you can have summer heat, you can have rain and you can have harvest, but you cannot have them simultaneously.

In the same way, you can bestow the badge of fool, and you can bestow the badge of honor, but not simultaneously on the same person. Being a fool is not a seasonal occupation, it is a character description. In the Book of Proverbs, there are two classifications of people, that of fools and that of the wise. The fools are sinners pursuing their own ways; the wise are sinners pursuing a life of obedience to the Lord and His ways. To change basic standards of right and wrong in order to be more "inclusive," is like bestowing honor on a fool. That merely serves to enfranchise the fool in his foolishness, and to incorporate the ones bestowing the honor right in the middle of the pack of fools. Earlier in Proverbs, (14:12) we saw that there is a way that seems right, but actually leads to death. To choose the way of death, even if done ignorantly, is foolish. To bestow honor on a fool will merely encourage him to continue on his foolish way. Let's get wisdom.

PROVERBS TO LIVE BY

Proverbs 26:2

*"Like a fluttering sparrow or a darting swallow, an
undeserved curse does not come to rest."*

The first verse of this chapter dealt with what is not fitting, i.e. honor, for a fool. Today's text deals with what is unfitting for the innocent or wise person. Again, the comparison begins with "like." Most city folk do not spend a lot of time watching "fluttering sparrows or darting swallows" I too have become a city dweller, and my childhood memories of life on a farm are rapidly fading. However, one thing is fairly evident, whether we have actually observed it or not: fluttering sparrows and darting swallows are not coming in for a landing. They are on the move, and *perhaps* they are looking for a place to land. The thing that is not fitting for the innocent and the wise is an undeserved curse.

So, let's take a look. Is there a "curse" or a false accusation aimed at you—at me, looking for a landing site? If that is not the case right now, it has already happened and it will happen again. In this wicked world that is a foregone conclusion. Jesus warned us: in this world you will have troubles.

A barn-swallow just needs a barn to land and build a nest. A curse or accusation just needs a guilty person to land on. So, our first and primary protection is to remain innocent and live a life undeserving of the accusation. Does that mean if we remain "undeserving" the curse can't come? Not at all; we will have troubles including curses and false accusations, including, in some instances, even being declared guilty.

But Jesus' warning was accompanied by a great assurance: "I have overcome the world." So, at this point, He becomes your high tower, your Rock of refuge. He will be your strength, your encouragement, your vindication and in the end, the Judge of all the earth will declare you "not guilty" and you will be rewarded for your faithfulness. Remember, though we remain "in the world, we are not of the world." The future has never been brighter, or nearer.

Proverbs 26:4-5

"Do not answer a fool according to his folly, or you will be like him yourself. Answer a fool according to his folly, or he will be wise in his own eyes."

These verses give us two opposite answers to nearly identical situations. The fool has exposed himself and a response is required. A specific response may be right in case #1, and totally wrong in #2, and yet the two may be reversed at another time. Today it is right to answer a fool according to his folly, and tomorrow it is wrong to do so. How do you know when to "answer a fool according to his folly," and when not to? Our text seems to indicate that "this calls for wisdom." I do not believe there is any "textbook" answer to this kind of a conundrum. Wisdom does not come along with a PhD from Harvard. Proverbs 2:6 tells us the Lord gives wisdom and James 1:5 adds to this: "if any of you lacks wisdom, he should ask God, who gives generously. . ."

Let's see what we can learn about the two different approaches, and then ask and trust God for the wisdom needed to discern. It is one thing to discuss and debate issues, except at times when the antagonist is a "fool." If a person gets all uptight when shown a different perspective, he is a self-indicted fool. If you or I then get equally uptight and answer in that condition, we prove ourselves to be like the fool. Does anyone have a potential problem here? When the better part of wisdom is silence or a calm response, so be it.

There are times, however, when circumstances would indicate to answer according to the folly. Leaving his folly unchallenged the fool will believe that his folly has won out. In that case he may become more obnoxious than ever. Sometimes folly, and the fool propagating it, needs to be exposed for what it is. I, for one, desperately need to grow in wisdom so that when the occasion arises, I'll be prepared.

PROVERBS TO LIVE BY

Proverbs 26:7

"Like a lame man's legs that hang limp is a proverb in the mouth of a fool."

This was written in an era long before prosthetics, so the details would differ somewhat, but the word-picture is clear. Such a person's legs are useless to him for walking. How is that like a "proverb in the mouth of a fool?" A follow-up question then would ask "what can we learn from this proverb that will help us today." I've been asking myself that question, and I'll try giving at least one workable answer.

We get the picture of the legs that hang limp, and when we see someone who has lost the use of his legs, we can take that as an opportunity to pray for that individual and to thank God for His bountiful grace to us. It may also provide us an opportunity to be of service to a fellow earth-traveler. But that is not why Solomon wrote this proverb. The point was not legs, or health or infirmity. His point was to have us think about how that condition pre-figures a proverb in the mouth of a fool. All of us could probably plead guilty of acting or speaking foolishly from time to time, but that does not make us fools. In fact, comments like "Oh I'm so stupid, or I'm such a fool" should never cross the lips of one of God's redeemed children. A fool, according to numerous verses in the Psalms, is one who says in his heart there is no God.

What is a Proverb? It is a wise saying. A fool may know some wise sayings, and he may even quote them to others, but it does him no good, because as a fool, he has no intentions of applying the wise saying to his own life. How often do we as God's redeemed children, who are not fools, nevertheless still act the fool. At times we may take a proverb, or a Bible promise, and use it as a club to beat someone over the head with it. Yet we do not slow down enough to see what we are doing. The very proverb we use to correct another has never moved from our intellect to our character. We might just as well not even know the truth, if we won't let it penetrate both our heart and our mind.

Next time you meet someone whose "legs hang limp," ask yourself if that is a picture of your own life.

PROVERBS TO LIVE BY

Proverbs 26:8-9

"Like tying a stone in a sing is the giving of honor to a fool. Like a thorn bush in a drunkard's hand is a proverb in the mouth of a fool."

Several verses in this section of the chapter deal with the absurdity of wise sayings, or proverbs, in the hands (or mouth) of a fool. A foolish person simply does not know how to deal with wisdom. In Bible-College we taught a fellow-student a non-sense phrase in a language he did not understand. It was sometimes hilarious to hear him use that phrase because, being non-sense, it was always inappropriate. No harm done. But the situation in this proverb is much more serious.

A stone tied in a sling will never hit its target and will certainly hurt the one trying launch the stone, and likely some others as well. Try to imagine doing this to David as he faced Goliath. King Saul and his army officers gave great honor to David, and rightly so, because he was no fool. He was God's kid, doing a yeoman's job. To honor a fool by giving him an important message to deliver will be about as effective, as tying a stone in a sling. The message will be tainted or garbled or worse, and it will end up a disaster. This message is to any who would consider entrusting something to a fool who is unable to deliver. Don't do it!

The next verse changes the imagery but continues the same theme. Here the fool picks up a thorn-stem with his hand, perhaps to use it as a walking stick. Not smart! He may be seeking to deliver the same message he was honored to be entrusted to deliver in the previous verse. There is still nothing wrong with the message, but he just does not get it, he does not understand, it is foolish to expect him to deliver beyond his capacity. If he will pick up a thorn-stem as a walking stick, there is not much hope for him.

I well remember giving someone a few minutes to speak at a seminar I was conducting, without properly vetting him first. He undid in a few minutes all I had done to build up to that point. I'm still not sure who the real fool was, and I still wish I could find someone else to blame. But I did learn a lesson that day. It is foolish to trust a fool—or a stranger, which brings us to the next verse.

Proverbs 26:10

"Like an archer who wounds at random is he who hires a fool, or any passer-by."

This proverb opens a slightly different angle to the same problem as the previous verses. Let's focus here on discernment or the exercise of better, or good, judgment. Not everyone is equally adept at discerning character traits in others, but all of us need to be working at it. If we are going to be involved with other people, and we all should be, we absolutely must learn to "read" people. This is not at all judgmentalism, far from it. Judgmentalism looks for failures, short comings, mistakes etc., and ascribes guilt or worth and value accordingly; discernment looks for abilities, preferences and, suitability and then use that information to enhance and promote the best use of talent.

The archer in this picture is not shooting at a specific target, he just shoots at whatever he sees. In that process he is likely to hurt a lot of people—perhaps not intentionally, but at least carelessly. Why would you want someone like that on your team? He is unpredictable, he is unreliable, he is a danger to himself and others, and in the end any association with him may turn out to be counterproductive. It must be obvious to many of us that for this kind of discernment we need wisdom, divine wisdom. It is a good thing that if/when we are suddenly confronted by a need to make a quick evaluation, we can shoot up a quick prayer for wisdom; it is better yet to be prayed up before ever facing such an urgent decision.

Wisdom is not listed as one facet of the nine-fold fruit of the Spirit. It is, however, like the fruit, a work of the Holy Spirit in the life of an obedient child of God. Just as Jesus "grew in wisdom," Luke 2:72, we need to be growing in wisdom daily. James promises to those who ask for wisdom that it will be given generously. A part of the receiving, however, involves the hard work of learning. Some of that learning may come from our own mistakes and trials and errors. Could it be that some lessons can best be learned through making errors and then correcting them? Think about that.

Proverbs 26:12

"Do you see a man wise in his own eyes? There is more hope for a fool than for him."

After all we have seen in Proverbs to this point, one would be forgiven to think that the worst thing in all the world is to be a fool. Not quite! This verse assures us that to be a conceited know-it-all is even worse. Hmmm. Have you ever met a person who seems to think that he knows just about everything there is to know, about everything? Have you ever met such a person in your own church group? In your own family? In your own bathroom mirror? Take another look; that is where people like that seem to hide out. If you ever meet one like that in your own bathroom mirror, take courage, for that person there is hope.

I told a friend of mine recently that there are a lot of things I don't know, the trouble is, I don't know what they are. When that truth is recognized as a reality and not just a joke, that insight becomes a crack in the door to let new information come in which immediately becomes an opportunity to learn something. That in turn can then lead to becoming wise. There is a vast difference between a wise-guy and a wise man. A wise-guy, or a know-it-all, will likely never claim out rightly that he knows everything—he just acts like he *thinks* he knows everything. For such a person there is little, if any, hope.

Chances are many of us have at times acted like we know—if not everything, at least more than is we do know. There is still hope. Where hope dies, is when "in our own eyes" we believe we are wise. That blinds us to any need for deeper wisdom. Let us learn to be wiser than we think we are, and for this we will need God's evaluation, not our own. Search me, O God, and know my heart . . . and lead me.

Proverbs 27:1-2

"Do not boast about tomorrow, for you do not know what a day may bring forth. Let another praise you, and not your own mouth; someone else, and not your own lips."

In chapter 26 we had several foibles of the foolish, but chapter 27 begins with some evidentiary marks of the wise. These are some markers we can safely use in self-evaluation.

First, there is the matter of boasting in general. Perhaps it is because of home upbringing, or perhaps because of certain successes already experienced, but there are some people just more prone to boasting than others. Seemingly, some are not fully aware that is what they are doing. However, we must *be* aware; examine yourself, even ask a trusted friend "do I do that?" If so, stop it! Remember 1 Corinthians 4:7; "What do you have that you did not receive?"

Next, our text specifies boasting about tomorrow. It is good to make plans for the tomorrows of our life, but they must always be submissive plans. Don't talk about your plans as accomplished feats; you can't even control your present, much less your tomorrows. James 4:15-16 says "you ought to say 'if it is the Lord's will . . . As it is you boast and brag. All such boasting is evil.

Then the text says: "let another praise you." The first application of that would be to not extol yourself or your accomplishments. Such self-exaltation quickly becomes very odious. Be wise! If you want to be recognized for a job well done, OK, but let someone else do it. Now, take "let another praise you" in another sense and say *allow* others to praise you. If someone wishes to praise what you did, just a simple "thank you" works fine. Some people tend to counter with excuses for why it wasn't better, and that diminishes the friend's intention. Allow them to say what they want to say. You can work on your own self-improvement later. For now, be wise!

Proverbs 27:5-6

"Better is open rebuke than hidden love. Wounds from a friend can be trusted, but an enemy multiplies kisses."

A true friend will praise you when that is appropriate, and we like it, especially when we are the recipient of that praise. It only stands to reason then, that when appropriate we should also do that for the friend. I recall telling a friend how much I had appreciated his solo during the choir concert. I did not say or imply that it was my favorite part of the concert, it wasn't, but it was a good contribution to the whole effort, and I told him that was perhaps the best I had ever heard him perform. My comments were an encouragement to him, as intended. For me to have kept quiet would have been tantamount to "hidden love."

Nobody likes to rebuke a friend, except maybe mean fools, but if we want to have and be a true friend, a rebuke may at some point be necessary. A gracious compliment can be very encouraging to someone who is "on the way," but a kind rebuke, or caution, can be corrective to help keep someone "on the right way." According to our text, of the two, a rebuke can serve a better purpose in the long run. To be sure, to rebuke a friend is a tough assignment, and should only be done in tandem with a lot of prayer. I recall a gentle rebuke by a friend when I was age 16, and to this day, though we now live a few thousand miles apart, he remains one of my very best friends. I am open to a rebuke from him any time he sees I need one.

The text continues: "Wounds from a friend can be trusted." If he is a true friend, and you will know if he is, what he is offering is what he perceives to be in your best interest. Trust him, he is not trying to hurt or even destroy you. The friendly neighborhood fool will heap compliments—if not literal kisses, because he really wants your downfall. He is just pretending to be a friend with his insincere affirmations and glib justifications of your incorrect plans or procedures. Ask God to give you a true friend, and then also seek to be such a true friend.

Proverbs 27:7

"He who is full loathes honey, but to the hungry even what is bitter tastes sweet."

This is another proverb that is easy to understand on the surface, but also has some deeper significance that is more difficult to apply to life. Every person's appetite changes in proportion to the amount of exercise or physical activity they are involved in. A person who is fully sated has no desire for dainties; he is just too full. Compare that to an inmate in a Nazi concentration camp who never got enough to eat. OK, those camps were shut down, but conditions in some third world countries are far too similar. Most of us have no first-hand knowledge of that, but we get the picture.

No doubt, many American "couch potatoes" need to get out and get some physical exercise for healthier living. But let's look at our spiritual health. When I first started into pastoral ministry, occasionally people would leave a neighboring church and come to try ours, because they 'were not being spiritually fed'? Others too would leave our church for the same reason. But really? Was that the problem? Upon closer examination, many of those people were spiritual couch potatoes; they got no genuine exercise.

Now, I am not talking about being in the church building every time the doors are open; I am not talking about going out and door-knocking, like some cults are required to do. In fact, I am not talking about organized church activity at all, no matter how good some of that may be. I am asking each of us, how much of last Sunday's sermon teaching have we even considered applying to our own lives by the end of the week? Applying it to life is not the same as remembering the three main points of the outline. *Spiritual exercise begins with personal life application.* We don't need to tell the Lord how good or how bad the sermon was, He already knows that. Exercise begins with evaluating before the Lord how my life measures up to the teaching of the Word. Once we begin to do that, we will be amazed at how rapidly and how greatly the quality of the sermons will improve. Even the rebukes of Scripture and the conviction by the Holy Spirit will become sweet as honey. It all depends on the appetite.

PROVERBS TO LIVE BY

Proverbs 27:10

"Do not forsake your friend and the friend of your
father, and do not go to your brother's house when
disaster strikes you—better a neighbor nearby than a
brother far away."

Life on this planet is all about relationships, and wise people will seek to develop as many as possible, and then to maintain them. Sadly, in a mobile culture like ours, this becomes more and more difficult to do. But a meaningful and fulfilling life is built on relationships, rather than on possessions and accomplishments. Of course, it will take wisdom to build right and good relationships. Wise people need to hang out with wise people, and let fools hang out with fools.

Recently I was hospitalized for a few days with a minor malady, and when I came home my neighbor good naturedly scolded me for not letting them know, because "we were worried about you. We are available to look after your house or take care of your wife, or whatever you need." (My nearest brother lives about 1500 miles away.) I knew mine was not a life-threatening emergency, but he didn't. So better a neighbor nearby than a brother far away because of those kinds of constraints. Now, turn the coin over, and it is the neighbor who needs "a neighbor nearby." To have a good neighbor, one must be a good neighbor. That is how relationships work, but they must be properly cultivated. Calamities come in all shapes and sizes and are always unpredictable as to the time they strike, so a wise person will nurture and grow relationships wherever and whenever he can, and then maintain them.

Furthermore, there are spiritual concerns as well. My brother knows the Lord, whereas my neighbor may not. How can I point him to where the real life-answers are, unless we have a good relationship? Jesus told us to let your light so shine before men that they may see your good deeds and praise your Father in Heaven. Matthew 5:16. That light may not be visible when I go to "witness" to him, unless it first shines while we trim our respective hedges, mow the lawn or talk sports. Our text is not another commandment; it is just wisdom.

Proverbs 27:19, 21

"As water reflects a face, so a man's heart reflects the man. The crucible for silver and the furnace for gold, but man is tested by the praise he receives."

A quick glance in a mirror will remind you who you are, just in case you had forgotten. It takes more careful scrutiny in a full-length mirror to show you whether or not you are externally presentable to the public. A look in the mirror may also tell you whether you look happy or sad or perhaps tired. With a little effort, we can change or mask what we see in the mirror, at least to a degree. But it takes a lot more to make changes to who you really are, and a regular mirror does not reveal the real you, either before or after attempted improvements.

Our text tells us that the person's heart reflects the real person, so how do we get a look at our heart? Open heart surgery won't do it, because the "heart" in the text is not talking about the body organ called heart. To see the real person who lives in the body, there is some testing required. This testing generally consists of trials and difficulties. Throughout Israel's wilderness wanderings, we read they were repeatedly "tested." Why? Certainly not so God could find out about them; He already knew, and He even told Moses, that after he had passed from the scene, Israel would quickly turn away from Him. The "testing" was so that they could see who they really were.

That is equally true for us. According to verse 21, one very revealing test is the praise we receive—or desire. If/when we want to know who we really are and what we are like, we must go to the Manufacturer's Manual for the proper operation of the product. Another name for this Manual is the Bible. So, when you notice a reaction or response to some external stimuli, check the Manual to see if that is the way it is supposed to function. First John 2:16 tells us "all that is in the world, the lust of the eyes, the lust of the flesh and the pride of life is not of the father but is of the world." How often do you look in the bathroom mirror, and how often in the mirror of life?

Proverbs 28:1

"The wicked man flees though no one pursues, but the righteous are as bold as a lion."

This chapter is loaded with warnings to the wicked or dishonest among us, that they will not "get-away-with-it." There will be life-long consequences that stretch out into eternity. The wicked flee even when no one is pursuing, (no one, maybe, but not nothing) because the one pursuer they still do have is their own conscience. Let me illustrate with an elementary experience. A 5th grade friend gave me a pair of nesting pigeons when the family moved to another community. A few weeks later when the eggs should have been hatched, another boy came to tell me "I didn't steal those pigeons." Hmmm, I wonder what prompted that. The silent pursuer, perhaps!

More than once, Isaiah tells us: There is no peace, says the Lord, for the wicked. No one can know the peace of God while trying to hide or cover up wickedness. We may not even try to flee the country or the community or even an offended person, but we will always try to flee discovery or exposure until the sin is dealt with. We know this, and yet so often we nevertheless keep trying to cover it up. All the while, the solution to the paranoia and the guilt is so simple, and so complete, it is stated in one sentence: "If we confess our sins He is faithful and just and will forgive us our sins and cleanse us from all unrighteousness. 1John 1:9.

When we are forgiven by God and cleansed from all unrighteousness, then we are declared "righteous." Our text says the righteous are as bold as a lion. Some translations use the word "confident" in place of bold. There is no more need to fear discovery or public exposure, because the highest Authority in the universe has declared us forgiven. Oh, there may still be consequences for wrongs done, we may still reap what we sow in this life, but we can be as confident as a lion which has no natural predators. No one can do us permanent harm. We are safe and secure from all alarms.

Let me ask you, are you enjoying the freedom of conscience and the confident assurance that Jesus purchased for you? It's yours for the taking, paid in full, permanently, eternally.

Proverbs 28:9

*"If anyone turns a deaf ear to the law, even his prayers
are detestable."*

Let's ask a few basic questions of this text: what is meant by "the law,"
what is meant by turning a deaf ear, and then what kind of person would
turn a deaf ear.

The Hebrew Scriptures in the time of Solomon consisted of the
Pentateuch, which of curse contained the Ten Commandments and
other "laws" regarding life in general as well as worship and sacrifices etc.
Collectively, these five books were known as "the law." In other words, it
referred to their entire Bible. By taking it in that sense today, it would refer
to the whole Word of God, not just the Ten Commandments. It includes
both the Old and New Testaments. It is all God's Word.

So, what does it mean to "turn away?" First of all it assumes a person
has it, or has access to it and/or its teaching. It does not necessarily imply
any overt rejection or denial of the Bible. One cannot turn away unless
one is turned toward it or is in its presence. It does not really mean a
repudiation of it, though of course some people do that as well, because
one who repudiates the Bible will not simultaneously pray to the God of
the Bible. It seems to boil down to simply ignoring it or living as if it were
irrelevant.

So, who is the "anyone" who might turn away from the Word of God?
In a word, that could be anyone. That could be any upstanding individual
in your community or even in your church. It would be anyone who lives
his "Christian Life" without any serious interruption or changes because
of something the Word of God says. To turn away may be to believe
what it says, but then not to act on it; it may be to avoid all appearance of
evil, without any change of attitude or character. Such a person's prayer
is "detestable" to God. Woah!! Is God really that concerned about little
secret things? You tell me.

PROVERBS TO LIVE BY

Proverbs 28:11-12

"A rich man may be wise in his own eyes, but a poor man who has discernment sees through him. When the righteous triumph, there is great elation; but when the wicked rise to power, men go into hiding."

Our text acknowledges that there are both rich and poor people, and that there are also selfish, egotists who consider themselves superior to everyone else, and there are also people with discernment. The egotists are not selfish because of their riches, they may merely use their wealth to "lord it over" the peons. They are egotists because of their impoverished character. There are of course also some rich people—some very rich, who are truly wise and discerning and so use their wealth for God's glory, they are just not in this text. The other category in our text are not discerning because they are poor, but because their lives have been given over to the pursuit of true wisdom. Our text is seeking to show that wisdom supersedes both riches and poverty or any other external accouterments.

The person who sees his wealth, or his advanced college degrees, or his/her good looks, as evidence of personal superiority, has very serious "I" problems. God does not see it that way, neither did Solomon. Back in chapter 4:7 we learned that "wisdom is supreme; therefore, get wisdom. Though it cost all you have, get understanding." That has not changed in the intervening chapters.

All the way through the book, the righteous and the wise are lumped together to where at times the words are interchangeable, and the wicked and the fools are lumped together in the same way. So now the text assures us that when the righteous triumph, the whole nation is blessed. It could be said that all citizenry is happier, more prosperous and safer. Psalm 33:12 simply says "Blessed is the nation whose God is the Lord." And, of course, the opposite is also true. Our text says when the wicked rise to power, men go into hiding. How sad. How opposite to God's design! How contrary to all practical experience and evidence! How antithetical to wisdom and common sense! If, what we see, makes us want to run and hide, let's run and hide in our prayer closet. God alone is the answer.

PROVERBS TO LIVE BY

Proverbs 28:13-14

"He who conceals his sins does not prosper, but whoever confesses and renounces them finds mercy. Blessed is the man who always fears the Lord, but he who hardens his heart falls into trouble."

Isn't God good? Think of His grace, His mercy and His love that has provided an eternity of bliss for those who will trust Him. We cannot thank Him enough. We have come to see that Proverbs is not a book about going to heaven, although the way of wisdom taught, if followed, will in some ways make heaven even better for us. But now add to that. Remember, Proverbs is written to enhance this life down here, and today's text is given to show us a definite way of improving life for us down here.

We have all tried to conceal some of our sins and should have learned that it is ALWAYS counter-productive. But I'm not sure we ever quite finish learning that lesson. Have you ever been stopped for speeding, and then tried to conceal that you were aware of that fact? I've learned that life is more enjoyable if I don't speed and get pulled over in the first place. But never mind the cops, be your own cop with the help of the Holy Spirit. He who tries to conceal any sin will not prosper. That's it! He won't. That is the warning, but it is followed by the promise. "Whoever confesses and renounces finds mercy."

Notice the two aspects: confess, which literally means to agree with God on whatever the sin or issue may be and renounce it. Determine that by the grace of God and in the power of the Holy Spirit I am now turning away from that sin. That is also called repentance. Jesus once said: apart from me you can do nothing, John 15:5. Since He was, and is right about that, we can't go it alone, but look at the rest of our text. "Blessed is the man who always fears the Lord, but he who hardens his heart falls into trouble."

I want more out of this life than merely avoiding the trouble, I want the blessing. How about you? Guess what, the blessing is there for the claiming. Bill Gaither wrote "victory is mine for the claiming." He was right. Victory is a part of the blessing promised in our text.

PROVERBS TO LIVE BY

Proverbs 28:17-18

"A man tormented by the guilt of murder will be a fugitive till death, let no one support him. He whose walk is blameless is kept safe, but he whose ways are perverse will suddenly fall."

This proverb continues the theme from verses 13-14, but with some specifics added. It is one thing to talk about concealing sin in general, but when you get specific and name the sin it takes on a greater significance. We can agree that a murderer who seemingly has gotten away with it will be a fugitive from the law for life—or until apprehended. But what if the sin has no legal implications, as is often the case in our permissive culture? Well, then one would not be a fugitive from the law but would still be a fugitive from a guilty conscience. Of course, it is all too possible to simply continue with un-confessed sin and thus harden the conscience, but that merely compounds the problem.

The warning that follows is *do not support* such a person in the sin. That is for the benefit of the sinner. He needs to hear the convicting voice of the Holy Spirit, so while we must not support one in his sin, we must maintain a life that is so much like Jesus Christ that it will help the sinner to come to repentance. That means we cannot be accusatory or condemning in our attitude—much less in our words. We need to support such a one toward repentance.

He whose walk is blameless is kept safe. Not superior, just safe—so long as the walk remains blameless. But none of us is infallible; none of us is sinless; all of us remain susceptible to fail and to fall. "If you think you are standing firm, be careful that you don't fall" says 1 Corinthians 10:12. Galatians 6:1 adds "if someone is caught in a sin, you who are spiritual should restore him gently, but watch yourself or you may be tempted." So long as anyone has a superior attitude, an accusatory attitude, a condemning attitude, we cannot possibly hope to be used of the Holy Spirit "to restore" one who has fallen into sin. Perhaps today you can help restore, but tomorrow you may be the one in need of restoring. Our safety is never in our own determination, but only in a close walk with the Holy Spirit who is Himself our safety.

Proverbs 28:20

"A faithful man will be richly blessed, but one eager to get rich will not go unpunished."

A faithful man in this text refers a person who is trustworthy, diligent, and reliable in his responsibilities, according to the Moody Bible Commentary. Every employer wants to have people like that on his team. The truth of the matter is that everyone can pretty much be that way by sincere effort and commitment if that is what they desire to be and to achieve. Those are the people who generally receive the pay raises and promotions, although this is where The Peter Principle often kicks, in and these people get promoted to the level of their incompetence. In other words, they get promoted above their level of skills, and so life becomes dreary and intolerable for them. So, what has gone wrong? Proverbs is a book of wisdom, teaching us how to live wisely and successfully in this life.

Here it is time to take another look at what it means to be blessed. First, blessings come from the Lord, and are not always expressed in better pay and prestige. Better pay and titles tend to feed our inner greed, and when that happens, the blessing of joy loses out. Our text says the "one eager to get rich will not go unpunished." The punishment may be just that almost imperceptible loss of joy and satisfaction we once knew. The job, the ministry, the church activity and even the hobby, may no longer provide the joy and pleasure they once did. What has gone wrong is the focus.

The blessing promised in the text is promised by the Lord and comes from the Lord. Therefore, our faithfulness needs to be first and foremost to the Lord. Ecclesiastes 9:10 tells us "Whatever your hand finds to do, do it with all your might," which is to say be diligent, trustworthy, and reliable, but with the primary focus and motivation being the Lord Himself. Colossians 3:23 puts it this way, "Whatever you do, work at it with all your heart, as working for the Lord, not for men." Do it diligently and faithfully, reaping the financial rewards leading to wealth, but keep the focus right. Otherwise, the punishment will be personal loss now in this life, plus a loss of reward in heaven—though not the loss of heaven itself.

Proverbs 28:23

*"He who rebukes a man will in the end gain more favor
than he who has a flattering tongue."*

Some people think of the concept of a rebuke in terms of being always
and only confrontational. "You are wrong, and what you are doing is
wrong, and the results will be disastrous." Such a rebuke may be necessary
at times, but it is extremely difficult to bring and more difficult yet to
receive. If such is our perception, then of course flattery would be much
more pleasant and the easier way to go. But the easy way is not always the
best way, and it is rarely the most profitable in the long run.

Here we are dealing with right and wrong. The one who needs the
rebuke is in some way wrong, and as I understand the text, he knows
he is wrong. He may have chosen that way because the other seemed
too difficult, and maybe because the wrong way promised greater profit.
Whatever the reason, the wise man can see it was a bad choice, and he
is able to intervene. Now he too must make a choice. Shall he do what is
necessary and right and rebuke his friend, though that may be difficult,
or shall he flatter his friend with insincere but soothing words. One can
perhaps visualize potential outcomes or applications.

Our text assures us that a necessary rebuke, when wisely given, will "in
the end," or in the long run, gain him more favor, than flattering words.
A rebuke may well begin with a sincere compliment, though never with
flattery, assuring the friend that you have his best interests at heart. You are
not there to prove him wrong or yourself right. Your "rebuke" might well
include questions like have you considered . . . or a reminder of a previous
experience. The object is to help him see that his decision was unwise, or
perhaps even dangerous. In the end, you will have gained favor with the
Lord, but also with the one whom you rebuked, because he will come to
see the wisdom in your rebuke. Flattery, in contrast to complimentary, is
always counter-productive in the long run.

It is not always an easy road we are called to travel, but it is always a
right road.

Proverbs 28:26

"He who trusts in himself is a fool, but he who walks in wisdom is kept safe."

There is a lot to be said for being independent, self-sufficiency, positive thinking, taking responsibility, self-help books etc., so how do we balance that with our text? In fact, doesn't that line up with Galatians 5:22, "the fruit of the Spirit is . . . self-control"? Obviously, God wants us to learn and to have self-control. For many of us, the self-control issue is the critical point of many of our struggles and difficulties. We do fine until we are confronted at our point of major weakness, and then we lose the self-control we thought we had. So, to reconcile that, we might first ask another question: what is the path of wisdom? After all, wisdom is the one over-riding theme of the whole book.

So naturally, the contrast in our text is again between the foolish person and the wise one. And the key in this lesson may be found in the word trust. The fool trusts in himself. That is, in his own resources and abilities, including, perhaps the wisdom already acquired. He is a little like the three-year-old, who vehemently proclaims "me do it myself." From a three-year-old, that may be kind of cute. The kid really believes he can do it, he doesn't know any better, he hasn't learned yet. And?!!!

We need to get back to our earlier question: what is the path of wisdom? Ultimately, all wisdom comes from God. He is all-wise, and He is the Source of all wisdom. He not only knows the outcome and resolution to whatever we face, He is already there. He has already lived through all my tomorrows. He already saw the place in my path where the rattlesnake is hiding, and I won't even know that a rattler is there until I'm confronted, so isn't it wise to walk and to step where He tells me it is safe. He just finished navigating the whole path. Sure, I am self-sufficient enough and have enough self-control to do my own walking, but it is better to do it with my eyes and ears open and focused on the One who is ultimately in charge. Of course, I can simply trust in my own ability, but since I haven't been through tomorrow yet, that would seem kind of foolish.

"A man who remains stiff-necked after many rebukes will suddenly be destroyed—without remedy."

The Book of Proverbs has repeatedly insisted that the wise will heed rebuke. This text seems to indicate that even the wise may not always heed the rebuke the first time, however. The truth of the matter is that we all, both the wise and the foolish, need to be rebuked at times. If we are wise, we need not wait for some outsider to rebuke us; we can accept the Lord's rebuke, given in His Word, or perhaps given by the quiet, inner voice of the Holy Spirit. The wise person will heed the rebuke however it is given, and thereby remove himself from the company of the "stiff-necked."

Yesterday's proverb dealt with the matter of any of us needing to give a rebuke; this text deals with the one receiving a rebuke. Every indication seems to be that the person in this text is not wise, but rather is a plain fool. To him who repeatedly rejects the rebukes is given a very strong warning indeed. Only the Lord Himself can give such a strong warning. We are not told just what that sudden destruction will be, and we don't want to find out. Hebrews 10:31 tells us "It is a dreadful thing to fall into the hands of the living God." The Apostle Paul talks in 1 Corinthians 4:5 about turning a man over to Satan "so that the sinful nature may be destroyed." We do not know precisely what that entailed, and again, we really don't want to find out for ourselves. The man in Corinth apparently finally heeded the rebuke and in the next letter Paul urged the church to receive him back into fellowship. We don't know what he went through to come back, but he came.

So where are we in relation to heeding rebukes? We don't like to give them, and we certainly don't like to receive them. But when they come, we must respond. And we have a choice—always. We can try to deny, to excuse, or to justify, we can get angry, we can resent, we can refuse to listen we can remain stiff-necked, but we can also be wise and listen and pay heed. If our choice is negative, so will be the results of that choice, and the ultimate might be some form of destruction. If our choice is wise and repentant the result will be increased wisdom and joy and restoration and blessing.

Proverbs 29:4

"By justice a king gives the country stability, but one who is greedy tears it down."

We know of course that God has established human government, and that since humans are imperfect beings, there is no perfect earthly government. Most of us would also agree that a government by the people is ideally better than an absolute monarchy or dictatorship. However, some basic principles of government are pretty much constant. In recent decades we have watched as democracies and our own constitutional republic have deteriorated into corrupted versions of what we were intended to be. Some of us would argue that the basic problem is that we have abandoned the biblical principles and the Judeo-Christian values of our founding fathers. Our text speaks to the issues of a king who rules justly verses one who rules for selfish greed. That principle applies equally to any elected congress or parliament with a President or Prime Minister.

Let me suggest that what we decry in our elected officials, many of us nevertheless practice in our own lives and spheres of influence or authority. Let me further suggest that the louder we denounce and criticize the corruption in our elected and appointed leaders, the more likely it is that we are hoping the noise will drown out our own hypocrisy. When confronted, many people rationalize that what we do in our homes and on our jobs is miniscule compared to the greed and graft of our government. In the final analysis, I don't think God is as interested in the size of our greed and graft and corruption as He is in the fact and the presence of it. In some states shoplifting items valued below a certain amount is a misdemeanor while in larger values it becomes a felony. The Bible does not excuse minor thefts or other sins.

When we condone or ignore any corruption in our own lives, we assist in tearing down whatever system or structure we are a part of and ultimately we assist in tearing down our whole legal and governmental structure. But are not the leaders responsible? Absolutely they are, and we are responsible for the leadership in our own lives and our own homes.

PROVERBS TO LIVE BY

Proverbs 29:7

"The righteous care about justice for the poor, but the wicked have no such concern."

To deal with this proverb we must first determine what constitutes "justice for the poor." We have a segment of society today that seems to believe justice for the poor simply means welfare, and so they keep doling out welfare to purchase those votes. Rather than providing justice, this can simply become a form of discrimination. Our text seems to be referring to legal justice and anti-discrimination as being matters of personal concern. However, so long as we see "the poor" as a class of people, there will be no true justice for them. We must see them and help them as individuals who are created in the image of God. More and better laws do not produce "care" in the true sense of the word.

Such personal concern should be a given in our culture, especially among believers in our Lord Jesus Christ. We read of Jesus "When he saw the crowds, he had compassion on them, because they were harassed and helpless," Matthew 9:36. We may not have the depth of compassion that Jesus did, but His compassion is available to us. Compassion must then be cultivated and nurtured by the Word and personal, specific prayer. This whole matter is not so much a national political matter as it is a personal spiritual matter.

In this regard, our text divides respondents into two categories; the righteous and the wicked. The righteous care about the *people* (who are poor.) The wicked have no such concern. It seems to me that we must absolutely differentiate between the condition and the people. When we deal compassionately with the people, the condition will disappear. Of course, there are ministries and organizations doing an admirable job of caring, and we must applaud and support that. But our text is not calling us to evaluate and appraise what others are doing, so much as it is calling us as individuals to evaluate ourselves. A few basic questions may help us: Am I a righteous person who cares? Am I a wicked person who has no such concern? Am I claiming to be a righteous person without the evidence of caring to back it up? Am I willing to ask God to give me a heart of compassion like His own? That is why He came that 1st Christmas.

Proverbs 29:11

"A fool gives full vent to his anger, but a wise man keeps himself under control."

There is an old saying that says: it is better to keep quiet and be thought a fool than to speak up and remove all doubt. I wonder if some version of that saying was around in Solomon's day. It is sure on-theme with our text for today.

There is an interesting teaching in Ephesians chapter 4, on anger. Verse 26 says "In your anger, do not sin." That does not mean it is OK to sin when you are not angry, nor does it say that anger itself is a sin. The verse goes on to tell us to "not let the sun go down while you are still angry." You can't do anything about sun-down, so deal with your anger quickly; do not carry a grudge. Anger is a very powerful emotion, and therefore difficult to control. While some are naturally much more mellow than others, anger has an ability to take over. That is when we are most likely to let it take us into sin. As Dr. John Haggai would say: "Stop it!"

Our text says: (only) "a fool gives full vent to his anger." Why would anyone, even though he is very angry right now, rant and rave and say every negative thing he can think of? Because he has lost control and is acting the fool. If something happens to make one angry today, what does that have to do with something that happened two years ago? Nothing? Then why bring it up now? A fool gives full vent to his anger; he lets it all out. There is a thought in psychology that suggests screaming at and kicking or punching a pillow to get rid of your anger. That may be better than to do the same thing to a person, but what has the poor pillow ever done to you!

Our text tells us that a wise person "keeps himself under control." In this text, the wise person probably got as angry as the fool did, but while the fool gave the control of himself over to anger, the wise person kept himself under control. He probably expressed his anger but did not let it control him. Because God knew that most, if not all of us, could not maintain that degree of self-control by ourselves, He assigned the resident Holy Spirit to produce and develop self-control within us. It is His to develop, and ours to display it.

Proverbs 29:25

"Fear of man will prove to be a snare, but whoever trusts in the Lord is kept safe."

In our text, fear of man of course does not refer to any threat of physical harm, although in our violent culture such threats abound. Our text is referring more specifically to a fear of what others may think or say or do. Really, this would spring from deep personal insecurity. This means we can never really relax and be our natural selves. We are always on guard and ready with a disclaimer, in case anyone has taken offense. Everything you say, do or even think can become so guarded that it becomes nearly impossible even to express an honest opinion.

Such fear, such paranoia, will most certainly cut into our trust in the Lord. One cannot simultaneously harbor a fear of man and a trust in God; a respect for man, yes, but fear, no. A healthy respect for others and their differing opinion, including even anti-Christian views, will keep us from infringing on their personal freedoms, and a vibrant trust in the Lord will keep us from violating their rights. If God allows people to disagree with Him, who are we to do any less.

A dear Christian brother, who is also a friend, holds to certain views which are diametrically opposed to mine. I just don't discuss those issues with him, not because I harbor a fear of man, but because I believe God still has a work to do in his life—and in mine. I try to agree with my friend when I can, and when I disagree, I try to do it gracefully and as unobtrusively as possible. And so, we remain friends, and perhaps in heaven we will be next door neighbors. Wouldn't that be something!

Whoever trusts in the Lord is kept safe. What a Hallelujah promise! Some would encourage the super-timid to assert themselves. Be bold, learn to speak your mind. That may have its place, but the opposite of fear is not boldness and courage, it is love, according to 1 John 4:18. "Perfect love casts out fear, and the only perfect love is God's love. Translating that into the language of our text it comes out as a bold, confident trust in the Lord. And it works, at least it is in process of working in my life.

Proverbs 30:5-6

"Every word of God is flawless; he is a shield to those who take refuge in him. Do not add to his words, or he will rebuke you to your face."

The four rhetorical questions of verse 4 can serve as an introduction to these verses. Also, Isaiah 40 (a great chapter to read today) expands on the greatness of God where verse 18 asks, also rhetorically: "To whom then will you compare me?"

Now then, in the light of God's incomparable greatness, and our inability to ever begin to comprehend Him, let us never presume to question or doubt anything He has said. His word is flawless, it is never in doubt, it is never inaccurate. We may indeed find at times that what we had understood Him to say, turns out to be inaccurate. So, we were wrong in our initial understanding of what He said. No news there. Because the current meanings of words change over time, (so much so that it is fair to say our language changes over time,) is one reason for the multiple new translations of the Bible. That is also why it is appropriate and logical that one may prefer one translation over another. But the word of God never changes; it is flawless, it is perfect, it is sure.

Because "every word of God is flawless, [therefore] he is a shield to those who take refuge in him." No one knows in advance what a day will be like, what it holds in store for us, whether rough or smooth, whether tough or easy, but we can safely take our refuge in Him. He is our shield. He will protect us, whether IN trials or THROUGH trials or FROM trials He protects US, all of us who take refuge in Him. Therefore, we must be careful to never add to His words. We may do that in subtle ways. For example, I can never say what God will do in any given situation unless He has already said that He will. We have many promises that we can claim in every circumstance of life, but I cannot claim that He will do for me precisely what He did for you. He is God. He is Sovereign. And He always keeps His word. So, we finite people must be careful not to add to His words, nor to take away from them.

Proverbs 30:10

"Do not slander a servant to his master, or he will curse you, and you will pay for it."

Again, this proverb is a precursor to a Scripture written later, this one in Romans 14:4, which reads *"who are you to judge someone else's servant? To his own master he stands or falls. And he will stand, for the Lord is able to make him stand."*

At first blush it might seem that the prohibition here is meddling in other people's affairs, and that is certainly valid as we see in Proverbs 26:17. It is never wise to meddle in things that are none of our business or to interfere in other people's affairs. Unless they ask for it, they probably don't want our advice. But the word used in our text is slander, and that has connotations deeper than mere meddling. This has the idea of false accusations or speaking disparagingly of one who is accountable to another. The Moody Bible Commentary suggests the idea of speaking against someone furtively, whether true or false.

In our current church culture, that could piously be couched in terms of a prayer request. It might go something like this: please pray for so and so, because it seems he may have been guilty of XYZ. That should get the wheels turning. All right! You didn't really lie or even falsely accuse, because you said he *may* have, but in the minds of hearers he has been painted with the guilty brush. You merely made yourself appear superior and beyond reproach. Our text says: "don't do that." It may cost you more than you bargained for; you are not beyond reproach in this.

In this text the issue involves a servant and his trusting master; in God's economy the issue takes on a more significant tone. The corollary text in Romans (14:4) also uses the word master with a lower case "m" but the connotation clearly includes that of a servant of THE Master. Either mortal or divine, we must remember that final payday is not next Friday. "To his own master he stands or falls, and to his own Master he stands or falls." As do you and I. He will stand because the Lord is able to make him stand, and us too. So, let's not try to tear anyone else down, even if that should happen to us.

Proverbs 30:32-33

"If you have played the fool and exalted yourself, or if you have planned evil, clap you hand over your mouth! For as churning milk produces butter, and as twisting the nose produces blood, so stirring up anger produces strife."

Throughout the book, the contrast has been between the wise and the fools, between wisdom and foolishness. As we grow in wisdom by the grace of God, we more and more depart from foolishness. But it is a life-long journey, and all the way along it is possible to momentarily slip back into foolishness. One thing that will help us stay on track in following after wisdom, is to remember that actions have consequences. We may sing with confidence and boldness that Calvary covers it all, my past with its sin and foolishness, Calvary covers it all. Still, in this life, actions have consequences. And it is true, Calvary does cover it all. "My guilt and despair, Jesus took on Him there, and Calvary covers it all."

The Book of Wisdom was written to teach us wise living down here and thereby avoid "playing the fool." However, having in fact played the fool (again) it teaches recovery and return as well. So here, having foolishly exalted yourself, and who of us hasn't, STOP IT! Don't continue and perpetuate foolishness. You know deep down in your heart, that you are not what you want to be, nor what you are going to be, so don't pretend to be what (in this life) you are never going to be. I know on the authority of God's word that I am declared justified, righteous and perfectly sinless in Christ; I am just not there yet in practice. Therefore, since actions have consequences, and foolish actions have undesirable consequences, don't persist in and perpetuate foolish actions.

Referring to the picture in our text, if you want butter, keep churning until you get it; if you don't want a nosebleed, stop twisting and churning, or you will get it. And if you want peace, don't stir up anger, or the war will be on. If you want peace anywhere, in church, at home on the job, don't stir up anger there or anywhere else. You cannot cause harmony in one place and discord in another because you won't have peace in yourself. Be wise!

365

PROVERBS TO LIVE BY

Proverbs 31:8-9

"Speak up for those who cannot speak for themselves,
for the rights of all who are destitute. Speak up and
judge fairly; defend the rights of the poor and needy.

We do not know who Agur of chapter 30 was, nor precisely who King
Lemuel of chapter 31 was. We do know who Solomon, the compiler of all
these proverbs was, but we don't know how much he really understood
about the Messiah, for whom he was waiting, was either. But when I
look at these verses on this last day of the year, I see Jesus, the Christ, the
long-awaited Old Testament Messiah. I do not see Him named or fully
understood, but I see Him in action. I see in this text that God so loved
the world and of all those in it who are destitute, including you and me,
that He sent Jesus, the Redeemer.

Who are those who cannot speak for themselves? There are many, but
I think first of little children. O how Jesus loved the children! I see also
the unborn or the preborn children. He loves them equally, and they are so
totally helpless. Jesus has already embraced them in His loving arms. Who
else are those who cannot speak for themselves? They are the destitute, the
disenfranchised, the ones who have never heard the name of Jesus many
who are living in 3rd world countries. Jesus loves them and wants a better
life for them, a life of justice and opportunity and righteousness. Do I also
want that for them? How badly do I want it?

Who will speak up and judge fairly and defend the rights of the poor
and needy? Jesus did, and is, and will, but He needs those who will be His
mouthpieces here and now on this earth and in this life. One time, God
asked "Whom shall I send, and who will go for us?" (Isaiah 6:4), and Isaiah
answered Here am I. Send me. And God said whom shall I send today, in
this century, and who will go for us next year . . .

CPSIA information can be obtained
at www.ICGtesting.com
Printed in the USA
LVHW051735140621
690185LV00010B/1118